THE COLOUR OF MY HEART

A True Story of Hope, Perseverance and Love

DENIZ 'SKIP' ÖNAÇ

The Colour of my Heart

ISBN: 9781838283858

Book Cover Design: Listening To Your Voice Publishing

Editor: David Önaç

Typesetter: Ruth Pearson

Proof-readers: Deniz and David Önaç

Contents

Dedication

I dedicate this book to anyone who has ever experienced
prejudice or suffered injustice on account
of their race, colour or ethnicity.

Author's Foreword

Writing this true story of my life experiences in Jamaica, from 1971 to 1985, has been a new and fascinating experience. Most of my training and career has been spent within the world of Physics and Mathematics, and although I previously co-authored two successful Physics textbooks, this is my first foray into the narrative domain. Many of the episodes within this book have already been told, and retold, for the enjoyment of close groups of family and friends over several decades, and I have often been asked if, and when, I might record them for posterity.

But several factors have recently motivated me not to further delay the process of putting them into written form. Undoubtedly, if left too long, there is a risk that some memories can fade, and at times it has been necessary to consult those who shared the experiences with me to aid the accuracy of the account. More significantly, however, a diagnosis of cancer towards the end of 2019, and shortly after successful treatment for that, the experience of a minor stroke, have both served to focus my mind on putting pen to paper. Given that my recuperation also coincided with the onset of the global Covid-19 pandemic, and the unparalleled restrictions that this imposed upon normal life in the UK from early 2020, this season of confinement at home seemed the ideal time to start the task!

To my surprise, after I had struggled somewhat with the first chapter, the writing process became much easier, and the rest of the story flowed quite naturally; before I knew it, I was having to make difficult decisions about what *not* to include, and settled eventually on what is now contained within the 17 chapters of this book. Given that this first manuscript consisted of over 85,000 words, and took several months for me to laboriously type out on my (rather slow) desktop computer, I have been quite surprised at just how much additional work it has taken to get the book from that first version into its final form.

I have spent countless hours editing, re-writing, re-structuring, checking facts and details with various people, debating the best way to express my values and beliefs authentically and honestly, deciding exactly which of my many musical experiences to recount, deliberating whether to translate Jamaican *patois* more literally or idiomatically - not to mention the frustration of unsuccessfully approaching countless literary agents and publishers!

As already stated, this book is a true story, but it has nonetheless been necessary to change some names to protect identities, to ocassionally alter the chronology of events for dramatic purpose, or to embellish or amplify selected incidents to serve the narrative. It is also undoubtedly the case that, during the last 35 years, I may have forgotten or even accidentally modified certain details. Should this have occurred despite my best efforts, as the author, I apologise for any such unintentional errors or omissions. Overall, I have endeavoured to create a story which captures the profound, transformational effect that the island and culture of Jamaica had on my life. It is no understatement to say that I was never the same again, and my life would have been greatly the poorer had I not had the experience. My hope is that in reading this story, you might enjoy the humour, experience the drama and excitement, and empathise with the characters' lives and loves, but that, most of all, you will celebrate the fact that the colour of all human hearts is the same.

Deniz (Skip) Önaç BSc(Hons), Dip Ed, CPhys, MInstP

Editor's Foreword

I echo my father's sentiment in his Author's Foreword, since my acting as Editor for this book is rather new territory for me, too. Although my career has thus far been within the Arts (in Music, to be precise), within the arena of Literature, I've never taken on anything remotely like the task of editing an entire book! And this is not just any book. It is the story of a period in my father's life which played a definitive role in shaping him into the man I so admire, and, in so many ways, aspire to be like. The rewards of this task have been so worthwhile, that to describe all the benefits truly and fully in words would be quite as challenging as the actual editing!

Almost all the stories contained within this book, I have heard my father tell many times in person, after a fantastic Caribbean meal, or during a game of dominoes, or for the encouragement and exhortation of myself and others, or in the happy company of life-long friends, or while on long car journeys. He tells the stories well, with vigour, and authentic excitement, and just the right tone. The pacing and narrative arc are always somehow masterful, the content compelling, the exploits inspiring, the contrasts powerful, and the humorous elements are of the kind that make you laugh right to your core - and even though I've heard some of these stories 50 or 100 times, I never tire of hearing them again, a sentiment shared by many others.

This relates to one of my priorities as Editor. I wanted to make sure the way my father was expressing himself in prose went beyond just communicating 'the content of each episode as clearly as possible', and conveyed something of the *life* these stories seem to have when heard in person. During editing, I encouraged my father to retain repeated turns of phrase which 'sounded like him', including writing the text in a way which showed some of his emphases, and I similarly recommended that more of his real character be communicated in the final version of the manuscript, like his impulsive nature, which really did (and still does!) lead him into the most peculiar situations. My father has had an incredibly *interesting*, varied, exciting and fulfilling life, and it is exactly his characteristic impulsiveness that has driven him into many of his exciting encounters! It seemed right, then, to use this book as an opportunity to record him, as well as his selected scenes.

With my father's background not being in the Arts, I was rather encouraged and surprised by just how well the overall story seemed to flow (even in its very first version) - though, perhaps I ought to have expected as much from such a good live storyteller. It also emerged that skills required for my specific area of artistic expertise, musical composition, were partly transferable to the editing process. In many ways, I appraised my father's manuscript in the same way I would one of my own pieces, paying close attention to the relationship between structure and content; refining materials; checking the pacing; balancing contrast and consistency; always hoping that things like clarity of expression would serve higher goals, like communicating something significant about the human condition. As someone more experienced in the Arts, I therefore tried to aid my father by fine-tuning what was already there. This involved things like steering a sometimes too 'scientific' approach to prose towards something more natural, without undermining the major role that the Sciences have played in my father's life, as well as more rudimentary concerns like making the whole text more clear, concise and consistent.

My father and I edited this book together, going through the entire manuscript multiple times in different ways over a period of almost a year, making changes as we found, debated, agreed on (or compromised on), and resolved each issue - from the tiniest of corrections to considerations at the largest scale. In our many sessions, I often quoted "Truth is stranger than fiction!" when we were discussing solutions to problems, and the tendency during the editing process has in fact been to move everything even closer to the fullest account of the original events. Every time I insisted on digging deeper in conversations with my father, details which he had left out (with the good intention of serving the narrative) simply had to be included, again and again - and the more and more this happened, the more any 'manufactured' embellishments (again, well-intentioned) seemed not to belong, and were removed. This sometimes also involved lengthy discussions where I requested that my mother join us at the computer to supply further depth and detail for those parts of the story where she was either present or had direct knowledge of the events or context. My mother is vital to the story recorded here, and her contributions during the editing process provided material which made so many parts of the story more comprehensive, revealing, accurate and 3-dimensional.

Another recurrent concern during editing was to capture a sense of how my father's opinions and values change over the course of the narrative. Attentive readers will notice that it is not just that the story charts my father's gradual Jamaicanisation, but that the prose itself develops as the narrative progresses - that is, the *way* the narrator 'talks' to the reader to some extent reflects and corresponds with how my father's character develops within the narrative. This is related to how issues like race, class and era are approached. For example (after still more lengthy discussions) hopefully we have found a pragmatic balance between content which must necessarily represent the 1970s and 80s authentically, and an acknowledgment of the perspective of a post-2020 readership - though, despite our efforts, the proverb 'you can't please everyone' may still apply. But I do believe this book can say *something* of real significance to everyone. At the time of writing, it seems to me that there is a saddening polarisation and tribalism within popular culture, and my father's immersion in, and utter *devotion* to, a culture different to that of his birth for over a decade seems nothing short of inspiring. But simultaneously, this story is realistic that any such engagement takes real time, effort, self-critique - and mistakes! I long for a modern world in which the default response to mistakes is more gracious, and our efforts will have borne some fruit if my father's book can be a refuge in this regard.

My admiration for my father is presumably becoming clearer and clearer throughout this Editor's Foreword, and of the further potential items I might list, I must mention his ability to apply himself to all sorts of tasks, and to complete them *very well*. Now retired, he really just is 'one of those people' who seems to be able to do almost anything on a car, or to fix a household appliance, or to add a perfectly-working plumbing extension to the house's existing system, or, why not, just build an entire house from scratch in his 60s (yes… literally!). So, it was fascinating for me to see in this story the other side of such confident and diverse competence. This book charts the development of the skills (now so second-nature to him) which he had to learn - from scratch - such as auto mechanics and sound recording, as well as growth in domains such as teaching and leadership. It was important that some of these learning curves be described in substantial detail. So, long passages of prose which chronicle these developments have been retained.

This book is funny, too. For all I have said, the editing process hasn't been easy, and shouldn't be romanticised! There have been many long days, late nights, arguments, debates on recurrent themes, the inevitable encroachment of editing hours into other parts of life, the competing priorities of any intergenerational endeavour... and on top of all that, taking this book through to completion has itself been a *huge* learning curve for both me and my father. But after difficult editorial decisions, we would often find ourselves laughing, really laughing, within minutes; sometimes this occurred, beyond rational control, *during* the most difficult moments of the editing process - and it is my hope that, in its final version, this manuscript communicates something of the joy and humour of my father's life experiences, and that this is infectious. I hope you will laugh at the more comical episodes, and that as you do, you might experience the same lightness of spirit that I do when I see my father throw his head back in uncontrollable laughter, or when he dismissively brushes off a current problem with a chuckle, because he's been through enough experiences (some recorded here) to laugh at the future. I think we could all do with more of the kind of confidence that lets us laugh at the future, not because our prospects are easy, but because we have seen people like my father exemplify such circumstance-free laughter, and therefore, know that such laughter is also possible for us.

Dr David Önaç PhD, MPhil, MMus, MA(Cantab), LRSM

Tribute from Dr Phillip O'Connor

This literary and timely work is a labour of love from Mr Deniz Önaç.

Among other relevant and applicable themes, it focuses a powerful lens on some of his experiences, obstacles and opportunities, and allows us to gain a more in-depth understanding and appreciation of the life of this amazing former Physics and Head Teacher we affectionately call 'Skip.' In great detail he takes us through some of his personal experiences of adventure, struggles, disappointments, rejection, and loss; as well as stories of love, faith, trust, acceptance, non-discrimination, resilience, integrity, character and professionalism. Through all these, he reminds us that God has an ultimate plan for our lives that 'all things work together for good'.

Warmest congratulations to Skip for writing this masterpiece. Your book is inspiring, authentic, reflective and practical. It informs and reminds us of your journey of faith and trust, from England to your time and experiences in the Caribbean and Jamaica in particular. Your wholehearted contribution and humble service to Gospel Music, Education, Christian ministry, Scouting and the amazing influence you have had on thousands, will always be remembered, appreciated and indelibly memorialised not only in these pages but more so in the hearts of your readers. '*The Colour of my Heart*' will undoubtedly inspire, motivate, challenge, encourage and equip its readers to overcome personal setbacks, and celebrate their own unique stories and experiences. Thank you, my brother and friend, for giving this body of work to the world; may it obtain the wide readership that it abundantly deserves!

Dr Phillip J O'Connor EdD, MA, BA, TDip
Academic Lecturer, Teacher, Preacher and Inspirational Speaker.

Tribute from Dr Clifton Reid

The achievements of Deniz Önaç, 'Skip', this giant of a teacher, on whose shoulders so many of us stood when beginning the climb up the Jamaican socio-economic ladder, are legendary, rich and enviable.

Skip's story, captured in his book, "*The Colour of my Heart*", chronicles the fantastic journey of a white volunteer teacher recruited by the British organisation, Voluntary Service Overseas, (VSO), which began in 1971 in Frankfield, a deeply rural community nestled in the Hills of Clarendon, Jamaica. It was supposed to be just a one-year stint but, thankfully, extended to 14 very short years which provided the rich experiences which his readers will thoroughly enjoy in this riveting and inspirational account of that portion of his life's journey.

At Frankfield, Skip quickly endeared himself to his many audiences... Physics and Mathematics students, Electronics Club, Scouts, Sonic Salvation Gospel Band members, Science Exhibition team members, their parents and extended families. To his awe-struck students, Skip's mantra... captured in the local dialect, "*Evryting a Physics*" [sic]... was a potent, motivational tool that worked like a charm. It was what we turned to when faced with a seemingly, insurmountable problem. Difficult subjects and, indeed, preparation for life itself, suddenly became less daunting. So inspired were his young Science students that, during his tenure, we won not just regional Science Competitions but also the prestigious, national Secondary Schools Science Exhibition on several occasions. Not surprisingly, his Physics Department became legendary and he went on to co-author two text books, 'Physics for the Caribbean' and 'Physics for CSEC Examinations'. Also through his efforts and initiatives, Scouting flourished with hikes, camps, bush cooking, abseiling and orienteering; what wonderful days those were!

I can't wait to live again those Golden years, seen through the eyes of my Physics and Life-Teacher, Scoutmaster, career advisor, mentor and friend, Skip.

Dr Clifton Reid, MBBS
Life's Spring Medical Centre, Mandeville, Jamaica.

Tribute from Alvin Day

The peculiarly wonderful author of this book is a man I have known and admired since I was a fifteen-year-old in High School. Back then, he had only one name, Skip, because we, his students, could not correctly pronounce his actual name, Deniz Önaç.

Turning now to Skip's story, I present you with two scenarios to consider. If either one holds true for you, then you simply *must* read this book.

Firstly, you are often saddened that the world is so divided by discriminating prejudices, based on such factors as race, colour, creed and national origin. If so, '*The Colour of my Heart*' provides a refreshing breeze of hope. It shows in fine fashion, the kind of kinships, friendships and lifelong experiences that can enrich your life when you connect sincerely with persons who are different from you.

The engaging stories of this book show how tasty the cake of life can be, when you mix in the eggs, flour, salt, sugar, vanilla and other spices, even as they go through the fire together. Whether you are the vanilla or the salt, you alone cannot make a beautiful cake all by yourself. Skip's life, embracing diverse cultures, customs and cuisines, clearly shows that there is hope for the world. Furthermore, this book will fascinate you with effervescent life experiences that transcend the dark realities of the nightly news.

Secondly, you would rather have a life of adventure in which you live "out loud" and enjoy every breath of oxygen that you have time to inhale. Rather than living in doubt, afraid of risking greatness, you would prefer to look back at your life and glow with the memories of the mountains you climbed and the seas you crossed.

The riveting stories in this book show a man who did all of that and more, by taking others along with him, and building a powerful legacy through his own humble greatness. Reading this book will not only make you smile deep down, quite often, but it will also ignite in you a passion to embrace life in a way that cannot be thwarted by lack of money, time or the permission of those around you who might doubt your intentions and personal power.

Alvin Day, BA(Spanish), BBA
Motivational Speaker and author of '*If Caterpillars Can Fly ~ So Can I*'

Tribute from Dr Floyd Antonio

I am truly honoured and excited to be afforded the opportunity to pen a few words in tribute to this wonderfully inspiring, life-story. I am confident that my contribution to this literary endeavour will help set the stage for what will undoubtedly be a glorious and enlightening experience for all who read *'The Colour of my Heart'*. Included below are a mere selection of my sentiments about the author, Mr Deniz Tarik Önaç, affectionately called 'Skip'.

I first encountered Mr Önaç in the early 1970's when he served as my Form Teacher at the then Frankfield High School Comprehensive in Clarendon, Jamaica. This tall, long-haired, young teacher walked with a distinctive bounce. He was an ex-pat which was not unusual at that time since there were many other such persons teaching at our High School, especially from countries in Europe. What was unusual however was that many of those foreign teachers had the most interesting of names such as John Crow, Savage and Önaç (pronounced 'Ernatch'). It was, however, much easier for all of us to just use his Jamaican pet-name, 'Skip'. He taught the science subjects but demonstrated special perspicacity in Physics. It soon became obvious that everybody loved my Home-Room Teacher, Skip, whether he was involved in a game of soccer, taking Scouts on exciting adventures or bringing trophies back to 'Compre' (as the school was affectionately known). As far as I know, his Physics classes always took the top spot in practically every annual, national science competition that they ever entered.

During my final year as a student at 'Compre', I eventually became a part of the *Sonic Salvation Gospel Band* which Skip founded. From then until now, our brotherly love and friendship have continued. Our adventures and experiences are so many and varied that I will have to leave most of the details for my own book about 'true friendship'. I must mention, however, that Skip was the one who opened my eyes to the concept of music royalties when he encouraged me to join the Performing Rights Society in the UK some 40 years ago. He was also instrumental in helping me to sharpen my song-writing skills and we co-wrote many songs together. Some years later, Skip was the person who invited me to join his staff as a Music Teacher when he left Jamaica to serve as High School Principal at Kingsway Academy in the Bahamas.

I therefore present to some and introduce to others, someone who is well educated, polished and polite yet who is kind, respectful and considerate towards other human beings. Skip is not only a Physics Teacher, soccer player and Scout-master; he is also a skilled mechanic who was able to bring his mini-bus back to life after it was stolen and stripped down to a mere shell. Furthermore, Tarik (as I sometimes, affectionately, call him) is an excellent drummer, songwriter, choir-director, sound and studio engineer, clearly demonstrating that he is both versatile and flexible. When he speaks the Jamaica *patois* you will possibly swear he was born in that island. The same can be said about his tenure in the Bahamas. He has served or helped literally thousands of people, in both Jamaica and the Bahamas. This is the same awesome person who would selflessly divide up the small honorarium received after numerous Sonic Salvation Gospel Band concerts. There were occasions when he himself would be left with nothing at all, not even so much as would be needed to fill the petrol tank of his Ford Transit mini-bus which served to transport us to and from our concerts. As one of his closest friends, I am perhaps the only person from that little town of Frankfield, in Jamaica, who surreptitiously saw him kiss the girl of his dreams, before she later became his wife.

My hope and conviction is that this tribute will give you a deeper appreciation for his story, '*The Colour of my*

Heart'. The world in which we find ourselves at this time is rife with hatred and prejudice, especially racial prejudice. The motto for the country of Jamaica is: 'Out of many, one people'. In all my many and varied experiences while being around my friend, Skip, there has never been any doubt in my mind that this man typified the very essence of this Jamaican dictum.

While Skip is as fair as my white paternal grandmother, his darling wife, Joan, is a gorgeous lady whose complexion is as dark as that of my maternal grandmother. Their mixed-race son, Dr David Önaç is, himself, now married to a beautiful, fair-skinned, young English lady. I think that David's heart must be the same colour as that of his father, Skip, who had no reservation about marrying Joan because his heart had (and still has) a certain colour. I am in no doubt that as you read this book you will not only be entertained, but that you will, above all else, discover what the true colour of your own heart is, as well as what it should really be.

In the dead of winter a few years ago, when I travelled to England to bury my father, it was my friend Skip who met me at the train station with warm gloves and a hot drink. The Skip that I had known all those years had not changed, despite returning to his home country many years before. Myself and my wife Rosalie heartily congratulate our brother, Skip, for putting together this enlightening, informative, entertaining and life-changing offering. I therefore encourage everyone to buy, read, promote and give this book as a needed gift. I declare that Skip's true life-story will play its part in advancing God's kingdom here on earth.

Floyd Antonio PhD
Pastor: The Citadel Inc.
President and Founder of Carigospel Inc.

Acknowledgements

Firstly, I would like to thank God for His amazing, saving grace, for bringing me safely through my recent illness and allowing me to complete this book before all the many memories faded and were lost forever.

Next I would like to express my heart-felt appreciation to my wonderful wife, Joan, the inspiration for this story, for her love, faithfulness, support and patience. Without her Christian witness, my own conversion would never have happened. Over the past few months, she has provided invaluable help in reminding me of the details of many of the incidents and adventures that I have penned. Thanks also for giving up our family dining table which, for the last year, has been permanently hidden from sight by a laptop, a printer, lots of connecting wires and a mound of papers, photos, books and writing devices. They will soon be moved - I promise!

Then I must acknowledge the deep gratitude I owe to my son, Dr David Önaç, for the amazing job he has done as Chief Editor of the entire story. Without his keen eye and gentle but ruthless editing, my writing would have been more verbose and error-prone, less concise and, undoubtedly, less interesting. Thanks, Dave, for a brilliant job! And also, to my daughter-in-law, Elena, for her proof-reading of the final manuscript and her insightful suggestions for the artwork on the outer cover.

I am also indebted to my dear, lifelong friends, Floyd, Phillip, Alvin and Clifton for their very touching tributes and for their encouragement and advice throughout this project. I trust I am genuinely worthy of the many, glowing accolades you have offered.

Special thanks are also due to Alvin for his invaluable help in checking the accuracy of the *patois* and for his final proof-reading of the entire manuscript. Also to

Ian and Phillip, for reading through early versions of the text and offering many helpful suggestions; Martin and Joy for their help with my trying to secure a publisher; and to Joy for organising the recent, live, Sonic Salvation Gospel Band interview on the Jamaican radio station, Love 101 FM.

Thank you to all my brothers and sisters from Sonic Salvation Gospel Band for their amazing musical talents and enthusiastic encouragement, I pray for God's blessing on each one of you. Without your being such a vital part of my life, one of the foundation stones for the whole story could not have been laid. A special, heartfelt salutation to those band-members now deceased: Grace, Prince, Zyn and Dennis - may each of you rest in heavenly peace.

A huge thank you to my publisher, Ruth Pearson, of *Listening to Your Voice Publishing,* for her faith in what I have written and for everything she has done to make this project a success. May God bless your publishing company and help it to grow from strength to strength!

I would also like to express sincere thanks to my former student, Paul Roberts, for creating the photo which has been used on the front cover of the book. It is one of my favourite pictures and illustrates perfectly the theme of this story.

Finally, to all my readers, a huge, heart-felt thank you for your support in purchasing a copy of *'The Colour of my Heart'*. If you get but a fraction of the enjoyment from reading it as I got from personally living the story, the book will have achieved its aim.

God bless you all,

Deniz (Skip) Önaç

THE COLOUR
OF
MY HEART

A True Story of Hope, Perseverance and Love

Chapter 1: The Big Adventure

I suppose it all started in early 1971 during my final year of study for a BSc Hons degree in Physics at University College, London (UCL).

After my second year in virtual isolation, living in digs in East Finchley, and the daily nightmare of travelling on the hot, dirty, crowded Northern Line tube to central London and back, I was once again living within walking distance of UCL at Commonwealth Hall, near Euston Station. This was ideal in more ways than one; no public transport was necessary to get to and from lectures; no cooking was required on my part since the hall of residence provided both breakfast and an evening dinner daily (which was fortunate since my culinary skills were lacking, to say the least); I had lots of friends all located in the same building; and, most importantly, in the basement hall was a large grand piano and more than enough space to leave my entire drum set, permanently set up and ready to play.

During my first year at Commonwealth Hall, I had become close friends with Trevor, an absolutely amazing pianist who could play from memory just about every hit song ever written, and our 'jam sessions' had led to my securing the ultimate student job - working with him as a cruise ship musician during each of the long summer holidays while I was at uni! As an impoverished student, typically existing on only a lump of cheese and an apple every lunchtime, earning some much-needed money on the cruise lines would enable me to make the most of what London was offering. Now that Trevor, too, was residing again in the same hall while studying for his postgraduate degree in Chemistry, we could once again play music together on almost a daily basis and deepen our friendship.

So I continued happily with my Physics course, more than satisfied with the opportunities that had come my way thus far, and was looking forward to an exciting future.

* * *

All around me, everything seemed to be in a whirlwind state of flux. Age-old cultural traditions were being challenged left, right and centre, 'free love' was in abundance, flamboyant designer clothing was all the rage, and, in particular, the popular music revolution was in full swing. Coming from a relatively simple, rural background, I was now determined to take every advantage of being right in the heart of it all in England's most exciting city.

Now in the final year of my undergrad degree, it was imperative to use whatever time I had left to go to live gigs and concerts to see top bands such as the Rolling Stones, Jimmy Hendrix, and Deep Purple, to attend all the latest musicals showing at the big London theatres, such as 'Jesus Christ Superstar' and 'Hair', and to get personally involved whenever possible in UCL productions such as 'Oh, What A Lovely War!' Life was hectic but exciting, sleep was often in short supply and, predictably, academic studies began to slide gradually into second place. It wasn't that I was no longer enjoying the course I was doing but rather that so many other unmissable experiences also needed to be fitted into my increasingly busy life.

Two-and-a-half years earlier when I first made the massive leap from the gentle, rural life of Grindleford, a small village in the beautiful Derbyshire Peak District, to the throbbing hustle and bustle, the lights and theatres and restaurants and huge buildings of a seemingly never-ending metropolis, I was a very different person. My dress was conservative at best, and I remember attending my initial first-year lectures meticulously attired in suit and tie. However, this phase didn't last long and as I became more

2

and more involved in London's cultural offerings, firstly the suit was put out to pasture, next the shirt and tie were hung in a transparent plastic bag for future use and, subsequently, all were replaced by the then more typical student attire of jeans and a polo-neck sweater.

Once rescued from the clutches of compliance and conservatism, everything had changed; my outlook, my interests, my beliefs and my attire. I had culturally metamorphosed. Now, I was attending third-year lectures having a distinctly hippy-like appearance, sporting flower-patched jeans, sandals with hidden reindeer-bells to announce my entrance, and deliberately uncombed, shoulder-length hair, epitomising open rebellion and carefree non-conformity. (Fortunately, my obliging mother understood my need to be fashionable and had reluctantly agreed to sew the necessary flowery patches onto the jeans of her dear, first-born son).

Then there was Liz, a blonde, very attractive 20-year-old who was training to be a nurse at the nearby University College Hospital. We had been dating for over a year, our relationship was deepening and we were spending more and more time together. Together with my best friend, Chip, and his girlfriend, Lyn, who was also training as a nurse, we made the perfect foursome.

Chip, a fellow northerner from Dewsbury, was also in the middle of his final year doing Physics at UCL and so we had plenty of common ground to stimulate our conversations. Apart from the more serious, in-depth analyses of quantum mechanics and special relativity, one of our favourite conversation topics over late-night coffee and toast was the inequalities inherent in the UK's north-south divide at the time. The majority of our year group at UCL had clearly benefited from the nation's most qualified teachers and all the fantastic facilities offered by the fancy private schools, largely located in the southern part of the country. With our relatively modest state-school backgrounds from the wild northern wilderness, we therefore felt it necessary to do our best to redress the balance, whenever possible, by 'taking the mick'. Summoning our very best imitations of 'posh', southern accents, we would practice and refine suitable comments and phrases for use in conversation in the breaks between the next day's lectures, mercilessly mimicking those students whose accents we found most supercilious and irritating.

Chip, whose political leanings were distinctly left of centre, would, as usual, be attired in his long black worker's coat, along with a cloth cap to complete the left-wing image. While he tried to locate a suitable victim, I focused on summoning the necessary attention of the rest of the group by walking around to stimulate the invisible reindeer-bells in my sandals. After deliberately initiating the conversation with the adversary for whom we currently had the greatest disdain, we would tease, mock and provoke the wretched individual to such a degree that, within seconds, an inter-regional, verbal war had broken out between the northerners and the southerners. Fortunately, it never turned violent, and we could return to the next lecture satisfied and content in the knowledge that we had done our civic duty in trying to *properly* educate our southern friends.

It is interesting that Chip and myself, with our similar inclinations towards Physics and Mathematics, our outlandish attire, and our distinct leaning towards rebellion and non-conformity, chose to date two girls, both of whom were doing the same Nursing course and who both had a neat, delicately feminine appearance and gentle, pleasant personalities. Maybe it's the rule of opposites attracting, but some intangible force definitely bonded each pair together. Whenever we all found the necessary funds, we would be enjoying dances, parties, shows, concerts, eating out, or just happily walking by the Thames or around the streets of London. This was what life was supposed to be like!

By the middle of our final year, Chip and Lyn were making fairly frequent trips to Lyn's home in Wales, affording him the opportunity to introduce himself to her parents and to get to know her family. So it came as no surprise when, after one such trip, Chip broke the exciting news that he and Lyn were now engaged and planning to get married in the summer. To my delight, I was asked to be Best Man at the ceremony, whilst Liz was to be Chief Bridesmaid. Predictably, this announcement also served to bring my own relationship with Liz into sharper focus. We had been dating for over a year now and I knew that my feelings towards her were becoming increasingly strong. As far as I was aware, she felt the same way about me, so it occurred to me that perhaps I ought to follow Chip's lead and proceed with a marriage proposal of my own.

This, I realised, would be a massive step, with life-changing consequences. By then, my own mother and father had already been happily married for over 20 years and clearly viewed marriage as a lifelong commitment, 'not to be taken lightly or in haste'.

But was I ready?

Was my love for Liz sufficient to ask her to be my wife 'until death do us part'?

Was Liz's love for me deep enough to agree to be my wife, 'forsaking all else...'?

Where would we live and work?

If, by the mid-1970's, we had children, what if Liz wanted to become a full-time, stay-at-home mum? Would I have sufficient income to support the family?

Questions, more questions and even more questions. Unfortunately, however, I didn't have all the positive answers I craved. The only certainty was that I was now pretty sure I was in love.

One thing that concerned me was that, in spite of repeated invitations, Liz had always declined my requests for her to visit my home in rural Derbyshire to meet my parents and brother and sisters. Furthermore, in spite of my repeated hints that I would love to meet her parents and family in Scotland, she had never once offered me the opportunity. Was she afraid that my hippy-like attire and my long hair and my reindeer-bell sandals would all be a bit too way out and off-putting? At this rather precarious moment in my life, I felt unsure, doubtful, afraid even. What should my next step be?

I decided to consult Chip. He was, after all, my closest friend and he must have gone through similar questions in his mind before he and Lyn got engaged. Surely, if anyone had the answers I needed, it would be Chip. So after lectures the next day, we met in my room at Commonwealth Hall to analyse all my questions and, as good Physicists are supposed to do, consider all the possible answers. After this lengthy but encouraging conversation, I felt that a huge load had been lifted from my back. Furthermore, to help clarify the situation, Chip had agreed to talk to Lyn who, in turn, would talk to Liz. So far, so good.

However, the more I thought about it, the more I felt the need to go further, to take the initiative and do something absolutely transformational. It was time to create a new image.

So, without saying a word to anyone, I went out the next day after lectures, heading down Tottenham Court Road and then onto Oxford Street where I searched out the most exclusive-looking barber's salon I could find. If I was going to do this, it might as well be done properly! Quite clearly, I hadn't had a hair-cut for a considerable time so the look on the young barber's face was really a picture when I told him that I wanted almost all the unkempt, shoulder length hair to be *completely* removed and be replaced with an elegant, but still manly, *short* cut. This was no small task so, remaining as docile and motionless as I could, I kept my eyes closed as far as possible while he first hacked, then trimmed, shampooed and rinsed, dried and reshaped. Then, while patting down the hair above my ears, to my surprise, he actually cooed like a dove, before finally announcing that his masterpiece was complete. In total trepidation on seeing the vast pile of hair on the floor around the barber's chair, I eventually summoned the courage to look up.

For a moment, I wondered if someone else had inadvertently stepped between me and the mirror. Wow! What a transformation! I had re-metamorphosed back to respectability! Moreover, it actually didn't look too bad at all.

Surprisingly, my first thought was that my father, who had always intensely disliked my long hair, would be really pleased. And then, with some measure of fear and trembling, I began to wonder if Liz would like it, conscious of the fact that there was now no going back unless I was to wear a wig, which I definitely would not have dreamt of doing. The die was cast!

After profusely thanking the one responsible for my shearing, I immediately realised that now the excess hair was gone, I might as well complete the transformation and get some new clothes. Fortunately, Oxford street provided an almost infinite choice, and within half an hour (having never been a person who revelled in lengthy shopping expeditions), I had some new, very smart, maroon-coloured, velvet, flared trousers, a ribbed, close-fitting, green sweater (in those days, I was not only strong and muscular but also fit and slim) and a pair of really classy, dark red, Spanish shoes (to match the trousers). In truth, I was now a totally new creation; smart, neat, refined, handsome and dashing! I couldn't wait to see Liz later that evening.

* * *

7

As I walked back into Commonwealth Hall, I was stopped by the porter at the reception desk. In those days, Commonwealth Hall only had male residents and any visitors had to explain their visit to the porter before being allowed admission. Although I had lived in the hall for the last eight months and knew this gentleman well, he clearly didn't have a clue who I was and was inclined to believe I had somehow come into possession of an ID card belonging to one of the Hall residents (which, ironically, couldn't have been closer to the truth!). Eventually, after a lengthy discussion, I finally persuaded him of my true identity, then skipped up to my room on the fourth floor. Liz was due to come by in about an hour.

When I heard the knock on the door and called "Come in", I was standing Pharaoh-like in all my glory in the middle of the room as she entered. There was a brief gasp, followed by a scream and then a huge hug as she tried to take in the apparition before her, before asking "Deniz, is that *really* you?"

"I think so…."

"You look so different, I hardly recognised you."

"Hopefully, it's an improvement?" I pleaded.

"Yes, you look fantastic! Not just the hair, but new trousers and sweater and shoes…" and she gave me a little pinch on my arm just to make sure I wasn't an apparition.

I felt my head begin to spin and I suddenly thought 'you're not going to find a better time than this to ask her', and so, without any further thought, I plucked up all the courage I could muster and blurted out

"Liz, will you marry me?"

Now, it has to be said that, in following the logical order of things, I had failed miserably. I hadn't purchased an engagement ring so it was a bit pointless going down on one knee, and I had no idea if Chip had already voiced my intentions to Lyn, nor whether Lyn had had chance to talk

8

about it with Liz. It was all very spur of the moment, probably not terribly romantic, and clearly for Liz, totally unexpected. But I was on cloud nine and sometimes I didn't fully engage my brain before considering my actions.

Predictably, and devastatingly, my request was politely declined, which rather took the wind out of my sails and left me wondering what to say next. To her credit, Liz, summoning all her nursing skills, sat me down on the bed in case I should faint and, for the next couple of hours, very gently and quietly explained why. She was more than happy with our friendship, which she really valued and certainly didn't want to end, but at this point in her life, a permanent, marriage relationship was out of the question as her nursing career was only just beginning and so the timing just wasn't right. I listened mute, dumbfounded, and rejected, trying for the life of me to recall some distant quotation, probably from one of Shakespeare's plays that I'd studied while at secondary school, about 'love spurned…', but couldn't remember the rest of it. This was the first time in my life that I had ever had one of my amorous advances brushed aside, and it hurt. Really hurt.

* * *

Chip dropped by later that evening, having heard via Lyn what had happened between Liz and myself. I remember being sat, still in all my finery, hunched over with my elbows on the work-desk, and my arms and hands taking the weight of my head. Chip did his very best to try and console me, offering gentle reassurances that Liz would almost certainly rethink her decision and change her mind, as our relationship deepened. But, somehow, I knew in my heart that this was not to be and, one by one, big tears started to run down my face, making a little pool on the desk below.

"She doesn't love me," I whispered, with each word accompanied by an even bigger tear-drop.

Chip put his arm around my shoulder.

"No… don't say *that*, Deniz. Maybe you just caught her off-guard."

"But she said so herself - she just doesn't love me."

I couldn't remember ever having cried since I was a toddler, so crying while sharing my innermost thoughts and deepest emotions with someone else was a new and embarrassing experience. And, back then, a broken-hearted man shedding tears just wasn't the social norm. Fortunately, it was just me and my closest friend, trying to make some sort of sense out of it all. But what can remedy a situation where love is freely given, yet not returned?

Chip reminded me of all the great times Liz and I had had together, the sharing, the fun, the laughter, the carefree abandon of young lovers. But we were not really 'young lovers', were we? The fundamental reality was that we were, at best, one young lover and a good friend. And I tried my best to smile as the tears ran over my upper lip and into my mouth. I just don't know how I would have coped without a friend like Chip. However, try as I might, I couldn't see any light at the end of the tunnel.

* * *

A good Physicist, confronted with unanticipated results from his experiment, sometimes has to back-track and try a new hypothesis or even a completely new approach. So, in view of the distinctly negative outcome of my marriage proposal, it was now clearly expedient to revisit my plans for the future.

At the start of my final year at university, I had seen an advert in one of the tube stations for an organisation called Voluntary Service Overseas (VSO) and fired up with altruistic enthusiasm for spending a year doing something

10

worthwhile with my life, had immediately submitted an application covering the period of my 'year out', which would commence that summer. However, I had heard nothing further and so assumed the application had been unsuccessful. Now I had to consider other alternatives.

One obvious option was to continue at UCL and do a postgrad degree in Physics. Dr Smith, one of my third-year tutors, had already made it clear that, should I be interested in pursuing this with himself as my supervisor in the Atomic Physics department, he would be very happy to receive my application. But although this was a very flattering invitation and despite having no reluctance about staying on at UCL, I somehow didn't feel that it was an academic area which had sufficient appeal for me to commit to doing a doctoral degree in, spanning at least a further three years.

I wanted to commit my life and energy to something which would really be of benefit to humanity; something inspiring, exciting and possibly ground-breaking - perhaps in an area such as Medical Physics. And so, I did the necessary investigating, and within a relatively short space of time, discovered an ideal postgrad course offered by nearby St Bartholomew's Hospital Medical College (Bart's). The course was under the leadership of one Professor Joseph Rotblat and involved attending lectures with medical students during the first two years, followed by research into one's chosen area of Medical Physics for the remainder of the course. Although I was a bit apprehensive about the amount of memory work which the two years of clinical lectures would involve, I was confident I could cope, and so submitted a neatly handwritten application to the Professor and left the outcome to fate.

Meanwhile, Liz and I continued to go out together and the four of us carried on, I suppose, much as before, enjoying all London had to offer. She and I were still the best of friends but clearly not 'young lovers', planning a future together. Our relationship had now settled into a phase of being more than platonic, while not really describable as passionate. I was probably still hoping that my impossible dream might morph into reality, even though that would have been a most unlikely outcome.

A few weeks later, I received a lovely reply from Professor Rotblat inviting me to come and see him to discuss areas of Medical Physics that I might be interested in pursuing. However, it rather caught me off guard as it appeared to imply I had already been accepted onto the course. Added to which, there was the issue of funding which, for me, was critical as my parents were already trying to cope financially with my brother now being in his first year at university, and my twin sisters likely to follow in about a year's time.

The actual 'interview' must have been lifted out of a fairy-tale; I was immediately put at ease by the Professor who welcomed me almost like an old friend and who was relaxed, congenial and clearly delighted with my enthusiasm. So much so that he offered me, right there and then, a place on the course as well as a full Science Research Council (SRC) grant for its entire duration!

To say that I was elated would be a gross understatement. At least my future potential career was now right on track, even if my love life had swerved off the road! In fact, now that I would be remaining in London for at least another three years, there might still be hope for me and Liz.

The rest of the academic year simply raced by. Finals came and went and, as I had suspected, I did nowhere near as well as I ought to have done. Life at both UCL and at Commonwealth Hall were coming to an end and the longest summer holiday of my entire life was already planned out in detail; Chip and Lyn's wedding, followed by two months' playing with Trevor on the 'Patricia', a beautiful new Swedish cruiser ferrying passengers and their cars to and fro between Southampton and Bilbao in Northern Spain; followed by a month cruising round the Mediterranean on a Greek cruise ship playing drums in a 4-piece dance band; prior to returning to Bart's to commence my postgrad studies.

Then, out of the blue, and amidst all the hectic post-finals activities including the Leavers' Party at Commonwealth Hall and the end-of-year Leavers' Ball at UCL, came the phone call that would change my life.

* * *

The VSO secretary had contacted me to come in urgently to the London Office. Further information would be available when I got there. To be honest, by then, I had totally forgotten about my original liaison with VSO nearly a year ago, so their unexpected phone call was a bit disconcerting and mildly irritating now that I had my immediate future all mapped out. However, I reasoned that it would only be polite to respond and at least find out what they wanted.

Since it was so close to the end of term, I was just about broke and so I decided not to take the tube but to walk to the VSO office which was about a mile away. It was a bright, sunny afternoon and I couldn't help thinking how much I was in need of a really nice trip to the seaside. All the dull, grey, London buildings would never be a substitute for a good dose of sun, sea and sand. On arrival, I was immediately ushered into the inner sanctuary to be greeted by three or four well-dressed gentlemen seated on the other side of a large, well-polished desk. I felt a little intimidated and rather glad that I now had a neat haircut and proper shoes instead of the reindeer-bell sandals.

However, I was soon put at ease and the 'suits' immediately got to the reason for the meeting.

"Thank you, Mr Önaç, for coming in so quickly,"

said a posh voice, mis-pronouncing my surname, as people always did,

"but a last-minute opportunity has arisen which we thought might interest you. One of our schools has informed us that, due to a late resignation, it is in desperate need of a Physics teacher for September. Unfortunately, you are the only person on our books, so to speak, who is not already assigned and who fits the bill."

I smiled slightly, mildly irritated by the use of the word 'unfortunately'.

"And where might this school be?"

"Well, I'm sure you would like it, if you enjoy sun, sea and sand - it's located in Jamaica, in the Caribbean."

My jaw must have dropped two inches and for a moment I was dumbfounded. My good friend and Venture Scout Leader, Ian, had recently returned from a trip to Tobago and I immediately recalled how envious I had been when he had related the details of his trip, including descriptions of the beautiful turquoise sea, lit up by dawn-to-dusk sunshine, the amazing coral reefs and the pristine white-sand beaches.

"The Caribbean?" I repeated.

"Yes, between England and America, but closer to America."

The lesson in basic geography having been duly terminated, the 'suit' continued,

"So, in a nutshell, we need to know if you are still interested. By the way, we generally ask volunteers to commit to a two-year stint."

My mind was now working at a furious rate. If only I hadn't already committed to the postgrad course at Bart's! But what an amazing opportunity - could any sort of compromise be reached? I stalled for a few seconds then suddenly had a brainwave. A two-year delay in starting my proposed course would probably not be feasible but the Professor might just agree to a one-year postponement.

"How long can you give me to decide?"

"I think we'd need a firm decision by tomorrow. With the request coming in so late, there's a lot to get organised in a relatively short time. I presume you do have a passport?"

I nodded in the affirmative. Fortunately, I'd had to acquire one for the first time I had played with Trevor on the cruise ships.

And with that, the conversation finished abruptly and the 'suit' in the middle held out his hand to indicate the meeting was concluded.

On leaving the VSO building, I rushed straight to Bart's and, realising rather late that I hadn't called in advance, let alone had an appointment, I breathlessly asked the receptionist in the medical research department if there was any possibility of seeing Professor Rotblat and, yes, it *was* an emergency.

I am sure that some people in this world would have rubbed my nose in the dirt when I put forward my proposal for a one-year deferment of my postgrad course to the Professor, having only just been offered a place on the course *and* an SRC grant to go with it, but the Professor, bless his heart, was not that type of person. He listened carefully and thoughtfully to all the reasons I had thought up in my hasty journey across London as to why my proposed one-year stint for VSO would be of infinite benefit to both myself as well as to his department, then stretched, smiled and simply said,

"OK. I understand. I'll save the place and the grant until you return."

I thanked him profusely and felt like giving him a huge hug but was a bit too shy to follow my instincts. Now I only had to convince the 'suits' at VSO to let me go for one year instead of the usual two.

Next day I reached the VSO office bright and early and was once again ushered into the inner sanctuary where the 'suits' were already assembled. Without further ado, I went headlong into my pre-rehearsed speech, detailing all the reasons why, although I would love to go for one year, it was not feasible to stay for two. They were not happy for a variety of reasons, but because of the lateness of the request from the school, time was on my side and they knew they would be most unlikely to find anyone else at this late stage.

> "Very well, Mr Önaç, (again mis-pronounced), it looks like we shall just have to compromise on this occasion and allow a one-year commitment."

I am sure that, had I believed in God at the time, I would have jumped up, waved my arms in the air and done a holy jig! As it was, I was so taken aback at how everything had worked out so perfectly that I just sat there, stunned, until the 'suit' in the middle held out his hand and informed me that all the details of the school, the travel, my accommodation, etc, etc, would be forthcoming in the next few days, and that was that!

Somehow, in the excitement of it all, I had forgotten all about Liz and further attempts at nurturing our relationship. I had also put on a back burner my intention of pursuing a postgrad course in Medical Physics. After a summer of weddings and playing drums, I was about to embark on the most amazing opportunity; something one only read about in books; the experience of a lifetime.

In just over three months, I was about to begin 'The Big Adventure'.

Chapter 2: Arrival

The summer of 1971 disappeared in the blink of an eye. So many things had to be crammed into such a short space of time.

Chip and Lyn's wedding in Wales was a grand affair and when they looked at each other, even the blind would have seen the depth of their shared love. I trust I did justice to my closest friend in my Best Man's speech trying, as best I could, to combine humour and a selection of jokes with various anecdotes from our fun times together at UCL, while not forgetting some genuinely heart-felt accolades. Liz looked spectacular in her bridesmaid's dress and, as we walked up the aisle of the church together, I couldn't help thinking how nice it would have been had *we* been the bride and groom. But that was never going to happen and when I left the wedding reception, it was the last time I would ever see or hear from her. I don't know if she ever married anyone else, and the memories of all the happy times we had spent together gradually faded.

Almost as soon as I arrived back at our family home in the picturesque Derbyshire village of Grindleford, I was off again to Southampton where I met up with Trevor for our two-month stint together, entertaining the passengers travelling back and forth between England and Spain on the cruise ship, 'Patricia'. That was also the last time I would ever see or play drums with Trevor, who ended up abandoning his PhD in Chemistry at UCL for a full-time career in music, working at the BBC. His decision came as no surprise.

And then, towards the end of the summer, having completed my work on the 'Patricia', I headed back home again to get things together for my next cruise around the Mediterranean. The month-long trip started in Italy, so the cruise company provided me with an all-expenses-paid flight from the UK to Italy - my first time ever in an aeroplane! I shall never forget that amazing experience, having taken off in typically dull English weather, but then, after rising above an enchanting, fluffy layer of white cloud, emerging into blue sky and beautiful sunshine. It was all completely magical except for the instant of touch-down when I literally thought my heart was going to stop.

The relatively old Greek cruiser was not a match for the 'Patricia', but the cruise itinerary couldn't have been better, with stop-offs at various cities along the Italian coast, then a couple of stops in Greece and tours of several of the beautiful Greek islands, then Istanbul in Turkey and finally Dubrovnik in what was then Yugoslavia. Best of all, I was allowed to eat in the same restaurants as all the passengers and got free passes for all the on-shore visits, so it was just like getting my own cruise holiday with all the perks, in return for playing in the band, which I enjoyed doing anyway! But before I knew it, we were back in Italy, ready for my return flight home to London and the train journey back to Derbyshire. I then had just a couple of days to get everything ready for 'The Big Adventure'.

I should probably say here that my parents, in general, and my father, in particular, were not overly enthusiastic about the idea of my gap year in the Caribbean. For 'Baba', as he was lovingly known by his four children, the most important thing was for me to complete all my university studies and secure a well-paying job at the end of it. However, this mindset had to be seen in the context of him having had his own studies interrupted by World War II and his future employment hindered as a result. For Mum, it was more a case of fear of losing my physical and emotional presence. Maybe her mother's sixth sense alerted her to the possibility of my future going in a rather different direction than even I could have imagined at the time.

Fortunately, I had been pretty well briefed by VSO as to what I needed to take with me and what it was wise to leave behind. One large suitcase and a small piece of hand luggage seemed a bit on the sparse side for a year-long trip, but I was advised that I would have my meals provided by my new hosts, have facilities for getting clothes washed, and that heavy coats and woollens would not be needed. So I focused mainly on appropriate things to wear for the teaching job, not forgetting a couple of pairs of drumsticks, just in case.

Before I knew it, I was at the train station, hugging Baba goodbye and trying to comfort Mum, who was in a flood of tears as I boarded the train to leave for London.

"Don't forget to write",
she sobbed, as I jostled the rather large, old-fashioned suitcase and a small leather briefcase containing all my documents through the narrow carriage doors. But despite the macho way in which I endeavoured to belittle my departure, I couldn't deny a tear or two in my own eyes as the train pulled away from Chesterfield station.

In a matter of hours, I was at Heathrow airport, boarding the huge plane for Kingston, Jamaica, and having finally got settled, both physically in my seat and emotionally in my heart, I gave a huge sigh of relief. Perhaps the summer had been just a bit *too* hectic! Having never before been away from home for longer than a couple of months, it was a big step, even for an adventurous 21-year-old and, as yet, having only a vague idea of what I had let myself in for, I was now experiencing an unusual degree of trepidation along with the excitement. However, there was no turning back now and so, as the plane thundered down the runway, I finally waved goodbye to England, home and family, friends, university, and my unfortunate love-life, to face the new chapter ahead.

Back in 1971, trans-Atlantic flights were pretty glamorous affairs. The seats were nice and wide, with ample leg-room and the food provided was tasty and filling. There had been virtually no security check at the airport, quite unlike what one is subjected to today, with all the indignity of having to remove one's belt and shoes and glasses and small change, and I had breezed through passport control just as a rock-star might expect. I was still fairly weary from all the rushing around of the last few days so, once I had completed my meal on the aeroplane, I was ready for a short nap and, before I knew it, was happily in dream-land.

The jolt of landing provided a somewhat rude awakening from all my fantasies, and the sudden glare of bright sunshine flooding through the plane window made me squint and shield my eyes. We had just landed in Kingston, the capital of Jamaica - I had slept the whole way!

Once the plane had come to a stop and I had retrieved my leather briefcase from the rack above me and stretched to get my blood flowing, I emerged, still somewhat dazed from our carrier, into the intense light and furnace-like heat of the Jamaican summer. At the top of the steps, I paused, spellbound by my first view of the deep blue sea which seemed to completely surround the airport. And raising my gaze to the distant horizon, I got my first glimpse of the majestic Blue Mountains, silently rebuking myself for having been asleep as the plane had been making its descent, and for missing what must have been a spectacular panorama. By the time I had descended the metal steps from the plane to the runway, I was already drenched with sweat. Then as we ambled across the tarmac, my ear caught the sound of unfamiliar, but very catchy, reggae music drifting across the airport and I immediately warmed to my new home. I had finally arrived in the Caribbean!

Having passed through customs and retrieved my old leather suitcase, I was met in the airport by an elderly rep from the British High Commission, which rather made me feel as if I were a diplomat or an ambassador.

"Welcome to Jamaica, Mr Önaç".

I mentally logged the fact that British people were clearly incapable of pronouncing even the simplest of foreign names and words.

"Good flight?"

"Yes, thanks. The food sent me to sleep though."

He smiled. A pleasant enough guy, I thought, even if he *was* a bit 'posh'.

On exiting the terminal building, we almost had to force a passageway through the hordes of would-be luggage-carriers, all of whom were shouting in what I later learnt was Jamaican *patois*, but what, at the time, seemed to me to be a strange foreign language with just the occasional, recognizable word. While some were dressed in attire familiar to me, others had long plaited hair and trousers cut off just below the knee, reminding me of pirates I had seen in films such as 'Treasure Island'. Their kind offers were politely declined by the suited rep, as we headed for a waiting, chauffeur-driven, black car. The driver, wearing a floral, short-sleeved shirt and whose accent clearly identified him as Jamaican, also greeted me with a cheery,

"Welcome to Jamaica!",

and off we drove along the fairly straight road on the narrow strip of land joining the airport to the mainland. Along the road, we passed numerous stalls, full of tempting-looking fruits such as oranges and pineapples, and rather large, green objects which I later learned were actually coconuts, quite unlike the somewhat smaller, hard-shelled versions which I had seen at fairgrounds back in England. At one point, and without any warning whatsoever, the car in front stopped suddenly to buy something from one of the roadside stalls. Our driver, unable to pass because of the oncoming traffic, slammed on his brakes and cursed the driver of the car, although, having never heard Jamaican swear-words before, I wasn't sure exactly what he said or meant.

While we waited to pass, I lapped up more reggae music blaring out from a small radio perched on a shelf at the rear of the stall and I marvelled at the skill and dexterity of the vendor, happily swaying to the music, who proceeded to cut off the outer green husk of one of the coconuts before lopping off one end, all at arm's length with a long, very vicious looking, sword-like weapon which I was duly informed by our driver was a 'cutlass'. I made a hasty mental note not to get into any argument with a cutlass-carrying local as I quite liked my two arms and needed them for drumming.

However, the man from the car in front who had presumably bought the coconut, seemed to be thoroughly enjoying drinking the juice inside and I was just about to ask if I could buy one for myself. But, before I had chance, we were off again, past numerous other stalls, each with its own deafening sound system and dodging out of the way of a huge truck whose warning blast on the horn would literally have woken the dead! Then we followed the rather bumpy, winding, narrower road through the eastern side of Kingston, which I thought to myself was probably not the best advert for visitors to the island, until we finally reached a rather more serene, manicured and landscaped area of the city, with some high-rise buildings and smartly dressed people actually walking on roadside pavements, made for the purpose. This, I was informed, was New Kingston, an area 'inhabited by more educated people' working in banks, insurance companies and the like. Definitely not the sort of 'posh' area a northerner like myself would be likely to frequent!

Finally, we reached our destination, also a rather 'posh'-looking building where I would apparently be spending a few days during our orientation briefings. I thanked our driver profusely for his obvious driving skills in adverse circumstances and for getting us to our destination in one piece, and he laughed and shook my hand, before saying in Jamaican patois,

"Noh problem, man. If yuh need anyting, jus check me out." [*That's ok. If you need anything, just let me know.*]

* * *

The orientation week was useful in a variety of ways. Firstly, all twenty or so VSO volunteers starting that year were present so, still recovering from a broken heart, I relished the opportunity of meeting nice girls who were from all over the British Isles. I made sure to ask for the contact details of the ones whom I found particularly attractive or interesting, and note them down in case I should forget. Maybe there was hope for my love-life after all!

Secondly, I got to meet Andy, who would be teaching Biology at the same school where I would be working, and with whom I soon became firm friends. He had also just completed his undergraduate degree at uni and now wanted to take a couple of years' break from studies and to broaden his horizons and experiences before he settled down back in England.

And then we had various visiting speakers, mostly Jamaican, to acquaint us with the island's history (including slavery and emancipation), culture (including art and music), local language (Jamaican *patois*), the education system (since most of us were going to work as teachers in local schools), religion (and all its ramifications for the society), politics (which we were strongly advised to steer well clear of), social mores and expectations (which we needed to be aware of to help us 'fit in'), etc, etc, etc. By the end of the week I felt that my head was almost bursting with information but, in fairness to the organisers, the sessions did cover a lot of very useful ground.

There were also a number of cocktail receptions, replete with exquisite Jamaican dishes, most of which tasted fantastic but were completely unknown to me, and delicious fruity drinks, spiced up with a dash of Jamaican rum. There was no question in my mind that I would ever go hungry or thirsty in Jamaica. I suppose these informal get-togethers were organised specifically for helping us all get acquainted, although some of the young male volunteers were clearly unaccustomed to the potency of the alcoholic content in the drinks and therefore were unable to take full advantage of the opportunity.

The overall head of VSO in Jamaica, in my opinion a perfect 'toff', was a tall, elderly, typical private-school-educated gentleman, who was dressed in very formal attire. He had probably served in the military, and spoke perfect Queen's English with a very 'posh' accent, epitomising the kind of southerner whom Chip and myself used to mock and provoke during our time at UCL. Whilst not being in the slightest unpleasant, he was obviously regarded by most of our VSO group as a bit of a relic of a bygone era; an era of masters and servants, gentry and serfs, educated and ignorant. And in the evenings, when free to socialise with each other, we would mercilessly attempt to imitate his mannerisms and speech and 'posh' accent.

We rapidly came to the facetious conclusion that the creature he most closely resembled was a tusked, spectacled walrus, and this image was immortalised in an amazing cartoon drawn by one of our group. This drawing was later used to front each edition of the Jamaican VSO newspaper which myself and Andy founded, duplicated and posted out to all the volunteers each month. Entitled 'The Walrus', it was made up of a collection of humorous articles submitted by the literarily capable amongst us. It was the perfect way to keep in touch, share our individual experiences, organise get-togethers and advertise anything which any volunteer contributor thought might be of interest to the wider group.

In no time at all, our orientation was concluded and we had crammed enough knowledge into our heads to fill an encyclopaedia. Finally, having been fussed over like we were still little children, who needed to be duly armed with emergency phone numbers should we be unfortunate enough to be robbed - or die - we packed our belongings, thanked our hosts for their unforgettable food and drink, and said our goodbyes to each other. In military-like precision we were then chauffeured off in multiple different directions to our new homes across the island, with Andy and myself travelling in the same vehicle, and being two of the last to leave. I was finally on my way to Frankfield, a small town in the parish of Clarendon, located almost exactly in the centre of the island.

'Frankfield High School (Comprehensive)', known locally as 'Compre', was, in fact, the first comprehensive secondary school in Jamaica and the brainchild of the then Education Minister, the Hon Edwin Allen. The school had been kind enough to hire a small minibus to travel to Kingston and ferry the two of us to our destination. This was driven by Hector, a rather large, almost bald Jamaican driver whose really friendly demeanour immediately made us feel welcome and who was more than willing to answer our many questions. After installing our cases in the back, we climbed into the second row of seats and, with a jerk and a sharp grating sound of clashing gears, we were off.

"Di clutch bad," he informed us, "but noh fret man, we wi get deh." [*The clutch is bad, but don't worry, we'll get there.*]

We barraged poor Hector with question after question:
How far did we have to travel?
How long would the journey take?

Were we both living at the same home?
What was our landlady like?
Was the school close to where we would be living?
How many students were at the school?
Why did trucks always blow their horns going round corners?
Was the weather always as hot as this?
Were the potholes in the road ever filled in?
Did local teachers teach in Jamaican *patois*?
What was that reggae song that was playing everywhere?

After travelling westwards along the relatively straight, fast two-lane highway from Kingston, through Spanish Town and Old Harbour to May Pen, we turned north towards Chapelton and Frankfield. Here the road was narrower, more winding, more potholed, and more bumpy. Houses and roadside stalls had gradually given way to dense green foliage, often covered with a canopy of bright red or yellow flowers. The flat, sugar-cane-growing plains on either side of the highway had now been replaced by steep-sided hills and valleys, also covered with dense undergrowth, quite unlike the grass-covered hills of Derbyshire that I was used to. And after passing through the small town of Chapelton we were now travelling along the side of the winding Rio Minho River, a small gentle trickle now, but which could become a huge torrent in the wet season, according to Hector. Just after Trout Hall with its lush orange groves (except, to our surprise, all the oranges were green!), we crossed the railway line, also making its way to Frankfield where it terminated. After passing through Commissary, we were almost there.

The approach to Frankfield, past one of the several local churches on the left, with the Primary School a short distance behind it, was not particularly striking and the Rio Minho, now someway further back from the road, had disappeared from view. When the minibus pulled over to the side of the road, we didn't realise at first that the house in front of which we had stopped was, in fact, to be our home for the foreseeable future. Mrs Daphne Broomfield (Miss Daph) and Mr Thomas Broomfield (Mas' Tom), relaxing in the warm early-evening air on some wrought iron chairs in the shade of the veranda, both stood up to greet us and Mas' Tom opened the wrought iron gate to let us into the yard. Despite his massive weight, Hector was clearly very agile and strong, and with Andy's suitcase in one hand and mine in the other, he followed us through the gate, dropped the cases by the front door and with a cheery wave, bid Mr and Mrs Broomfield,

"Good evening",

before wishing Andy and myself a very happy time at 'Compre' and shooting off into the rapidly fading light.

I was very conscious of there being no period of twilight to talk of in Jamaica; one minute it was light and almost the next minute it was dark. With the veranda light already switched on, however, even a cursory glance could discern that this was a very well-built 'block, concrete and steel-reinforced single-storey house which we later learnt had been built by Mas' Tom himself while he was still in the haulage business, prior to his recent retirement. Although I never asked him, I put Mas' Tom at about seventy, with Miss Daph a few years younger. Both were on the pale side of brown, both spectacled and both somewhat overweight. Miss Daph was wearing an attractive ankle-length dress, while Mas' Tom was in casual trousers with a leather belt to hold them in place on his rounded, protruding tummy, and a smart, short-sleeved shirt. After we had introduced ourselves and been warmly welcomed, Mas' Tom motioned for us to sit down on the remaining veranda chairs while Miss Daph prepared and brought us what must have been the most welcome, wonderful, iced drink I had had for a long time. Jamaican hospitality was surely tops!

After exchanging a few pleasantries, she suggested that if we were hungry, our evening meal was ready and waiting, and motioned for us to go inside. The house was spotlessly clean, with colourful, shiny tiles underfoot, creamy white painted ceilings above, various religious paintings on the walls, and at the end of the very large entrance room, a polished wooden table, partially covered with a white tablecloth, already set out with numerous covered dishes and shiny steel cutlery set for two people. Miss Daph helpfully explained that the big dish contained 'rice and peas', while a smaller dish contained 'curried goat'. Then there were various other dishes of 'avocado pear', 'fried breadfruit', and 'boiled yam'. I hadn't a clue what all these delicious-smelling foods were, but by this time I was so ravenous that I didn't pause to enquire further. The food was absolutely fantastic, and both Andy and myself thanked our lucky stars that we were being accommodated at the home of someone with such exceptional culinary skills. If all our meals were going to be like this, I would have to watch my waistline!

After we had finished our evening meal, topped off with hot, Blue Mountain coffee, sweetened with condensed milk, Mas' Tom showed us to our rooms, helped bring in our cases and, after apologising for Andy and myself having to share the same toilet and shower, located between our two bedrooms, he and Miss Daph retired to their bedroom on the other side of the house and left us to our own devices. There was so much to talk about, but we were both exhausted from the heat and the journey and so decided to forgo unpacking and any further conversation until we had rested. I grabbed a quick, deliciously cool shower and literally flopped down onto my bed. Before I knew it, I was sleeping like a log and when I awoke, it was already the afternoon of the following day.

Chapter 3: New Perspectives

We had arrived on Thursday evening and school was due to reopen after the long summer holiday on Monday. That gave us three days to settle in, although since it was already Friday afternoon, more like two-and-a-half days. I knocked on Andy's bedroom door to see if he was awake yet and could see from the advanced state of his unpacking that he had clearly got up some time ago.

"Good sleep?",
I asked, having slept like a log myself.

"Yes, great, apart from an invisible mosquito buzzing around my face all night in search of a suitable meal, and the majestic music of a friendly cockerel crowing at the unearthly hour of 6 o'clock, followed by the inane braying of a really sociable donkey on its way to the local market...yes, *brilliant* thanks!"

I was tempted to tease Andy by asking if he had minored in melodrama at uni. At that time, I had rather fixed notions about the relative rigour of different university courses and had made up my mind that undergrad Biology was much less demanding than Physics - so naturally, Andy must have had lots of spare time to do other things. Trying hard not to laugh and resisting the temptation to wave a red flag at an angry bull, I commiserated on his unfortunate loss of sleep and asked instead,

"Do you fancy a walk into the town?"
"Yep, but Miss Daph has had breakfast on the table for about five hours now and I wouldn't want her to think that we normally didn't have a morning meal."
"O.K., I'm ready whenever you are."

* * *

Our mid-afternoon 'breakfast' was again very carefully covered with a white tablecloth, presumably to prevent any flies getting there first. Everything had been meticulously placed in the centre of the table, each different item in its own, white, porcelain dish. A thermos flask of hot coffee was at one end, along with a small jug of sweet, condensed milk. I later learned that cow's milk was rarely used because it tended to go off in the heat, before it got to a refrigerator. Being a person with a very sweet tooth, who would normally shovel copious amounts of sugar into a cup of coffee, the 'sweet milk' suited me down to the ground, once I had become accustomed to its slightly different taste.

For our first breakfast feast, we had 'fried liver', cooked in a gorgeous brown gravy, with boiled 'green bananas'. This was yet another novelty, since I had simply assumed during my past 21 years that all bananas were yellow, just as I had assumed all oranges were orange. Then there were delicious 'fried Johnny-cakes' and 'avocado pear' (clearly an entirely different species to sweet, English pear). But my favourite was the 'fried plantain'; slices of the inside of a yellow and black, banana-shaped fruit, but larger and sweeter than the bananas I knew, and fried in hot oil until the outside became slightly crisp. I could have eaten a basket full!

Miss Daph was at the back of the house washing some clothes in the outdoor sink. The back yard was a somewhat dismal affair, with no lawn or paving to speak of and generally not at all up to the same immaculate standard as the house itself. Most of the yard's surface consisted of packed-down soil which, I thought, would become an absolute quagmire when it rained heavily. The general philosophy of the property appeared to be 'don't worry about what isn't in public view'. However, the rear of the property was no concern of mine, so having expressed our heart-felt thanks for such a wonderful breakfast, at which she glanced at the wall-clock just inside the back door of the kitchen and 'tutted', we informed Miss Daph that we were going to walk into the town and have a look round. She insisted on providing us with a protective sheath of advice about what to do and what to avoid and gently reminded us that dinner would be ready at 6 o'clock, which made me feel slightly guilty about having been the cause of such a late breakfast.

To get to the centre of the town, we had to cross the bridge over the Rio Minho. This was an ancient steel structure, badly in need of some paint and consisting of a labyrinth of huge girders above and below the single-width roadway. It must have been situated at least 20 feet above the trickle of water below it, since this was the 'dry season'. As we were to witness, however, during the 'rainy season', this little trickle could become a dangerous, raging torrent in a matter of hours. With no separate pedestrian walkway as such, it was wise to time one's crossing to coincide with the absence of any vehicle, particularly large trucks.

Immediately after crossing the bridge and passing Chang's General Supplies Store, which lived up to its name by selling almost everything under the sun, from groceries and haberdashery to clothing and agricultural supplies, we were there in the 'town centre'.

This encircled the sign-posted junction of three roads, the first to Nine Turns, the second to Spaulding and the third, back along the way we had just walked, to Chapelton. On the right was the new clothing store, with large glass windows enclosing mannequins adorned with all the latest fashions, above which was the brand new cinema. Together with the supermarket a little way up the road to Nine Turns, and the bakery and gas-station just past the cinema on the Spaulding road, these fairly recent innovations were all the creations of local businessman, 'big dog' Campbell, who lived in a huge multi-storey house opposite the railway station.

I couldn't help thinking that, for a so-called, little 'backwater' town in the heart of rural Clarendon, Frankfield was something of an anomaly; olde-worlde in many ways, but endowed with many of the mod-cons that we had observed in the 'posh' New Kingston district of the capital. The town was an anachronistic confluence of different eras: produce-laden donkeys tied to a rail just below the fancy indoor cinema; an air-conditioned supermarket next to a bamboo shack selling trinkets; a curious mix of vehicles of all ages and models from both sides of the Atlantic; buses filled with passengers travelling from one town to another, but piled to twice their normal height with bags and suitcases precariously balanced on the roof-rack; and a melting pot of people of all colours and races, some barefoot and wearing no shirt, mingling with others attired in gentleman-like, three-piece suits such as the wandering Jehovah's Witnesses.

Looking round at all the different groups of people, I was reminded of the Jamaican motto, '*Out of many, one people*', which we had been introduced to during our week's initiation ceremony. In spite of all the differences between Jamaica's Frankfield and my birthplace in England's Peak District in Derbyshire, I felt strangely at home here. And, somehow, I had every confidence that I would fit in.

We continued for a few yards along the Spaulding road, past the fancy clothing store and on to the bakery, just before the gas (petrol) station. The smell emanating from inside the bakery was too enticing to resist, even though we had only just finished gorging ourselves on our mid-afternoon 'breakfast'. After eating a couple of hot, freshly baked patties, washed down with an ice-cold ginger beer, I concluded that anyone who had never eaten a genuine Jamaican patty was really missing a treat. The real treat that we were about to experience, however, was that around one of the gnarled wooden tables inside the dimly lit bakery was a group of aggressively and vehemently loud men, engrossed in some sort of game, which I soon learned was Jamaican dominoes. Andy and myself went over to the table and watched, fascinated, as the game progressed.

"Yuh play, sah?" [*Do you know how to play, sir?*] asked one of the domino players, looking straight at me, while simultaneously smacking his remaining four dominoes with all his might and bravado onto the table, one after another, in quick succession.

"SIX LOVE!", he bellowed as he 'bowed out' and sealed his victory, pushing back his seat and swivelling round so that any onlookers would be in no doubt as to who had won the game.

"What a man play BAD, man!" [*What a guy! He plays amazingly well!*] sighed one of the losing team.

"Soh wah ya-ah seh? Unu wahn play?" [*So, how about it, would you like to play?*]

"White man kyahn play dominoes!" [*White people don't know how to play dominoes!*]

"Wah ya-ah seh? Mek dem learn di game, man! Move over! [*How about it? Give them the chance to learn how to play! Move aside so they can sit down!*]

Much to our subsequent regret and embarrassment, Andy and myself were clearly obliged to sit down in the two seats now vacated by the unfortunate losers. This was to be our initiation ceremony into the game of Jamaican dominoes, and I nervously noticed that the watching crowd had already swelled in number.

"Losers buy di nex round." [*Whoever loses the game will buy the next round of drinks.*]
We nodded our agreement, although in the circumstances, it appeared that we had little choice.

"White-man gainst black-man. But noh fret, man; we jus a match di domino-dem, fi give unu a chance". [*White team against Black team. But don't worry, we will simply 'match' the numbers on the dominoes - to at least give you a chance of winning.*]

Anyone not born or raised in the Caribbean must initially find it very difficult to understand the significance of a game of Jamaican dominoes. Given my mathematical background, I just could not figure out at first why such an apparently 'simple' game could involve so much passion and fervour, and so much elation at winning a coveted 'six-love'. But as I was soon to learn, not only is the game anything but 'simple', but it also serves to bridge the social spectrum and enables people from all walks of life to come together for an enjoyable couple of hours whenever and wherever a set of dominoes is available and any sort of makeshift table can be found. And woe betide anyone who should imagine that social status is any guarantee of winning!

In all fairness, our opposing duo did everything possible to make our very first domino experience as useful a learning experience as possible. Analysing the game as a good Physicist should, I gradually realised that by observing and remembering how both your partner, as well as your opponents, play, you can, *in theory*, have a pretty accurate knowledge of who has which 'cards' [dominoes] after two or three rounds. With this knowledge, one no longer merely has to 'match', but can play more strategically with one's partner, with a greater likelihood of winning. But, alas, we were obviously like non-swimmers thrown in the deep end. And game after game, our two opponents out-manoeuvred us and left us holding unplayable, 'dead cards' and, most infuriatingly of all, they actually knew precisely which dominoes we had left in our hands, almost as if they were holding our 'cards' themselves.

Utterly humiliated at our own 'six-love' experience, we duly bought the next round of drinks and, like dogs slinking away with their tails between their legs, vacated our seats for more learned colleagues to continue in our stead.

"Good game, man. Til nex time…"

I decided there and then that if there was one thing I was going to master during my short sojourn in Jamaica, it was the game of (partner) dominoes. As a Physicist, who ought to be able to use his knowledge to devise winning strategies for numerical games, I was determined not to be humiliated like this in future.

With this new resolution firmly rooted in my mind, we endeavoured to make as inconspicuous an exit as possible from the bakery, deciding on the spur of the moment to continue along the Spaulding road towards where we had been told the secondary school was located. Leaving the gas-station behind us, we passed the woefully ramshackle (yet amazingly productive) wood-yard belonging to the local preacher, Baba Miller, on the right, and then the short path leading down the river bank from the road to the stepping stones across the river. This benign, almost fairy-tale-like crossing clearly posed no problem with the river as low as it was at present, but I wondered out loud how the residents of the Cow Pen community on the other side managed to get across, whenever the river was in flood.

Although the road had been surfaced with tarmac at some time in the distant past, it was now embellished with some massive potholes which most vehicles, travelling at the usual, apparently statutory high speed, tried to avoid, by meandering along and swerving from one side to the other as necessary. There was no pavement of any sort for pedestrians, so the relative narrowness of the road made the journey somewhat precarious, particularly if the vehicle was a large truck. For the next 200 yards, the road had been carved out of a shale cliff on the left, while being bounded on the right by 'Long Wall', a solid, vertical structure rising about 15 to 20 feet above the river bed, which sustained the integrity of the road and hopefully

35

protected it from being washed away when the river flooded. In the event of meeting a large vehicle on this stretch, one was therefore left with little choice but to either hug the cliff on the left, or Long Wall on the right, hoping and praying that one would not lose a limb in the process. With my Physicist's hat on, I tried to estimate the chances of not breaking a leg or worse, should it be necessary to jump over the wall down to the river below to avoid the alternative of being crushed against either the cliff or the wall.

Not familiar with the volume of traffic on this road, we decided to traverse this death-defying section with a certain degree of urgency, while marvelling at the many, small, unaccompanied children we passed on the way, who seemed relatively unconcerned. Then, wiping the sweat from our foreheads, we returned to a more dignified pace up a gentle rise where the road widened, and along by the Teachers' Flats on the left, just before the school's playing field. Long before reaching the flats, however, we heard the thump and shrill of a massive, old-style juke-box, blasting out the very popular current reggae hit, 'Cherry, oh Baby'. I paused and stood listening to the song, fascinated by the reggae rhythm.

"I've got to learn that beat."
I said with utter conviction.
"At least the teachers living in the flats won't need to buy a radio or record player",
Andy countered, while shielding his near-side ear and grimacing at the sheer volume of the music. We had no idea who lived in the flats and whether they were local or ex-pat teachers, so decided against calling in to introduce ourselves and, instead, continued along the road by the playing field until we came to the school gate. This rather grand, tubular steel structure, with the unmistakeable sign, 'Frankfield High School (Comprehensive)' overhead, was opposite yet another bar, this one without music. Not that it

36

needed its own sound system anyway, as the music from the bar we had just passed, opposite the Teachers' Flats, was still very clearly audible, echoing back and forth off the steep sides of the Frankfield valley.

I wondered to myself why the word 'Comprehensive' was in brackets and later learned that this was at the behest of NW Clarendon's local politician and then Minister of Education, the Hon Edwin Allen, who lived just a short distance further along the main road. His vision, through this flagship school, was to create a new type of secondary school throughout Jamaica, free for all local children, (in contrast to nearly all the fee-paying, secondary schools and colleges at that time) and which would provide the children with a wide-ranging curriculum to give them all the opportunities they needed to succeed in life. Perhaps the brackets were indicative of the fact that it was still an experimental educational idea and a novelty in Jamaica, which was yet to be fully accepted.

The large school gate was wide open, so we decided it was as good a time as any to go and investigate our new work-place, which was more or less invisible from the main road. While walking up the rather steep, tarred drive-way leading to the school, we paused to look back down over the play-field and towards Frankfield town, now largely hidden by masses of rich, green foliage. The field was clearly used as a multi-purpose sports area and had already been marked out with white lines for a full-size football pitch, with a very attractive 400-yard, six-lane running track around the perimeter.

I couldn't help thinking how beautiful it all looked, and how similar the terrain was to the Derbyshire hills and valleys where I had grown up. I couldn't wait to get out hiking and exploring my new environment.

On rounding the sharp bend at the top of the school drive, the first block to come into view was the single-storey Technical Wing with its various offerings including metalwork, woodwork and welding. These areas were all heavily fortified with thick steel bars in lieu of louvres in the windows, and even thicker steel rods welded in a metal framework to serve as the heavily pad-locked, grilled doors.

"No need for a visit to Fort Knox!",
quipped Andy as we peered through the bars into the dark interior. But I felt slightly miffed that, only a short time ago, I had unfortunately *not* been afforded similar learning opportunities during my seven years at the Lady Manners Grammar School in Derbyshire, where the only practical subject on offer at the time was woodwork, and even that was only available for the more academic pupils via an after-school club every Friday evening.

We were now in the centre of the school on the upper level of the car park, facing the lower level which we later learned was referred to as 'the quadrangle'. In almost every direction were classroom blocks, two or three stories high, together with a large, open-sided auditorium extending right along one side of the upper parking area. We were just about to search for the Science Laboratories when we noticed an elderly, white haired man with wrinkled, light brown skin and wearing army-green, baggy trousers and an orange, cotton shirt, open down the front, walking across from the car park entrance towards us. Although his face may have looked quite benign and friendly, the stark reality was that in his right hand he was carrying a two-foot long and very dangerous-looking 'cutlass'.

We had no idea who he was or what his intentions towards us were, so, defenceless as we were, and sensing the very real possibility of an imminent armed robbery, my brain immediately engaged emergency gear and I looked round quickly to see which direction might offer the best chance of escape. Although I had never excelled in sprint races, I reckoned we had a decent chance against the old man if it came to making a get-away run, except that we were more or less encircled by buildings and he was approaching from the school driveway entrance to the car park, which would probably have been our best exit. I felt my heart beating overtime and, for an instant, had visions of a newspaper headline detailing the dismembering and demise of a young, expatriate British Physics Teacher before he had even had chance to start work when, to our immense relief, the old man's face broke into a huge grin as he said,

"Soh yuh is di new teacher-dem from Englahn. Yuh come early sah. Mi nah expec nobady tideh." [*So, you're the new teachers from England are you? You've arrived early. I wasn't expecting anybody today.*]

And that was our introduction to school watchman, Mas' John, one of the friendliest and nicest people you could ever hope to meet. When I asked him about the reason for the machete, he laughed and simply said,

"All sort a tief can come yah, an ah mus ready fi dem". [*All sorts of thieves can get in here, and I have to be ready for them.*]

I felt distinctly glad that I had not been mistaken for a thief and that I could breathe normally again. We asked Mas' John about the whereabouts of the Science Labs, but he was in no hurry and said with another grin,

"Nuh fret, man! Ah will show yuh evryting". [*Don't worry guys! I'll show you everything.*]

And so, for the next hour we had a detailed, guided tour of every part of the school, with Mas' John using his massive bunch of keys to gain entry to any locked areas, and offering explanations and answers to our many questions. The school certainly offered a wide variety of subject areas, including technical, commercial, scientific, vocational, artistic, and many more.

The only problem was that, alas, there was no *separate* Physics Lab! Although Andy and myself had bonded well so far, I could foresee the myriad logistical problems and practical difficulties that would ensue from having to share the same lab for both Biology and Physics. But fortunately, it would only be for a year, so I would just have to manage.

Chapter 4: New Experiences

Everything seemed to be falling nicely into place and, before we knew it, Monday had arrived. For once, we were both up early; in fact, almost at the crack of dawn. It was a beautiful day with a clear blue sky, just a touch of breeze, and duly orchestrated with every sort of bird and animal sounds imaginable, all heralding the start of a new school year.

After another of Miss Daph's amazing breakfasts, and dressed in smart trousers with polished leather shoes, colourful short-sleeved, cotton shirts, and matching ties, we set off for our very first day at 'Compre'. Having been duly advised on our induction course about the merits of using scented deodorant to help cope in the heat, we must have smelt like two lavender trees! I was the proud bearer of a brand new, brown leather briefcase containing a couple of current British GCE Physics textbooks, a writing pad and a variety of pens, while Andy carried just a small pouch, too small to hold any books at all.

The road towards the town centre was already bustling with children; hundreds of them, all heading in the same direction. Many pupils were arriving early since it was first day of school, and the boys were dressed, spic and span, in smart, long khaki trousers and shirts, while the girls were a sight to behold in their light blue tunics with immaculately pressed, pleated skirts, short-sleeved, white blouses, and the most beautifully braided hair patterns or neatly bowed, light-blue hair-ribbons. As for the children's shoes, they literally gleamed in the sunshine, making our own, carefully polished footwear appear relatively dull in comparison. I wondered to myself what ungodly hour they must have had to get up at, in order to do their ironing, braid their hair, get dressed, polish their shoes and eat breakfast to all be ready for school, which started at 8 o'clock. What I didn't know at the time was that many of these same children had, in fact, already travelled several miles *on foot* that morning from a multitude of surrounding villages in order to reach Frankfield, and that when school finished, they would then have to retrace the same journey to get home. Amazingly, this daily feat of endurance did not diminish their unquenchable thirst for knowledge or their wonderful enthusiasm for learning.

As we had expected, we were immediately the centre of attention;

"Good morning Sir"

(spoken with the most wonderful smile).

"Are you from England, Sir?"

(spoken so respectfully and in perfect Queen's English).

"How do you like Jamaica?"

"Which church do you go to?"

(and with typical agnostic evasion, I simply smiled in answer).

"Are you going to be teaching at the High School?"

(with such an appealing look, I wouldn't have wanted to teach anywhere else, even if I had had the choice).

"Can you tell me your name, Sir?"

"What will you be teaching?",

one little girl asked, smiling and innocently stroking my arm, presumably fascinated by my fair skin colour.

"Why is your skin so fair?"

(Andy's blond, wavy hair evoked lots of similar comments).

"Are you married, Sir?"

(with that delightful directness that is characteristic of Jamaican children).

"Have you got any children?"…

On and on went the questions, with the crowd of mainly 11- to 12-year old children now gathered around us getting bigger and bigger with each step as we reached the town centre.

I observed that nearly all of these local children from the Frankfield area were either black or of much darker brown complexion than Miss Daph and Mas' Tom. And it was a completely new experience for me to be mingling with and talking to so many people of different colour to my own, and caught me a little off-guard. Having grown up in the 1950s and 60s in rural Derbyshire with only white boys as my schoolmates and friends, and with my general propensity for blonde girlfriends as a teenager, I began to realise that my definitions of what characteristics and features made a boy 'good-looking' and what hair-styles and facial appearance rendered a girl 'beautiful', might now need some considerable revision. It suddenly dawned on me that I was now even thinking of all these boys and girls with their dark skin, appealing inquisitiveness, amazing politeness, beautifully braided hair and cute smiles, almost as if they were members of my very own family - what a cultural awakening!

So with this very positive introduction to our future students, we carried on past the bakery, the gas station, Baba Miller's wood-yard and the path down to the stepping stones and, with so many children filing past Long Wall where the road narrowed, vehicles actually had to come to a standstill until the majority had passed. The reggae music was still blaring out from the juke box at the entrance to the bar opposite the Teachers' Flats and, as someone who had never really learned to dance (from a young age, I was usually on stage helping provide the music rather than dancing to it), I smiled with a certain degree of envy at the way the children swayed so naturally to the music as they passed the juke box. When we started up the school drive, the now enlarged stream of children looked like a blue, white and khaki ribbon laid out on the long driveway, as far as the eye could see.

By the time we reached the top of the school drive, a little breathless and starting to feel a bit sticky from the heat, we were glad to be rescued by one of the senior members of staff who gave us a most courteous welcome, shooed away the flock of children, and escorted us into the nearby staffroom. As members of the Science team who apparently used one of their own prep-labs as their general meeting room, we hadn't been allocated our own desks in the staffroom and so spent the better part of the next hour standing around, shaking hands and getting introduced to everyone, all of whose names I almost immediately forgot.

The young staff of about 80 men and women was a truly amazing mixture of colours, races, nationalities, and specialities - almost a mini United Nations! Most were in their twenties or thirties, with about two thirds Jamaican and the remainder from England, Canada, America, South Africa, Guyana, Honduras and elsewhere. Andy and myself were the only two VSO volunteers which, in a strange way, worked to our advantage as we soon learned that the pay and conditions of most of the 'ex-pat' teachers was significantly better than that of the local Jamaican teachers, which caused a certain amount of resentment. Since VSO teachers only got a small monthly allowance, this placed us at the base of the salary pyramid and earned us a certain degree of respect for our perceived philanthropy. At least no one could accuse us of being in the Caribbean just for the money!

Then it was introduction time in the auditorium, with all the teaching staff crammed onto the platform, while the 1,600 or so students stood in neat rows, youngest at the front and oldest at the back, rather like sardines in a tin. As each teacher's name and teaching speciality was called out by the Principal, Mr Latty, there was a respectful murmur of approval and excitement from the student body as the individual stood and identified themselves. As expected, my name gave the usual problem with pronunciation and I vowed I would have to devise some method of overcoming this ongoing issue.

The assembly concluded with a short prayer followed by the first verse of the Jamaican National Anthem. Having previously only heard the British National Anthem, this was a totally new experience; the lyrics had a rather different emphasis, and it was very noticeable how its wonderfully inspiring words and catchy melody were sung proudly and lustily by all the students:

Eternal Father bless our land,
Guard us with Thy mighty hand,
Keep us free from evil powers,
Be our light through countless hours.
To our leaders, Great Defender,
Grant true wisdom from above,
Justice, Truth be ours forever,
Jamaica, land we love.
Jamaica, Jamaica, Jamaica land we love.

After the whole-school assembly, it was form-time. I had been assigned a Grade 10 GCE group of girls and boys aged between 15 and 17 and our form-room was on the second floor, directly above the staffroom. As I ought to have expected from 17-year old teenagers (but as a new teacher straight out of university and with no formal teacher training, had yet to learn), these older students were determined to put their young Form-Teacher through his paces, unlike the blissfully innocent youngsters with whom we walked up to school a couple of hours before. After all, I was barely five years their senior.

The boys, in particular, were full of tricks designed to test whether or not I could outwit them, jokes to determine the limits of my sense of humour, and strength-tests to see who was really the strongest physically. They had some unforgettable 'pet-names' such as 'Peter Rabbit', 'Lanzo', 'Fern', 'Spenga' and 'Burri-warrah'.

45

On the other hand, by this stage in their transition from cute little girls to beautiful young women, the girls were generally more mature and demure, and tended to keep out of the way when the boys got a bit too rough. Instead, they tended to cluster together in small groups, chattering and watching and making occasional wry comments.

Fortunately, I survived my 'initiation' period and we all soon became good friends.

The first day of school was deliberately shortened to allow for a full staff meeting after lunch when, much to their delight, the students were all sent home early. The meeting was held in the library which was designed for about 40 students rather than 80 adults, so everyone was tightly crushed together with barely room to breathe. After persuading the staff to reintroduce themselves, Mr Latty pressed on with his rather lengthy agenda. It was stiflingly hot so I had to try the best I could to stay awake. Much of the discussion related to the previous year's exam results and the possible reasons why a given subject had fared particularly well or badly. The Science Department seemed to have done quite well, so at least that sounded hopeful. Staff in other areas blamed their relative lack of success on a variety of causes, ranging from lack of equipment to the lower-than-average academic calibre of the students who had taken their subject.

The forceful manner in which any discontent was voiced by staff members rather caught me off guard. Although they were talking to their Principal, some of the established teachers such as 'Sugar' and Lucy, in particular, did not mince words, and appeared quite unfazed by voicing their strong opinions in front of a rather large audience. Mr Latty, in complete contrast, was polite and surprisingly gentle in his responses to criticism directed at any deficiencies in school equipment or provisions. And I was particularly impressed by how diplomatically and calmly he dealt with criticisms of a more personal nature, endeavouring to pour oil on any wounds and foster a sense of unity amongst the staff. As a new teacher, I felt it was not yet time for me to be voicing any strong opinions of my own and so I just sat and listened.

In the week that followed, I had ample opportunity to better acquaint myself with the boys and girls in my tutor group. Their inquisitiveness knew no bounds and they wanted to know every detail of my life, my interests, my beliefs and my values;

"Would I marry a black woman?"
"Did I believe in God?"
"Why didn't I go to church?"
"Did I like reggae music?"
"Would I have someone black as my best friend?"
"Did I believe in corporal punishment?"
"Did I always tell the truth?"
"Did I believe in sex before marriage?"

Wow! These questions were tricky to answer and all of them quite profound. But their more serious questions were all asked politely and with deep interest in my answers as they, no doubt, endeavoured to formulate their own values and beliefs. One belief, however, they all held in common: education was a means to an end, a route to a better job and higher salary. So along with all the good-natured frivolity and jokes and horse-play, there was an underlying seriousness about their purpose for being at 'Compre'. They were there to succeed.

It's amazing how perceptive teenagers are. In less than a day, most of them had sussed out the good teachers from the bad, the staff who really cared and those who didn't. And if you knew your subject and were willing to go the extra mile to help your students succeed, they would do everything in their power to make your life enjoyable. I suppose I must have fared pretty well on their comparison

47

charts because, apart from the very occasional, cheeky retort from a student, any behavioural problems in my classes were fortunately absolutely minimal. I was enjoying my new job and since I was the only Physics teacher in the entire school, teaching a subject which was only offered to the most academically able students, I was also fortunate to get students who, for the most part, really had an interest in what they were learning.

Sharing the lab with Biology was definitely an issue, however, which I urgently needed to resolve, so at the first opportunity, I sought a meeting to discuss the matter with Mr Latty.

The Principal's Office was small, cramped and dimly lit by a rather tiny window, with just a solitary, framed picture of Mr Latty in full academic regalia on the opposite wall, partially obscured by a tall filing cabinet. The solitary desk behind which Mr Latty resided was piled high with numerous stacks of file-folders and official-looking papers which almost hid him from sight. He was of light brown complexion and smartly dressed in full suit and tie (in spite of the absence of any sort of cooling mechanism in the office except an old fan which creaked and groaned as it rotated on its base). I couldn't help wondering how he managed to look so cool and collected in the summer heat. After standing and vigorously shaking my hand, he smiled, looked me straight in the eye and speaking slowly and thoughtfully, gave me a very touching, heart-felt welcome. His glasses somehow made him a rather benign figure, and his unusual accent, which to my ears sounded slightly 'posh', made me wonder if he had studied in England at some point. His unpretentious civility and the genuine warmth of his greeting immediately made me feel at home.

After various preliminaries through which he endeavoured to make sure I had settled in well at the school and had everything I needed, we got down to business as I laid out all my pre-rehearsed arguments about the difficulties of sharing a lab with Biology and the urgent need for a separate Physics Lab. Mr Latty listened politely and patiently without interrupting, occasionally nodding in agreement before repositioning his glasses in the correct position on his nose. Quietly and carefully, he then explained how the problem had arisen. The long and short of it was that some areas of the school were still incomplete and that the current two-storey Science block had, in fact, been designed to have a Physics Lab as its third storey. More importantly, however, he pledged that now that he had a new, full-time, resident Physics Teacher, he would do everything in his power to see that the building would be completed and equipped as soon as possible. I couldn't really have asked for more, so I thanked him profusely and after another handshake I left him with his piles of folders and papers and returned to the Science block.

Being without a Physics Lab was one thing but the problem was compounded by an almost complete absence of any meaningful Physics equipment to use for practical work or for demonstrations. I therefore had to improvise with whatever was to hand and spent many a long evening using old reels of resistance wire to make resistors of known value for simple electricity experiments; cutting up steel, copper and brass rods, (begged from the Metalwork Department) to use in heat-conduction experiments; and constructing small, wooden light-boxes and lovingly sawn and sand-papered sheets of plywood (scrounged from the Woodwork Department) to serve as pin-boards for light experiments. In fact, I was doing so much begging that I was getting quite a reputation as a perpetual scrounger with the teachers in the workshops who, although always civil and generous in their donations to the impoverished Physics Department, also had limited supplies to use with their own students.

* * *

One day, out of the blue, Mr Latty appeared in the doorway of the shared Biology and Physics Lab, right in the middle of one of my electricity practicals with the Grade 10 students, mainly from my own tutor group.

"Good afternoon, Mr Önaç (incorrectly pronounced). May I join your class for a minute to see if these clever boys and girls can explain any Physics to their Principal?"

He came in anyway, without affording me the chance to respond, and proceeded to walk around in all his grandeur, interrogating the students as to what they were doing and why, looking through their Physics notebooks (which, fortunately, I had thoroughly marked and annotated the previous evening), and occasionally giving a satisfied smile when a student gave a particularly convincing response to one of his questions. I hovered around in the background trying to listen in to the dialogue and hoping with more than a little apprehension that my students would not let me down.

I need not have worried; this was my first taste of the amazing way that Jamaican youngsters could hold their own in such a situation, exuding confidence and intelligence, no matter whom they were addressing. To their credit, my tutees proceeded perfectly diligently with their experiments, behaving immaculately and answering Mr Latty's questions with complete confidence and respectfulness. I felt so relieved and thankful, I could have burst with pride. After his brief scrutiny of the practical session ended, Mr Latty beckoned me to join him at the side of the room.

"I have some good news for you, Mr Önaç",
(still incorrectly pronounced)

"The building work on your new Physics Lab will commence at the start of the Christmas holidays. We're hoping it will be ready for use early next term."

I'm sure I almost fainted and I think I would have given Mr Latty a huge hug, had he not been the Principal.

"You've made my day, Mr Latty! I can't believe we're getting the new lab so soon." (and then, rather cheekily) "You must know people in the right places." Mr Latty gave a wry smile.

"Yes, I thought you would be pleased. But I won't hold you up now as I can see you and your students are busy. They seem to be understanding what they are doing and enjoying your lesson. Have a very good afternoon."

And with that, he was gone.

For a brief moment, while one of the boys assumed the temporary role of lookout in the doorway until Mr Latty was at a safe distance across the car park, all was calm and quiet... then the class erupted, with all the students crowding around me, excited and shouting;

"How did we do, Sir?"

"You didn't think we'd let you down, did you Sir?"

"Was Mr Latty pleased with us?"

"What did he say to you, Sir?"

"Are we getting a new Physics Lab?"

I made a vain attempt to quieten things down, but realised I was fighting a losing battle. The horse had already bolted.

"You were absolutely... (I paused for dramatic effect) ...*fantastic!*"

I could almost see the glow on their dark faces. And, perhaps, for the first time in my teaching career, I began to understand the value of *praising children for doing well*. When the cheering finally subsided,

"Now show me how quick you are at packing everything away. It's almost time for the bell."

That night, I decided to take time out from book-marking and lesson preparation and making apparatus; instead, Andy and myself went out to one of the nearby bars for a cold beer and to enjoy the incessant reggae music blasting from the statutory juke-box.

It was an appropriate time to celebrate.

Chapter 5: Outside the Classroom

I think Mr Latty must have liked me; he always greeted me so enthusiastically, talked to me as if I were an old friend and, as we gradually got to know each other better, even tried to pronounce my name correctly! The more I got to know him, the more I liked him and respected his unswerving devotion to ensuring the success of 'his' school.

About halfway through the first term, he called me into his office one day and, after the usual salutations, he took up a file folder that was on his desk, opened it and said,

"It says here on your *curriculum vitae* that, during your teenage years, you were very involved with Scouting and even achieved your Queen's Scout Award. Have you ever given any thought to giving something back to the organisation?"

I was caught a little off-guard and, wondering where this conversation was leading, I shook my head.

"We used to have a very strong Scout group here at the school, but it disintegrated when the teacher who was leading it left for greener pastures. I was wondering if you might consider re-forming the group?"

"Well..." I responded with a certain degree of hesitation, "it sounds like an interesting idea but, as far as I am aware, the school has no equipment for essential Scouting activities like camping and outdoor cooking and orienteering, and no store-room where all the equipment could be safely kept."

"How about if I provided you with some initial funding to get you started and a temporary store-room until we can construct something more permanent? I was thinking you could also get some fund-raising going by putting on film-shows using our school projector. I know you will get a very positive response from the boys (there was no such thing as Girl Scouts in Jamaica in those days) and it would give you the chance to make a valuable contribution to our extra-curricular programme."

Mr Latty beamed at me and that was the end of the conversation.

I was well aware that the Phys Ed teachers, in particular, put in many after-school hours training the football and athletics teams and that various members of staff were involved in other after-school activities such as music and drama, but then, I was already a frequent evening visitor to the school for my equipment-making expeditions so I felt I was already making a significant extra-curricular contribution. Mr Latty, however, had already assumed my positive response to his request and so it appeared I didn't have a lot of choice; I'd just have to now fit Scouting into my already busy life. I tried to wear a positive expression on my face as we shook hands, and as Mr Latty thanked me profusely for everything I was doing at the school.

And so, the new 17th Clarendon Scout Troop was born, with me as the guinea-pig Scout Master.

* * *

Mr Latty's intuitive assessment of the likely response from the boys was, of course, spot on, and within a couple of weeks I had so many boys signed up that I had to split the group up into four patrols and choose Patrol Leaders and 'Seconds'. Not surprisingly, most of the eight leaders ended up coming from my own tutor group as I knew these boys better and had seen on a daily basis how they responded in a variety of situations. Peter Rabbit, Harry,

54

Dave and Kenneth, ably assisted by Moraise, Ikey, Charlie and Jeffrey, took to their new leadership roles with pride and excitement, revealing within the next couple of weeks that I had definitely made the right choices.

When I acquainted the troop with the age-old Scouting tradition that the Scout Master was generally referred to as 'Skip', I had unwittingly and quite unintentionally determined the pet-name by which I would henceforth be known in Jamaica. It didn't take long for the Scouts that I taught to start calling me 'Skip' in lessons, then other students caught on and, before I knew it, even Mr Latty was addressing me as 'Skip' in whole-school assemblies. After that, many parents of students and other local people simply assumed that it was my actual name, referring to me as 'Mr Skip'. It was clearly pointless to keep correcting this rather touching error and so I just accepted that my new Jamaican name was to be 'Skip'. Moreover, use of this new name, once and for all, eliminated the problem of the mispronunciation of my actual surname, so who was I to complain!

As the Scout group flourished, we needed to include more adventurous and exciting activities, and camping expeditions far from the Compre sports field were an obvious choice, especially since many of the boys had never really travelled much further away from the school than the Clarendon parish border. This proposed activity, however, required tents, cooking equipment, ropes, lanterns, games and much more. To raise the necessary funds would need a massive investment of time and energy on my part. While considering all the implications of this added commitment to my already hectic schedule, however, I had a flash of inspiration - which I henceforth referred to as 'The Contract'. I would spearhead the fundraising and all the associated organisation but, in return, the Scouts would have to do two things, both of which I knew, instinctively, would facilitate my further integration into the Jamaican culture.

Firstly, the Scouts would be required to become my personal mentors in my attempts to learn and speak the Jamaican *patois*. Secondly, they would be required to teach me how to play dominoes.

Needless to say, my initial attempts to speak the local dialect were an unending source of hilarity and amusement, but I was determined not to give up, even when my efforts were greeted with unconcealed derision by some of my adult Jamaican friends. Little by little, I accumulated the vocabulary, assimilated the various idiomatic expressions and familiarised myself with the contextual and social implications of speaking in the local dialect. The role-reversal (I was now the student and my students were now the teachers) was an outstandingly successful venture and I owe my 'mentors' a great debt of gratitude.

I shall never forget the first time I was able to use my new language skills to my advantage. One bright Saturday morning, I had decided to pay a visit to Mandeville, a nearby town in the parish of Manchester. All of a sudden, while I was walking down the main street in the town, I was verbally attacked for no reason at all (except, perhaps, my skin colour?) by a dark-skinned man with long braided hair and a rainbow-coloured waistband, whom I assumed was a 'rasta-man'. Determined not to be intimidated, I stood my ground, looked him straight in the eye and responded in my very best *patois* by asking him what his problem was. The man looked totally aghast for an instant, but then, to my amazement and delight, he immediately apologised and offered his hand as a sign of brotherhood and friendship. My efforts with the *patois* were starting to bear fruit!

The domino lessons were also a hit from the word 'go' and my young teachers set about their task with great gusto, explaining the various nuances of the game, including the importance of remembering how and what each person has played, the crucial bond between a player and his partner, and the art of 'bowing out' to conclude a game in style. I soon realised that playing dominoes was almost like an art-form and that although being good at Maths might be helpful, it was by no means an assurance of success. A photographic memory, quick thinking, interpreting correctly the playing style of one's partner, and the ability to keep one's cool under intense psychological pressure (people took the game very seriously!) were just as crucial, if not more so. Most important for me, however, was that attaining a good working knowledge of the game enabled me to integrate more easily into the wider society. With the help and encouragement of my young teachers, particularly Harry, Spenga and Clifton, I was slowly being 'Jamaicanised'!

Fund raising for camping equipment, in particular, was also a novel learning experience. I discovered that reel-to-reel copies of fairly recent 'hit' movies were available to rent (at minimal cost) from a small distribution centre in Kingston, so every couple of weeks I would make the return journey from Frankfield to Kingston by public minibus to collect whatever was available at the time.

If you have never travelled on a Jamaican minibus, especially in a rural area, you have missed the unforgettable opportunity of witnessing the dark art of cramming as many as 30 people into a space designed for only 15 - like stunts to gain a place in the Guinness Book of Records by squeezing as many people as possible into a telephone box. The drivers race with each other in their attempt to get to each pick-up point first, squealing their tyres round every bend in the road, while continuously blowing their abnormally loud air-horns lest an equally mad, unseen vehicle should be approaching from the opposite direction. Should you be fortunate enough to get a proper seat, you will find that your knees frequently become a substitute seat for whoever might topple over in your direction whenever the minibus negotiates a sharp bend;

"Beg pardon, sah." [*Pardon me, sir.*]

"Tek time, driva!" [*Take your time, driver!*]

"Mi sure wi a goh dead in a dis ole brock!" [*I'm sure we're going to die in this old broken-down wreck!*]

"Lawd God, ha mercy pahn wi." [*Lord God, have mercy upon us.*]

"Di road dem bad, eh sah?" [*The condition of the roads is awful, isn't it?*]

The wretched passengers, all soaked in sweat, gasping for air, and unable to find any comfortable position in which to stand or sit, continue grumbling and cursing for the entire duration of the journey. But before you know it, you have reached your destination. Fortunately, I didn't have to make these journeys too often as I considered my life to be too precious for that, even for the sake of fund-raising for 17th Clarendon Scout Troop!

It didn't take me long to realise that action films attracted the largest student audiences, so films like 'The Magnificent Seven' and 'Bullet' were ideal for fundraising. While the more artistic Scouts were assigned the task of designing and making posters and fliers, and those with salesman skills were given the responsibility of promoting the film-show and organising the pre-sale of tickets, it was the job of the Patrol Leaders and Seconds to get the double classroom above the staffroom ready for *The Tuesday After-School Film-Show*.

This involved opening the dividing screen, moving all the desks to the sides, setting the chairs in rows, closing the metal window louvres to get the necessary blackout, and standing guard at the two entrances with suitable collection jars to collect entrance money from those who had not already bought tickets. How the unfortunate members of staff situated in the staffroom vertically below managed to think, let alone do any marking, I shall never know, because the noise generated by the process of setting up and getting ready, was horrendous! But much to my surprise, not a single member of staff ever complained. Meanwhile, I focussed on the technical part as chief projectionist, setting up the projector and screen with all the cabling to the wall sockets and speakers.

If setting up was noisy, however, the response of the student audience to the more exciting parts of the film was unbelievable! Accustomed, as I was, to the virtual silence during film showings at cinemas back in England, it was difficult, if not impossible, to believe the volume of the shouting and screaming from the 200 or more students packed like sardines into the double room, which occurred during something like a car-chase scene. The students totally immersed themselves in the on-screen action and it was as if they were literally taking part in what was happening, while verbally expressing their excitement and enthusiasm. By the end of the film-show, everyone was drenched with sweat, hoarse with shouting and screaming, but happy as ever! Fortunately, many of the Scouts lived relatively close to the school and we never had a problem of anyone slinking away afterwards rather than helping to clear up the room, so it was always left neat and tidy for the next day's lessons.

Mr Latty's fund-raising suggestion certainly bore fruit, and within a few short weeks, we had raised enough money to buy four large, green patrol tents from Scout HQ in Kingston, four sets of 'billy-pots' for cooking from local hardware stores, and four essential sets of 'bone' dominoes.

We were ready for our first camping trip.

* * *

In order to get to the destination, I had in mind, however, we needed transport and I soon discovered that

59

to hire a minibus for getting there *and* back would be impossibly expensive (the school not having a minibus of its own at that time). Fortunately, a solution was just around the corner, provided I limited this first trial excursion to myself and the four Patrol Leaders. I had decided that I needed a vehicle of my own.

An 'old banger', a maroon-coloured, Singer Vogue estate car that I eventually managed to haggle down to 200 JA$, fitted the bill perfectly. Or so I thought. But at that time, the only other car I had ever owned was an old Ford van which I had acquired as a student in London and which had been stolen about three months after I had bought it, too soon for me to have had the opportunity of getting to grips with even the most basic auto mechanics.

In its favour, the Vogue's paint-finish and bodywork were quite reasonable if you didn't look too closely, and all the lights worked, as well as the all-important horn. Also it was distinguished by having a fairly smart interior with leatherette seats for the driver and four passengers, and equally important, a decent amount of space behind the rear seat for carrying gear and equipment. But, having spent its best 10 years or so lurching in and out of potholes in the road and skidding around blind corners at high speed, the tyres, brakes, ball joints, wheel bearings, window-winders, clutch and engine were all pretty much knackered. However, on my meagre VSO monthly allowance, it was the best I could do and I reckoned that if I drove it gently, dodging the numerous potholes, and took my time going round corners, it would hopefully hold up until the next long school holiday when I would have the chance to address some of the mechanical problems, provided I put myself through a crash-course in auto mechanics in the meantime.

Granted, the car wasn't quite a Rolls Royce, but then it wasn't as if I needed something flashy to carry a pretty girl around in (I was still girlfriend-less). Furthermore, I was pretty sure the Scouts wouldn't complain, particularly if it was being used to ferry them around on an exciting camping trip. Housing a car in a locked garage was almost unheard of in Frankfield, so there was no choice but to park it on the roadside outside the Broomfields' house and, in any case, I reckoned the likelihood of anyone wanting to steal my 'illustrious' vehicle was as close to zero as one could get. So everything seemed to be falling into place, ready for the camping trip of a lifetime.

* * *

I had been in Jamaica now for close to three months but, as yet, had never had the opportunity to enjoy the beautiful seven-mile long, white-sand Negril beach at the western end of the island nor the enchanting coves and waterfalls of the North Coast, around Discovery Bay and Ocho Rios. Since Frankfield was pretty much in the centre of the island, the closest beach was at Discovery Bay, driving on minor roads via James Hill, Cave Valley, and Brown's Town. I had no plans for the upcoming Christmas holiday so was happy to set aside a week for our proposed trip. The Patrol Leaders were unbelievably excited about the idea and immediately set about planning menus, determining what food we would need to carry and doing all sorts of odd jobs to earn a bit of spending money for the trip. Fortunately, the Vogue had its own, quite sturdy roof-rack because there was no way that five people, all their personal gear, the huge volume of food, two tents and all the necessary camping equipment, was going to fit *inside* the car. I had decided to cover the petrol costs myself, but the boys all chipped in with food items like a massive bunch of green bananas, some very large yams, multiple tins of sardines, and a substantial number of tins of condensed milk for making hot drinks with home-grown coffee and cocoa. I hadn't really given much thought as to exactly

61

where we might camp - as usual, throwing caution to the wind - but I was hoping that we would be able to find somewhere suitable without too much trouble.

Before we knew it, I had completed my first term at Compre and our departure on our North Coast adventure was imminent. The parents had put their confidence in me to look after their teenage boys for a whole week but I really hadn't given much thought to the magnitude of this responsibility. Just prior to climbing into the driver's seat, however, I did one last check to see that everything was shipshape and duly noting that the car, now loaded with four big, strapping boys and all the food and equipment, inside and on top, was about as low on the springs as it was possible to be without the tyres rubbing on the wheel arches, I made a silent plea to a God I didn't believe in for safe journey... and we were off.

The minor road between James Hill and Cave Valley was about as bad as any road could be, with any tarmac having long since disappeared and huge caverns stretching from one side of the road to the other. I drove as gingerly as it was possible to do so, since the car was leaning over so far on passing through some of the deeper potholes that I honestly thought it was going to topple over. But we made it through the obstacle course, and once past Cave Valley we were on better, properly tarred roads, and could travel at a more appropriate rate. Now heading towards Brown's Town in the parish of St Ann, I noted a significant change in the scenery and vegetation. More akin to my own home county of Derbyshire, back in England, the hills and valleys here were more gentle and grass-covered instead of being hidden by thick undergrowth and vegetation.

We had all decided to travel in our navy-blue Scout uniforms, and when we eventually stopped in Brown's Town to pick up a few provisions from the road-side market, we realised what a good choice we had made. Everywhere we walked, we were greeted respectfully, almost reverently even, as most of the vendors seemed to assume that we were trainee soldiers from the Jamaica Defence Force and didn't even charge us for what we were buying! Of course, once the boys realised this, they took full advantage of the mistaken identity, deliberately drawing attention to themselves by marching in military formation and barking out commands to each other to complete the image. We all had a good laugh when we were once again on our way, with the boys teasing each other about who had done the best impersonation of a sergeant major or who had not been able to march in step. I couldn't have wished for a better group of lads.

Before making the long descent to Discovery Bay from the hills above Brown's Town, we stopped for a moment to take in the spectacular view. I couldn't believe the perfect turquoise colour of the distant sea, so alluring and so different from the cold-looking, grey waters around the British coast. It was a perfect, sunny day with just the hint of a breeze and with the sweet smell of *Poinciana* blossom wafting through the air. I thought, gratefully, how very fortunate I was to be spending my VSO year in such a beautiful place.

On reaching Discovery Bay, the main thing was to find a suitable place to camp. Having never set foot there before, I was not aware that the main beach, Puerto Seco, with a large, flat grassy area, stretching almost from the beach to the road, was completely encompassed by a tall security fence, installed by one of the bauxite companies who were responsible for its upkeep. What a perfect place to camp, assuming we could get the necessary permission!

Having ascertained who the person in charge of the compound was, I summoned Harry and Marky to accompany me to petition the said officer. After locating the administrative block in the nearby bauxite works, we were ushered in to a large office, luxuriously decorated and air-conditioned, prior to meeting the all-important gentleman. I couldn't have hoped to meet a nicer person; a congenial, well-spoken, smartly dressed Jamaican who, with a most endearing smile, bade us to be seated on a large, very soft settee by the window. Conversing with this obviously very well-educated person was clearly no time for practicing my *patois*, and so summoning my best Queen's English, I introduced myself as a VSO teacher and explained as best I could and with just a very minor distortion of the truth, that we were doing a training course for Scout Leaders and that we were in need of a suitable place to camp for a few nights. He thought for a moment and then, to my utter amazement, asked if the grassy area inside the compound would be suitable for our needs. We would be welcome to use the toilet block, the tennis courts and all the other facilities after the staff had left each evening. The only downside he could see was that the compound was locked each evening so we wouldn't be able to get in or out until the next morning. I assured him that the added security of being inside the locked compound more than made up for any inconvenience getting in or out during night-time hours, and then, with some degree of trepidation, I asked what the cost would be. I think Harry and Marky were even more surprised than I was when he smiled and said,

> "No man, we wouldn't charge you, but just try and keep the place tidy. I'll pass by and see how you are doing on Wednesday."

I made a mental log to make sure we would have a really top-notch meal ready for his visit; that was the least we could do to try and repay his kindness. I couldn't help thinking that if there *was* a God, he really must be a pretty nice sort of a chap to have allowed things to work out like this. We really couldn't have hoped for more.

The next few days were like a foretaste of heaven - at least, what I assumed heaven must be like! The water was deliciously warm and crystal clear, with small, apparently fearless, rainbow-coloured fish darting back and forth, and with no stones or pebbles underfoot. Relaxing on the beach, a carpet of beautiful, soft, warm, pink sand, was better than lying on a perfect bed. Moreover, we had free use of all the water-slides, diving boards, water-floats and other facilities. And to top it all off, there were some sturdy picnic tables dotted around the grassy area where we were camping, on which we could play dominoes, dominoes, and more dominoes, each evening, until we got so tired that we were nodding off in the middle of a game.

For me, the only two downsides were the burning power of the sun which I had to deal with by wearing a light coloured T-shirt during the hottest parts of the day, and the mosquitoes which descended on us with ferocity as the sun started to set. Fortunately the boys were experts at fighting these pests with smoke from our fire and by burning 'mosquito-coils' which we had purchased in the Brown's Town market, so apart from getting a few bites now and then, I was able to cope.

For Wednesday's inspection visit, we really pulled out all the stops, making sure the camp-site was immaculately clean and neat, and preparing a kingly Jamaican feast for our guest. I marvelled at how good the lads were at 'bush-cooking', as if they had been doing it all their lives, because the meal they put together was absolutely first class. It was clear that our guest was suitably impressed and stayed talking for some time after we had all eaten. When he spotted a set of dominoes on one of the picnic tables, and I (rather foolishly) challenged him to a quick game, he could not resist the temptation. It was me and Harry versus him and Marky but, alas, in spite of all my lessons, I was still a relative novice and we were soundly beaten (although not quite with the ignominy of getting a 'six-love'). He found my efforts somewhat unexpected and laughed with an appreciative nod on the odd occasions when Harry and myself won a game.

"The boys been teaching you then?"

"Yes, they're doing their best, but the more I play, the more I realise the depth of the game."

"And we're teaching him *patois* as well," Marky chipped in.

"Well, that will be a new one. Most people from 'foreign' come only for the sun, sea and sand, so it's refreshing when we get someone who actually wants to absorb some of the local culture. How are you getting on with the *patois*?"

I suddenly felt a bit nervous, remembering the ridicule my efforts had received from some of the staff back at Compre.

"It's more difficult than I imagined but... mi a try mi bess!" [*I do the best I can!*]

He laughed again, but not at all in a demoralising or supercilious way and encouraged me not to give up.

"If you would like to come back again anytime, just contact me beforehand,"

and he handed me a rather 'posh' business card. That kind of offer didn't come along every day of the week so I was rather overwhelmed by his kindness. In spite of our relatively short acquaintance, I felt I had made a new friend who epitomised Jamaican warmth, friendliness and hospitality.

After that, the week simply whistled by. I had been advised that it was worth visiting the nearby Green Grotto Cave just past Runaway Bay, so as a treat for the boys on the Thursday afternoon, I thought we would take a drive out and visit this pirate hideaway from times past. Based on our experiences in Brown's Town market, we decided to go, once again, in full uniform, in an attempt to get some sort of concession on the entrance fee. And once again, we benefited from the amazing Jamaican generosity towards uniformed groups by the young lady in the entrance booth who, with a gorgeous smile, waved us through *for free*!

The cave was much bigger, drier and airier than I could have possibly imagined and must have been a great hiding place and living area for its pirate occupants. Its history was made even more fascinating by our excellent young guide who undoubtedly embellished the stories of pirate life to such an extent that anyone, given half a chance, would have wanted to become a pirate themselves! The boys loved new and exciting experiences like this and such activities, quite apart from their intrinsic educational value, served to strengthen further the friendship bond between us. I was almost thinking of the boys now as being part of my own Jamaican family; a substitute for the family I had left on the far side of the Atlantic.

Our trip came to an end all too soon and it was time to repack the Vogue, although, having consumed such a vast quantity of food during our stay, there was significantly less stuff to take back than we had come with. The journey home was uneventful and, despite the state of the minor roads we had to navigate, the Vogue did me proud in reaching Frankfield in one piece. There were, however, some ominous noises coming from various hidden areas and it was clear that now my 'holiday' was over, I had to do some rapid learning of auto mechanics in time to try and resolve at least *some* of the noises before school resumed. I had decided that the best place to work on the car was in the relative security of the teachers' car park outside the ground-floor Chemistry Lab in the security of the school compound (with Mas' John and his cutlass to guard it), rather than on the roadside outside the Broomfields'.

So, you can imagine my utter amazement when I arrived up at the school to see the laboratory block looking significantly taller than when I last saw it. We now had a third storey and I had a new Physics Lab! *And* an adjoining prep-lab!

It was almost unbelievable that the 'extension' had been erected so quickly. Good old Mr Latty - he had been true to his word!

I parked the car and excitedly climbed the two flights of stairs to reach the third storey and inspect my brand-new domain. What a fabulous Christmas present even though there was a lot of work still to do to furnish and equip the future Physics Lab.

I could hardly have wished for more!

Chapter 6: One Becomes Two

The weeks between Christmas and Easter simply whistled by. I had now been roped into playing on the staff football team, no doubt partially because of the prevailing misconception that most Englishmen were automatically capable footballers and partially because of my size. However, having spent my student days at Lady Manners Grammar School playing only rugby, I possessed few or no football skills, and so was eventually relegated to the defence section of the staff team. Whenever Compre had a match with a staff team from another school, I considered my *raison d'etre* to be: (1) tackle as hard as possible any opposing forward who came my way with the ball, (2) try my best to gain possession of the ball from the unfortunate victim, and (3) give the ball a massive kick towards the opposition's goal-mouth where, hopefully, it would be utilised by one of our forwards. Although I never scored a goal for our team, the fairly frequent games did engender a good spirit of camaraderie between the Compre players and enabled me to get better acquainted with some of the male members of staff. The games also provided great amusement for the many student spectators present who loved to tease me afterwards about my (lack of) potential as a future Jamaican football star.

True to his word, during the week-long, half-term holiday, Mr Latty wasted no time in seeing to it that my new Physics Lab and prep-lab were painted and properly finished off. I had no idea what his plans had been for the furnishing; all I can say is that, during the short break, and entirely without my knowledge, an army of workers must have descended on the building. They had installed floor-level cupboards and drawers underneath a resistant, Formica work surface around the entire perimeter of both the main laboratory and the prep-lab. Then they had fixed wall cupboards, strategically positioned between the louvre windows, on the walls above. White porcelain sinks, sunk into the work surface, had also been situated around the perimeter of the main lab. All the necessary plumbing for water and waste were *in situ*, along with gas-taps, already connected in to the Science block's propane gas system. There was even an extra sink and gas-tap under the window in the prep-lab, and a 6-inch high, sturdy wooden platform to elevate the teacher above floor level had been installed in front of the black-board in the main lab.

But the thing that really hit you when you walked into the room were the beautiful, polished, wooden benches for students to sit around, and a similar teacher's bench on the platform at the front (also with its own dedicated sink and gas-taps for class demonstrations). Each bench had a set of matching wooden stools with contoured seats. The benches, in particular, must have been made by some very fine Jamaican craftsmen because they were as solid as rock, extremely heavy, with very thick tops and massive vertical legs and bracing joists, to eliminate any sort of vibration when students were doing experiments.

The first time I walked in to my newly-completed 'palace', I must have just stood there gaping like a fish out of water for several minutes while I took in the majesty of what was there before me. I certainly felt like I hardly deserved all this grandeur, and where had the funding come from?

Maybe Mr Latty had spoken to the then Minister of Education, Hon Edwin Allen, who lived fairly near to the school and who would obviously have wanted his 'flagship' school to be the envy of the island's entire educational system. I was well aware by this time of the extent to which 'politics talks' and if one knew the right people in the elected government, it was amazing how quickly schools could be built, roads fixed and funding be found for any number of projects in the local community.

In truth, I couldn't have cared less about the ways and means by which my 'palace' had been constructed and furnished. I finally had my own specialist teaching area and prep-lab, completely separate from the Biology Lab. And the view from my 'castle', up on the third storey of the Science block, was spectacular.

The first thing I felt it was appropriate to do was to go and convey my heartfelt thanks to Mr Latty.

"How is the new laboratory, Mr Skip? I trust it meets your expectations."

"It's fantastic, Sir! I just can't believe how they got everything finished off so quickly."

Mr Latty beamed.

"Now I'm sure you will be wondering about getting it all properly equipped."

He was already one step ahead, as usual!

"Yes, I have already made a 'wish list' for what we need, but I fear it will be very expensive, as Physics equipment doesn't come cheap."

"Could I ask you to go and have a talk with the Bursar. Tell him what you need and the likely cost and I'll take it from there. Do you think we can get most of it in Kingston, or will we have to get what we need from the 'Motherland'?"

Mr Latty smiled at his own joke.

"I think we can get a lot of it from Kingston, but some things will definitely need to be ordered from England. Would you like me to put an overseas order together?"

He nodded in the affirmative.

"By the way, how is the Scout Troup progressing?"

"It's actually going really well, thanks Mr Latty. So far we've managed to buy four tents out of our fund-raising."

Mr Latty nodded appreciatively and, always the gentleman, stood up to shake my hand.

"Have a very good day Mr Skip."

We managed as best we could for the next few weeks with the items I was able to procure from Kingston, together with odd pieces of Physics equipment which had been transferred from the Biology Lab. However, when the equipment in the overseas order from England arrived, we had to stack the half-dozen huge cardboard boxes along the corridor outside the new lab, which caused a distinct ripple of excitement amongst all my Physics GCE students and particularly those in my tutor group.

"Can we help unpack, Sir? We'll be really careful."

"Can I have one of the big cardboard boxes, please Sir?"

The boxes were so huge that I couldn't imagine how he would get it home. And so the next couple of evenings after school, I had a literal army of helpers, bursting with excitement and the thrill of a delayed Christmas.

Electric meters, rheostats and standard resistors were lovingly placed in ordered rows in various drawers, dynamics trolleys were neatly arranged in one of the two bigger cupboards, while the other was used to house the calorimeters, flasks, thermometers and Bunsen burners used in heat experiments. Some of the smaller cupboards were kept for apparatus used in light experiments, such as lenses, mirrors, prisms and light-boxes. Because of their size or vulnerability, I decided to keep specialised equipment like the Van de Graaff generator, the deflection-spot galvanometer and the CRT oscilloscopes in the prep-lab, but there was plenty of storage space for everything in one area or the other.

The new Physics Lab was now built, equipped, and ready to go! And I was determined that across the length and breadth of Jamaica the Compre Physics Department was going to be a force to be reckoned with, even if only for the few remaining months that I had left at the school.

72

Unfortunately, however, the day before we broke up for Easter, word must have somehow leaked out that I would be leaving Jamaica at the end of the Summer Term. My Year 10 tutees, in particular, accompanied by various students from other Physics classes, and a significant number of Scouts, had all requested a lunchtime meeting about 'the future', which I had agreed to host in the new lab. I had decided beforehand to allow the students to say whatever they wanted and to express their feelings openly but, once the meeting got underway, I rapidly reached the conclusion that, perhaps, I shouldn't have agreed to the meeting at all. One thing was clear as crystal; my tutees, in particular, perceived me as much more than just a Physics teacher; to them, I was the embodiment of a close confidant or possibly even a substitute father. The atmosphere was tense as the battle commenced.

"We understand you are leaving in the summer and we would be grateful if you could explain why."

I did my best to explain the commitment I had made to Bart's Medical Electronics Department back in London and the one-year agreement I had made with VSO.

"So who is going to teach us in Year 11 for our Physics GCE?"

I tried to bluff an answer by expressing my faith in Mr Latty's ability to procure a replacement.

"Did you leave your wife and children behind, and, if so, why couldn't they come out and join you for a while?"

I assured my inquisitor that I had neither wife nor children back in England. I was starting to perspire and loosened my tie so that I could unfasten the top button on my shirt. And then came some of the more emotional questions:

"How come you always keep saying how much you love us and what wonderful students we are? What kind of love is that if it doesn't include loving actions?"

Tears were rolling down her cheeks and I felt terrible. I had no answer.

"What will happen to the Scout Troop?"

I responded that I hoped very much that it would continue to flourish under new leadership.

"And what if a new leader cannot be found?"

No answer.

"Why didn't you tell us before, rather than leaving it until almost the last minute?"

The true answer to that one was that I had been ducking this situation for some time now in the hope it would just go away. It didn't.

"We trusted you to see us through to graduation. Why are you letting us down?"

No answer.

"Can you honestly say that your decision has nothing to do with you being in a small white minority in a largely black population?"

"Absolutely! You can trust me on that one."

"I don't think we can trust you on anything like we used to."

"You're no different from all the other foreign teachers!"

"And we thought you were *really* different."

I swallowed hard, hung my head and said nothing.

The questions went on and on and on, until our meeting had long passed the end of lunchtime. I was soaked with sweat, felt highly uncomfortable and extremely demoralised. It was time to bring the meeting to a close.

"Time for everyone to get to afternoon lessons now. Please? "

I smiled, but received only blank stares in return. This had been, without doubt, the worst hour I had experienced since arriving in Jamaica seven months before. I suppose I ought to have expected a negative response, but I certainly hadn't anticipated this level of hurt and disappointment in the students and was taken off-guard by just how much they already depended on me as their teacher. I wondered now why I hadn't just signed up, like Andy had done, for the full two years recommended by VSO, asking Professor Rotblat to hold the postgrad place for two years instead of one. The long and short of it was that I had been afraid of the possibility of him responding in the negative.

Fortunately, I had a 'free' period after lunch, so I slunk back my prep-lab like an animal that needed to hide in its lair, flopped down in my office chair, and started to wrestle with my thoughts and feelings about returning to London. What would a future there be likely to hold?

One thing I was sure about was that I was definitely not being drawn back by any lingering feelings for Liz. That relationship was definitely behind me.

But was I going back just to please my parents, particularly my father, by working towards getting a coveted PhD behind my name? Possibly; but I *was* genuinely interested in the postgrad course I had committed to and I couldn't have wished for a better Department Head than Professor Rotblat.

However, I was really loving teaching and my teenage students at Compre were as close to angels as one could ever hope for (most of the time!). Maybe remaining in Jamaica for another year ought to be considered?

And what about my new 'palace', the brand new Physics Lab that I had barely begun to enjoy yet? And all the adventures with the Scout Troop...?

After wrestling for the better part of an hour with the dilemma of deciding whether to return to England in the summer or remain for another year in Jamaica, I reached the conclusion that, in the final analysis, the most important thing was 'where would I be happiest?'

That night, over dinner, I shared my thoughts about staying or leaving with Andy to see what his opinion was on the matter. Having, by then, lived together for over half a year, we now knew each other really well and I increasingly held his opinions in high regard. Andy listened thoughtfully as I poured out all the pros and cons of going or remaining. Eventually, he responded,

> "If I were you, I would write to the Professor in London and find out whether or not he would be willing to hold your place for another year. His answer would narrow down your options somewhat and maybe make your decision a bit easier."

With no modern-day computer at my disposal or memory stick on which to save the letter, I have, unfortunately, no copy of the hand-written original but I think the gist of it was as follows:

> *Dear Professor Rotblat,*
>
> *I trust this letter finds you well and may I apologise for not having kept you better informed as to my progress with VSO out in Jamaica during the last seven or eight months.*
> *In a nutshell, I have been having a fantastic time! Although I wouldn't like to boast that I was 'born to teach', I thoroughly enjoy my work in the classroom and the various extra-curricular activities in which I am involved. Having been placed in a school with a Principal who has provided me with not only a brand new Physics Lab full of brand new equipment, but also a school where the students have an unquenchable thirst for knowledge and are polite, respectful and genuinely pleasant, I really have very little to complain about (except possibly the condition of the ancient car that I just managed to purchase out of my meagre VSO monthly allowance!).*

I know you are already aware that the VSO organisation has a strict policy of requiring all its volunteers to sign up for a two-year stint abroad and that, in my case, they only waived this requirement to facilitate my return to London to join your department after one year abroad. However, I can now see the wisdom in VSO's policy as it has become abundantly clear to me that, while the first year serves mainly as a learning experience for the volunteer, it is really the second year that facilitates making a useful contribution to the host country.

May I say that I hold you in the highest esteem for holding the place (and the SCR award) thus far and I realise that any request on my part for a further extension would seem almost impertinent. However, may I ask you to at least consider the possibility of my joining your research group a year later than we agreed previously, i.e. in summer 1973, rather than this current year, 1972. If you feel unable to reply in the affirmative, I shall understand.

I trust you are keeping in good health,
Very best wishes,
Deniz T. Önaç

I am sure my hand was shaking when I pushed the air-mail envelope through the slot at the top of the red postbox at the Frankfield Post Office on the morning of the first day of the Easter holiday. I had followed my conscience and done my best, but I had no intention of informing Mr Latty, my Compre students or my parents back in England about what I was intending until I had heard back from Professor Rotblat. There were no home postal deliveries so I had to keep visiting the Post Office each day to check for a reply. I felt almost like a young child, eagerly anticipating the arrival of a Christmas present.

But now it was imperative that I changed focus and got some work done on my poor old car during the two weeks of holiday ahead of me. Fortunately, my indefatigable 'Baba' back at the family home in Derbyshire had, at my request, managed to acquire a copy of the Haynes Workshop Manual for my Singer Vogue and had already posted this weighty tome out to me by air-mail, at great expense. The book had arrived a few days before my fateful meeting with the students (about my departure) but I hadn't really had chance to look at it yet.

Now it was time for some serious independent study which I hoped to be able to put into practice in trying to resurrect the car during the school holiday. I had never really ventured under a car bonnet in my entire life, so I must say that I was glad that my university degree had been in a subject area like Physics or Engineering which had equipped me with a fair understanding of technical issues. But woe unto those who venture solo into this domain, having neither any technical knowledge nor the practical experience! For each page that I read, I ended up with a page of questions in my 'mechanic's notebook', and I needed immediate answers from people who knew what they were doing and already had the practical experience.

My first foray into the domain of local mechanics, most of whom were loosely attached to the local gas-station, resulted in an embarrassing experience consisting almost exclusively of derision and mirth on their part. The basic problems were that, firstly, 'this wasn't the sort of work usually undertaken by white men' anyway and, secondly, how could a novice like myself, with no practical experience at all, hope to pick up in a flash the necessary knowledge that they had taken the better part of their working life to assimilate? Swallowing my pride, however, I decided to join in the fun by keeping the banter nice and light-hearted (while still asking the questions I needed answering). In the end, my persistence and good humour paid off and at least a couple of them started to be more helpful, particularly after I joined in the odd game of dominoes in the adjacent bakery. I think they respected the idea that I wasn't afraid to get my hands dirty or wear oil-covered work-clothes.

It quickly became obvious that I would need a professional set of mechanic's tools. So, the following day, with whatever cash I could scrape together, I took a minibus bound for Mandeville (fortunately only a 45-minute journey) and, on the advice of my new mechanic friends, headed for Lazarus's Tools and Light Engineering shop. A rather rotund, bespectacled, light-brown Jamaican, Mr Lazarus ran one of the most successful businesses in town, along with his son. When I introduced myself and voiced my intentions, the father warmed to me immediately and sought to help me in every possible way, selecting the most important tools and parts I would need for my immediate jobs. He had the most amazing memory I have ever witnessed and, without reference to any books or manuals, would call out the specification code for each item (containing at least a dozen numerical digits and letters) on 'our' list, for his son to go and locate in the cavernous warehouse at the back of the service counter. In less than an hour, we had got together everything I needed and he was calculating the bill, *in his head*! I was short about 10 JA$, but when I suggested I could hitch-hike back to Frankfield, and use my bus fare to make up the deficit, he simply laughed and said,

> "Dem tools is too heavy fi hitch-hike. Mek mi see what mi can do wid di total." [*Those tools are too heavy to carry on foot. I'll see what I can do about reducing the total cost.*]

And in a matter of seconds, he had applied various discounts which, using his own mental arithmetic skills, brought the total down just enough for me to still have the necessary bus-fare to get home. I thanked him profusely and made a mental note to patronise his shop in future, whenever the need arose. It was yet another example of the extraordinary generosity of the inhabitants of my new homeland.

I was now a fully equipped mechanic, raring to go!

* * *

Andy had brought with him to Jamaica a fair amount of cash with which he had also been able to purchase a second-hand car for himself soon after Christmas. He was clearly very keen on Julie, the rather good-looking English girl he had met on our induction course, and had decided that, over the Easter holiday, he would drive over to Westmoreland near the western end of the island where she was teaching and stay there with her for the duration of the holiday. So I was there at the Broomfield's with no 'youthful distractions' to take me away from my work on the Vogue.

Since it was getting on towards summer, the days were getting longer and brighter and I reckoned I could get in a solid 12 hours each day after an *early* breakfast (to the delight of Miss Daph) and before a late evening meal (long after she had retired to bed). The car was still parked up at Compre in the ground floor car park outside the Science block, where I had decided to leave it after we got back from our Christmas camping trip to Discovery Bay. This meant that I had to carry all my tools in a large cardboard box on my shoulder from the house up to the school on the first morning. It was a good thing I was young and strong as the tools were really heavy. However, I had no intention of repeating this on a daily basis; the tools would remain in one of my cupboards in the new Physics prep-lab at the end of each day's work. When I informed Mas' John, the school watchman, about leaving the tools each day, he simply shrugged and laughed, displaying all his smoke-stained teeth.

"Noh fret, Skip. Dem tools is safe, man. Any tief wid bad intention, will feel dis yah blade!" [*Don't worry Skip, the tools will be safe. Any thief with bad intentions will feel this blade here!*]

And he tested the sharpness of the cutlass that never left his side by gently running the index finger of his left hand along its razor-like edge. I was pretty sure that both the tools and the car would be as safe under his watchful eye and trusty blade as they would be anywhere, so I definitely had one thing less to worry about.

Fortunately, the car had come with a pretty solid jack but, on the advice of my new mechanic friends never to lie under a car, resting on three wheels and the jack, I took the obvious precaution of using the spare wheel and a few sturdy blocks of wood as a safety support.

I decided to start with the wheel bearings and brake pads since I had already purchased the necessary parts for these jobs from Mr Lazarus when I was getting the tools.

Getting the old bearing casings off was difficult, however, as these were designed to be a tight fit in their respective housings and were rusted *in situ*, probably never having been changed since the car was originally made. Eventually, it was a case of knocking the bearings out using a suitably large socket and a hammer. It was fortunate this job was on my to-do list as some of the bearings were in such a dreadful condition that it must have been a miracle we all got back from our camping trip in one piece! The good part, however, was that the new replacements were somewhat easier to 'tap in' and for each wheel done, with the benefit of hindsight, the next one was easier. By the end of the first day, all four wheel bearings had been renewed, and I was feeling quite pleased with myself. Furthermore, the new prep-lab was the ideal place for me to clean myself up, having a plentiful supply of clean water, liquid soap and paper towels.

Walking home that evening, I checked the school postbox as a matter of course, just in case the eagerly awaited reply from the Professor might be in the pile. This search was clearly premature as my own letter had probably not even reached England yet, but I was desperately anxious for a reply.

The next day, I decided to tackle the entire brake system, which included changing the brake pads, 'bleeding' the brake system and changing the brake sealing washers as necessary. For bleeding the system, I needed to enlist the help of Mas' John who was more than happy to 'pump the brake pedal', sitting in the driver's seat with a delighted grin on his face, while I lay under the car releasing the bleed nipples on each wheel. This might have been the very first time that old Mas John, who grew up in an era when cars were rarely seen, had ever had the opportunity to sit in the driver's seat of a vehicle.

Of course, with hindsight, I could have combined the previous day's job with the current brake job to avoid having to remove each wheel a second time - but with auto mechanics, you live and learn.

Now that these two major jobs were behind me, I felt that the essential safety of the car was no longer in jeopardy and so I decided to address some of the other issues. I had noticed on our return journey from the camping trip that the headlights had been getting gradually dimmer and dimmer as we drove along, so I had a suspicion that the alternator might have a minor fault. Furthermore, if this was not resolved soon, the battery would go flat and then the car would not be able to start. So, with relatively little effort, I slackened the fan-belt and removed the alternator from inside the engine compartment.

On further disassembly, however, it soon became apparent that the problem was anything but minor. The 'stator coil' insulation had almost completely burned out. This was totally unexpected and getting the replacement part would unfortunately involve a trip all the way to the Lucas Depot in Kingston. I had already decided that before tackling the alternator, I would spend a day doing a full oil and oil-filter change, putting in a new air filter and exchanging the old spark plugs for new ones. So, having completed these tasks, all of which were relatively quick and easy jobs, I then carefully wrapped up the alternator, which was really heavy and awkward. I had every intention of taking it with me to ensure I got the right part the following day and, making my statutory call to check the postbox on the way back, I got home as quickly as possible so I could get a good night's sleep and be ready for an early start. There was no letter.

Next morning, Mas' Tom was kind enough to lend me an old, but very strong shopping bag because, as he prudently observed, carrying a round, heavy object in one's hands on a crowded minibus, would not be a very easy task. Getting an early start was definitely preferable as it allowed me to have a seat near the back of the minibus for the whole journey and, after a relatively uneventful ride, we were in Kingston within two hours. I had no intention of trying to walk to the Lucas Depot with my heavy bag and, instead, called a taxi. Once I had established my credentials as a teacher, and flung a bit of *patois* into the conversation, the agreed fee became something rather more manageable and, after a 10-minute, hair-raising ride, I was at the Depot.

"Tanks man"

"One love, bredda",

and he was gone.

My immediate impression of the Lucas Distribution Depot was that it was more of a repair centre than somewhere to get parts and I waited for ages to get some sort of half-hearted service. When I unwrapped the alternator, showed the man the nature of the problem, and told him what I needed, he laughed.

"Yuh have two choice, man. Yuh can buy a bran new alternator for 600 JA$, or yuh can leave di ting wid me an mi will put in a new stator coil for 200 JA$. Wi noh sell parts." [*You've got two choices. Either buy a brand new alternator for 600 JA$ or leave it with me and I will put in a new stator coil myself for 200 JA$. We don't sell individual parts.*]

I stood looking at the man for several seconds, feeling totally dejected and deflated. 600 JA$ was obviously totally out of the question, and I couldn't afford even 200 JA$, since I had only paid 200 JA$ for the entire car! After a couple of terse exchanges, it was obvious that this offer was non-negotiable, so I rewrapped my alternator, dropped it back into the shopping bag and left, vowing never to return.

Then I had a brainwave; I knew already from my expeditions to Kingston to get equipment and materials for the new Compre Physics Lab, that there was an electrical shop in the King Street area which sold enamelled copper wire in various gauges. I would buy a long piece of enamelled copper wire of the appropriate thickness and, on my return to Frankfield, would re-wind the stator coil *myself*, by hand. Surely, it couldn't be *that* difficult!

To conserve precious funds, I decided to walk to the electrical supplies shop. But it was now mid-day and the Kingston heat was ferocious, so by the time I reached the shop, I was drenched with sweat. Fortunately, in complete contrast to the man I had just been dealing with at the Lucas Depot, the salesman at the electrical supplies shop was in a different league. He was willing to discuss my idea, suggesting any little extras I might need, and even took mercy on my dehydrated, sweaty state by offering me a cold drink.

I estimated that each coil in the winding was about 6 cm long and 5 cm wide and contained less than 100 turns. Each coil would therefore require about 22 metres of wire. Then there were three coils in each winding and one winding for each of the three phases, which brought the total length of wire needed to just under 200 metres. The whole lot, together with the necessary extras such as strips of fairly stiff insulation to slot into the grooves in the soft-iron armature prior to re-winding, cost less than 30 JA$. It was imperative that the 200 metres of wire was not kinked or bent or scratched, so the gentleman in the shop took pains to wind it in a very large, neat coil of about 100 turns, then wrapped around it with paper, held in place with tape.

"Don't let anyone sit on it in the minibus!"
I thanked him for both his helpfulness and his hospitality and headed to the closest point for getting a bus back home.

It was a terrible journey and by the time we reached Frankfield, I had cramp in both legs and a cricked neck but, thank goodness, my wire and the shopping bag containing the alternator were both safe. I must have been really tired because after my evening meal and a most welcome shower to remove all the Kingston grime, I hit the sack and didn't wake until 9:00am next morning. Fortunately VSO had not posted me at a school in the Kingston inferno - I would have been ready to leave after only a day on the job!

The next couple of days was a testimony to the Jamaican proverb,

> 'Tun yuh han, mek fashon'. [*Apply yourself to a task and use whatever resources you have to hand to make what you need.*]

I surprised even myself as to what it is possible to achieve when you really set your mind to it. I reckoned that if I slowly unwound the old burnt-out windings, making notes in my mechanics notebook as I went along, the process of re-winding would simply require following the notes in reverse. Fortunately, I had an empty Physics Lab at my disposal to lay out the new wire in a *huge* circle around the perimeter, and with due concentration, I managed the rewinding task in about 10 hours spread out over two days. When I had finished and all the wires were fixed firmly in position, with their ends soldered to the appropriate terminals, I couldn't help but congratulate myself on the results of my labour; it was neat, professional and every bit as good as, if not better than, the original winding that I had removed. I really felt proud of my achievements! Of course, 'the proof of the pudding is in the eating', but testing the efficacy of my work could wait until the following day.

I was so eager to see if everything was working properly that I was up at the crack of dawn and, after a quick breakfast, headed up to school. Installing the alternator back in the car was relatively easy, then it was just to 'tension the fan-belt', and I was ready to go. Mas' John who had been most encouraging, in an almost paternal sort of way over the last week, walked over to watch the outcome.

"Here we go, Mas' John" and I turned the ignition key. The engine roared into life and we both roared with enthusiasm!

"You fancy a little spin round? How about to Angel Bridge and back?"

Mas' John was delighted, and even more so when we stopped at the bar by the school gate to grab a couple of cold beers. But for me, the real test was that when I turned on the headlights, they were dazzlingly bright, even in the brightness of the day.

"Yuh is a good mechanic, Missa Skip. Betta dan all a dem so-an-so from in a di town. Well done, sah! Ah proud a yuh." [*You're a good mechanic Skip. You're*

86

better than all of those pretenders from in the town. Well done - I'm proud of you!]

Walking home that evening, I thought I might as well check for my letter at the Post Office. I couldn't even remember what day it was, with the time having slipped by so quickly, but my gut feeling told me that it was, by now, probably mid-way through the second week of the holiday. Sifting through the massive pile of letters in the box, (that always accumulated during the school holidays) I almost overlooked a white envelope with my name and address typed on the front and with the distinctive emblem of Bart's Hospital in the top left-hand corner. My hand was literally shaking as I rushed home and tore it open to see what it said:

Dear Deniz,

This reply to your letter will be very short because I know you will be anxious to pursue your plans for next year. I suspect you will be happy to hear that I understand your arguments fully and would not wish to put any obstacle in your way. I look forward to your return in the summer of 1973 when I can assure you that your place on the course as well as your financial support will still be waiting.

Very best wishes

(illegible signature)

P.S. Please send me a photo of one of your lessons in the new Physics Lab, whenever you get time.

It must have taken a full couple of minutes, sitting by myself at the dinner table, for the content of the letter to really sink in. Then my eyes moistened and I was finding it impossible to even make out all of Miss Daph's culinary delights set out on the table before me. I felt like a massive weight had been lifted off my heart. Everything was now falling into place for me to remain in Jamaica for a second year.

One year was about to become two.

Chapter 7: Settling In

I had more or less already decided that I would inform various individuals about my change of plans in a particular order: Miss Daph and Mas' Tom first (to eliminate the possibility of them getting a new lodger to take my place), then Mr Latty (before he recruited a new Physics teacher), then VSO to inform them of my decision (hopefully they would be pleased I was now keen to stay for the usual two years), then Andy (upon his return from visiting Julie), then my parents back in England (once all the extension arrangements were in place) and, finally, my students, tutees and Scouts at Compre.

Miss Daph was delighted that I wanted to stay on. Her children were all adults who had left the family home by this time, and in her eyes, I was a relatively safe pair of hands who was courteous, kept her house clean, made his own bed, wasn't too noisy and whose only fault was keeping irregular mealtimes (I could feel my halo glowing!).

I thought it would be appropriate to pay a visit to Mr Latty at his Principal's House up on the hillside above the school, rather than wait until school reopened for the Summer Term so, after a fairly leisurely breakfast, I strolled up to his home and after avoiding being devoured by two huge dogs, was cordially welcomed into his house.

"I thought you might have been sampling one of our lovely beaches, Skip, with a lady-friend, perhaps… Would you like a cold juice?"

"Thanks, Mr Latty. Yes, it is pretty warm. And no, I'm afraid I'm not really paired up with anyone at the moment."

"We'll have to see what can be done about that then…", (with a twinkle in his eye.) He beckoned to his wife and said,

"My dear, would you please bring a nice cold drink for Skip?"

"I thought it would be appropriate to let you know that I am asking VSO for my contract to be extended from one year to two and, assuming you've not already found a replacement, I would like to ask if I could stay on here at Compre for a second year."

Mr Latty looked at me quizzically and then smiled.

"So, Mr Skip, do you think the fish escapes the line so easily? You can be assured that I have taken no steps whatsoever to find your replacement, because I just knew you wouldn't be leaving us so soon anyway. After all - you've only just come!"

I gulped my drink and wondered inwardly how it was that all the jig-saw pieces were continuing to fit together so smoothly for my extended stay.

"Thanks, Sir. That's very kind of you."

We chatted amiably for about another half an hour before I left to walk home. That evening, just as I was about to start dinner, Andy arrived back from his trip to visit Julie. He was in very high spirits and had obviously had a great time. Miss Daph quickly supplemented the food portions as necessary so we could eat together. Andy was ravenous.

"That was good timing!"

I teased, as he piled very substantial helpings onto his plate.

"How's Julie? Did you have a good trip?"

After all the usual pleasantries were behind us, I broke the news that I had decided to stay on for the second year.

"I wasn't really expecting otherwise, but I *am* glad, Skip. It will give us a bit more time to get you hooked up with a nice girl."

I smiled and thought to myself that with both Mr Latty and Andy looking out for me, I ought to have very little problem finding that 'nice girl'. It was good to have Andy back again, but I wanted to write my letter to the VSO office in Kingston that evening, so I didn't stay talking for too long.

After this, the only remaining task for the holiday was to inform my parents of my decision. This would be both difficult and delicate and the letter needed to be very carefully worded. Whilst I could enthuse about the new Physics Lab and all my knowledge-thirsty students, I didn't want to put too great an emphasis on that, instead focusing more on the confirmation by Professor Rotblat of my place on the doctoral course for 1973, and how much I was looking forward to getting back into a top postgrad research department. This would help to alleviate any fears Baba might have had for my academic future. I think I achieved a good balance, so much so, that just before concluding, I decided to throw caution to the wind and ask my father if he would be so kind as to ship out my drum-set. Anticipating that this might cause him further apprehension about extending my stay in Jamaica, I made the case that I was aware of some forthcoming musical opportunities which required me to have my musical instrument with me, although I realised that this was somewhat stretching the truth. The drums were already in hard cases, but I knew that, Baba being Baba, he would get them all further encased in solid plywood boxes to completely insulate them from any possible damage. I did, of course, promise to pay for the shipping and insurance costs, though where I would find the necessary funds at that point in time, was another matter.

Once the letters to VSO and my parents were in the post, there remained only my students and the Scouts to be informed, but that could wait until school reopened on Monday. Furthermore, as someone who had a very mischievous streak, a plan was already formulating in my mind as to how I would trick them about my departure and get my own back for how they had made me feel at the meeting on the final day of last term.

We were now on the final weekend of the Easter holiday and, on a sudden impulse, I decided that, since I would be staying another year, I could further integrate into the local community by paying a visit to the nearby Frankfield Church of God. Not that I had suddenly had some sort of dramatic conversion or anything of the sort, having had no interest in religion since my compulsory attendance at Sunday School as a child, but I was just curious as to what rural church services in Jamaica were really like. So early Sunday morning, after a quick breakfast and shower, I donned a smart pair of trousers and a nice, short-sleeved, open-necked shirt and set off for the church which was just a short distance down the road. In spite of my protestations that Jesus himself probably wore sandals, and that they were the ideal footwear for the Jamaican heat, Miss Daph had insisted that I wear proper shoes and *not* sandals, and that was that! She was adamant, and clearly, there would be no further argument.

From the moment I set foot through the church door, I was treated like royalty, and I later learned that a visit from a white, ex-pat teacher to one of the local churches (except, perhaps, for the annual school graduation ceremony), almost never happened. I was courteously ushered to my seat, right in front of a fairly large group of elderly ladies who seemed to already know me as "Mister Skip". Then I was presented with a hymn book and a Bible and an order-of-service sheet. Before the start of the main service, there was a general welcome to everyone, but to say that I was singled out for special greeting would be a gross understatement.

> "This morning, brothers and sisters, I have great pleasure in welcoming, for the first time, Brother Skip, one of the most popular teachers at the comprehensive school. He has come to Jamaica all the way from England and he teaches Physics to our children."

The congregation murmured their appreciation. I looked round at the younger element present and was surprised to see a significant number of my own tutees, my Physics students and several of my Scouts. A lot of their parents were also in attendance and I soon discovered that, contrary to my own childhood experience in England, here in this little, rural Jamaican community, parents considered it a duty to actually *accompany* their children to church. The accolades continued:

> "Mr Skip, as you know, has been kind enough to take some of our children camping on the North Coast, giving up his own holiday time to make the trip. We are very grateful, Sir, for your kindness and dedication. May God *bless* you, Sir, and *protect* you and *provide* for all your needs. Can I get an '*Amen*' from the assembly?"

At this request, there were numerous '*Amens*' and a lot of clapping. I was beginning to get a bit self-conscious and felt my cheeks starting to burn.

> "Brother Skip - would you like to say a few words?"

I clearly had no choice and before I could refuse, I had been ushered up to the alter rail to shake hands with the person leading the service and to make my first-ever 'church speech'. I was desperately nervous. Put me in front of a lecture hall of students to talk Physics and I'll hold my own, but here in this beautiful little church with maybe 60 people present, at most, my tongue had stuck to the inside of my mouth and my brain had gone to sleep:

> "Er...Brothers and Sisters, I would just like... to thank you for your very warm words of welcome which made me feel almost like a long-time member of the congregation. I would like to congratulate you on the way you have raised your children to be so disciplined, courteous and loving. You must be doing something right!"

At this, to my surprise, all the elder members started to
clap.

"Er... It is my honour to be able to join you this
morning and I look forward to the remainder of the
service with anticipation. I live just a little way up the
road and sometimes hear some beautiful harmonies
coming from the church. So as a musician myself, I
am really looking forward to some wonderful singing
this morning. Er...Thank you again."

And I was led by one of the ushers back to my seat.

I suppose things could have gone a lot worse. A full
two hours later, the service was still in full swing, which was
something I definitely wasn't used to. But the singing of the
hymns was heavenly and I had to marvel at the seemingly
natural ability of so many of the congregation, both young
and old, to pitch instantaneous harmonies. Not having to
teach someone how to harmonise would be incredibly
useful if that individual was singing backing vocals in a
band. And the richness of the singing was truly awesome!
Hopefully, I didn't doze off in the hour-long sermon, which I
am sure contained lots of useful advice, particularly for a
non-Christian like myself. But overall, the church service
was a great experience and whether the prayers were
actually of any real benefit or not, it was still comforting to
have so many people offering prayers for my protection,
good health, prosperity and salvation.

* * *

My first lesson on Monday morning was with my
delightful Year 10 Physics group which included a
significant proportion of my tutees, so I thought it was as
good a time as any to tell them my latest news. At the start
of the lesson, they filed, almost like zombies, into the lab,
completely devoid of their former brightness and
exuberance. They had engaged in polite conversation with

94

me at the church service when their parents were present, but now, most of them deliberately avoided looking me in the eye. I could sense they were still hurting from our meeting in the Physics Lab at the end of last term so I really should have just told them without any further trickery or beating around the bush. But, to my shame, my mischievous nature gained the ascendancy and I stuck to my 'plan';

"I have some information about your new Physics teacher for next year."

Absolutely zero response.

"He's also a graduate of UCL in London, England, and... apparently he's young, free, single and disengaged."

I thought that might have evoked at least a smile, but there was nothing. I was starting to feel I was pushing this a bit too far.

"And would you believe it, his name is also Mr Skip."

I thought that they would have twigged to my trickery by now and I hadn't really got anything else planned to say.

"So... is he a relative or something?"

They had forgotten that no one knew me as 'Mr Skip' back in England.

"Well, I suppose you could say that."

It was getting harder and harder to keep a straight face. What other clue could I give them?

"And I understand he also plays the drums."

Some of them looked up. They knew I was a drummer.

"Is he your twin brother?"

I could maintain the façade no longer.

"No, you wonderful class of young Physicists, it's ME!"

For whatever reason, it still didn't sink in for several seconds, but then, like ripples spreading in a pond, one face after another lit up and then someone shouted,

"So you're not leaving us after all, Sir?

"No, I'm definitely NOT leaving."

But my response was completely drowned out by the explosion of shouting and screaming and stamping and clapping. Stools were knocked over as a wave of mad teenagers engulfed me, squeezed me and hugged me, all shouting at once. In fact, the noise was so loud that Andy, who was teaching Biology in the lab vertically below, had rushed upstairs to see if everything was alright.

"Some of us are trying to teach round here!"

But he could see that he would need more than water to quench this fire, and with a wry smile, having determined that there was no emergency, he returned to his laboratory.

When everything finally settled down and the students all found their seats, I noticed that some of the girls were crying, so I went over to try and comfort them, apologising for giving them any distress.

"That's OK Sir, these are tears of happiness."

* * *

A new secondary school teacher undoubtedly has to compile a catalogue of personal skills and learning experiences including an in-depth subject knowledge, good delivery, maintaining good discipline, consistency in dealing with different students, giving positive feedback, and so on. But we also need to realise that teenagers are still children, with all sorts of new feelings and emotions. Sometimes these surface in a flood of tears or even a fist-fight as the young person tries to come to terms with what is happening in their lives at that point in time. I'd never had any teacher training in the philosophy of education or child psychology up to that point, and I had learnt an important lesson that day: *long-term* commitment to children's education was crucial, and providing them with empathy and reassurance in stressful situations was just as essential as the attainment of intellectual skills and subject knowledge.

I simply hadn't realised how emotionally vulnerable teenagers can be, and hadn't at all anticipated just how big an impact my leaving or staying at Compre might have had on my students. Making a joke about this on that first morning of the Summer Term had certainly not been one of my proudest moments as a young teacher and, to be honest, my conscience was burning! Hopefully, what I had learnt about emotions and relationships that morning were lessons I would never forget. Fortunately, my students were not only forgiving, but also happy that I had decided to stay!

* * *

The letter from Baba, when it arrived a couple of weeks later, was predictably full of concern, disappointment, and sadness. He was worried about the effect a two-year gap in my academic studies might have on my further progress. Would I forget all my university-level Physics, requiring lengthy periods of relearning?

He expressed his regret that getting my final, postgraduate qualification would now be deferred for yet another year. And he was saddened that his first-born son would not be around to advise him on his latest projects in the garden and the family home. Such projects were always on a grand scale and built to create a lasting legacy - and many of his creations are still there today, enduring long after him! Furthermore, the family size was predictably getting smaller each year, with my brother already studying at university and my sisters now being in the process of putting together their own applications for further education. I suppose he was trying, in one way or another, to come to terms with the rapidly approaching 'empty nest' syndrome. For nothing mattered more to Baba than family.

In truth, there was some degree of merit in most of the points he had raised, but the die was now cast and I had no intention of changing my mind. To my surprise, however, he offered no objection to shipping the drums to me; perhaps he thought my being able to continue playing might remind me of all the musical opportunities I had had through drumming back in England, and that this, in turn, might help to convince me to return home sooner. Whatever his thinking, he had more than lived up to my expectations by packaging them in tank-proof plywood boxes, somehow ferrying them to Liverpool, and getting them shipped on the first available boat carrying freight to Jamaica. However, nearly 30 years after settling in England, Baba was still trying to master his second language, English, and always found letter writing to be a slow and onerous task. By the time his reply reached me, the boat had already docked in Kingston and unloaded.

As soon as I received the documentation, I asked two of my tutees, Harry and Marky, if they would be willing to accompany me to Kingston to help pick up the boxes, and having obtained permission from their parents and cleared our absences with school, we were off to the docks the following day. I realised afterwards what a good decision taking them along had been. I had made sure to impress on the lads the importance of being ultra-polite to whatever customs officer we might have to deal with, but as it all turned out, I needn't have said a thing.

The lady we had been assigned was a young and rather attractive customs officer whose job it was, firstly, to ascertain that the content of any incoming package was not contraband and, secondly, to determine what duty would be payable. While I used one of my large flat-blade screw-drivers (from my set of car-tools) to unscrew the myriad, long screws that held the lid in place on the largest box, the two lads set about 'chatting up' this young lady as if they had known her from primary school. Baba had made sure that the boxes were impenetrable to anyone but the most determined, so by the time I had removed the lid from the first box containing all the drum shells, stacked one inside the other, and broken the seal on the industrial-standard, grease-paper layer inside (to protect the contents from any possible ingress of sea-water), at least half an hour had passed. When the lady came over to view the contents, accompanied by her two young suitors, the charm offensive really got underway:

"This is our teacher, Mr Önaç, but we all call him 'Skip'."

"It's his Jamaican pet-name."

"He's a VSO *volunteer* teacher." (with appropriate emphasis)

"Good morning Mr Skip. I see you is a musician. How do you like our reggae music?" (I noticed that she spoke in a polished manner with just the odd injection of *patois*)

This was just the opening I needed, so wearing my most charming smile, and trying to throw in a bit of *patois* myself wherever possible, I replied,

"Good morning Miss. Yes maam, ah been drummin since before yuh bahn. An di reggae music, it sweet, sah!" [*Good morning miss. I have been drumming since before you were born, and I find reggae music very enjoyable!*]

The young lady doubled up in laughter.

"I see you is trying to learn the *patois*, Mr Skip"

"Yes Miss, and I have some excellent teachers" (pointing to the two lads).

"So what is in the other two boxes?"

"One have all di stan's an di other, all di cymbals." [*One has all the stands and the other all the cymbals.*]

She looked at her watch. This was now well into her lunchtime. Her questions then took on a more serious tone.

"You know what we call 'weed', Mr Skip?"

I nodded.

"How do I know that the small, unopened box is not full of weed?"

"But Miss, yuh really tink I is a rasta man?" [*But miss, you surely don't think someone like me is a rasta man?*]

She burst out into even louder laughter.

"Skip is a good Christian; he nuh even smoke cigarette-dem," interjected Marky.

"Oh, so you is a Christian?"

I had to be careful here. I was not going to tell a direct lie to a customs officer. But Harry interrupted before I was able to answer,

"Yes, Maam, Skip was with us at our Church of God in Frankfield on Sunday gone."

"So how you mean you is a *volunteer* teacher? I hear some of them white teacher from Englahn get better salary than our own Jamaican teachers - that noh right!"

"And I agree with you - that is not fair. But as a VSO volunteer, I only get an allowance of 60 JA$ per month."

At that, she raised her pretty eyebrows, but turning around, said nothing.

As she walked back to her office, closely followed by Harry, I could just hear him say,

"Skip do plenty for us. Him even use him own money fi tek us campin." [*Skip has done so much for us. He's even used his own money to take us camping.*]

"If anyone deserve a 'bly' [*break*], it's Skip."

After a few minutes she returned and handed me several documents.

"You can close up the box now and give this paper to the man at the gate."

"So you don't want to check that there's no weed in the other boxes?"

"It's OK. Your two friends have convinced me you are not a drug dealer. We normally charge duty on musical instruments coming into the country, but on this occasion, I have decided to make an exception. I hope you enjoy your stay in Jamaica."

I was so elated I wanted to give her a big hug, but thought it might not be appropriate in the circumstances so, instead, shook her hand and thanked her profusely as she got ready to leave for a late lunch.

"Skip wants to stay and live in Jamaica for the rest of his life! We're going to find him a nice Jamaican girl!" said Marky cheekily.

"A nice Jamaican girl like you, maybe?" I said impulsively.

She laughed, and despite my feeling a bit awkward about this exchange, I couldn't help thinking how attractive she was when she smiled.

"But what is this? Me did tink you was a good Christian gentleman, Mr Skip, but now you is trying to flirt wid me!"

After a wonderful lunch of patties, cocoa-bread (another delightful discovery) and ice-cold ginger beer at Tastee Patties, we headed home. I thanked the lads over and over again for their assistance. They had saved me from embarrassment in helping to get the duty waived as I didn't exactly have a lot of surplus money at the time.

"Now what's all this about 'finding me a nice Jamaican girl?' "

The lads just laughed.

* * *

I had already decided to keep the drums in the prep-lab as I didn't think they would go down too well with Miss Daph at my lodgings. Getting the boxes up to the third floor was a real trial of strength and it was fortunate we had Mas'

John to help the three of us push and pull them one step at a time. Over the next couple of evenings, I opened the remaining boxes and lovingly reassembled the drums, each shell with its respective skin. Then I set up the stands and cymbals and gave everything a good shine; they looked gorgeous, even though surrounded by Physics equipment.

Over the next couple of months, I kept looking round for any opportunity I could find to play with other musicians, but it soon became clear that the kind of musicians and musical styles that I had formerly been familiar with, were unlikely to be found in Frankfield. One day, however, while driving to Mandeville in the Vogue, I passed a pretty little cottage, quite separate from any other houses, about a mile beyond Spaulding. In the garden between the house and the road was a large wooden shed with no windows on the road side but, with my car windows down as usual, I could not help but hear the unmistakable, throbbing, sound of a bass guitar, a keyboard and a lead guitar, all playing reggae, coming from inside the shed. And the music sounded great! Without even thinking, but with great excitement, I stopped suddenly, pulled over, parked the car on the roadside and ran back to the shed. After knocking on the door around the far side and hearing a faint 'Yeh man' from within, I pushed open the door and was greeted by a literal wall of high intensity sound. When they saw me, the three musicians all stopped playing in amazement to size up the white man who had suddenly appeared from nowhere in the middle of their band practice.

"W'appen man! Yuh need a drummer?" [*How's it going? Does your band need a drummer?*]

Melvyn, the tall, dark, good-looking guy who had been singing and playing the bass guitar, laughed and turned to Clive, the guitarist;

"Yuh tink dis yah white man can lick a reggae beat, massa? [*What's the chance that this white man here can play a good reggae beat, guys?*]

"If im a try fi tahk patois, mek we gi'im a chance!"
[*Well, if he's made the effort to speak Jamaican patois, perhaps we should give him a chance?*]

And that was my introduction to the reggae band, soon to be known as 'Third Generation'. Although a policeman by profession, Melvyn, the band leader, was a born entertainer and could both sing and play really well. Clive, however, was undoubtedly the best musician, and whenever a dispute arose about which chord was required at any given place in any of the new songs being learnt, he was the final arbitrator. (When Clive eventually left Jamaica for the USA, he became the lead guitarist in the well-known soul band, Harold Melvyn and the Bluenotes.) Ash, who could play multiple instruments - keyboard, rhythm guitar *and* drums - was also a great musician and, over the next few weeks, taught me most of the reggae and calypso drum-beats that I would need to know.

Learning reggae and calypso was more complex than I had ever imagined. At first it seemed like the accented beats were all in the 'wrong' place in the bar, but I was determined to master this musical genre and refused to give up. It took several weeks for my brain to finally 'click' with these new and fascinating rhythms, but once I had them included in my drum-beat repertoire, I was hooked. Moreover, it was great fun, playing with the group of highly capable musicians who made up 'Third Generation'.

Chapter 8: Musical Adventures

I suppose it was inevitable that once it became common knowledge locally that, not only was I a drummer, but also now had my own drum-set available for use, requests would start to come my way to play at various church functions. In the early 1970's, Frankfield boasted at least six different churches, including the Anglican, the Methodist, the Baptist and no less than three different Church-of-God's. All six were able to offer beautiful, vocal renditions of traditional Christian hymns, as I had already experienced at 'my' local Church of God - but, they also each had their own, very catchy, Jamaican worship songs. And all the church leaders knew full well that if they hoped to attract more children and teenagers (with their parents) to swell their congregations, it was imperative to get an appropriate ratio of contemporary worship songs to traditional hymns, particularly at 'conventions' which typically took place two or three times a year. If a particular church was fortunate enough to have a keyboard or a guitar and competent musicians to play them, this was a great asset. To have these instruments accompanied by a live drummer, would be the icing on the cake! And so it was, with a certain degree of consternation, that I was soon frequently playing 'gospel drums' in various local churches on Sunday mornings or at church conventions, while playing 'reggae drums' at stage shows and in clubs with Third Generation band most Saturday nights.

In view of the inner conflict I was experiencing as a consequence of the obvious clash between my two, diametrically opposed, musical worlds, I was more than surprised when, after a few weeks of playing for church services and conventions, the idea of forming my very own *gospel* band (quite separate and apart from Third Generation reggae band) began to formulate in my mind.

And the more I tried to dismiss the idea, the stronger it became. I found this situation somewhat perplexing, since the very notion of an agnostic like me spearheading a band focusing on religious music, seemed to me to be totally contradictory. However, by this time, I had got to know several, very talented, young church musicians, most of whom I was actually already acquainted with because they were the same students whom I was teaching at Compre. When I casually asked one or two of them if they might be interested in playing in a gospel band, it was as if I had lit a bonfire!

With myself on drums and, by then, conversant with all the basic Caribbean rhythmic patterns, the percussion section of the band was basically taken care of (although I would soon be joined by Spenga, another of my Compre students, playing the bongos to further enhance it).

Then, there was Glen, already a highly accomplished Church of God guitarist, currently in Year 10, who lived in the nearby village of Pennants. From a young age he had been playing the lead guitar and chord patterns for a host of Jamaican gospel tunes, and any that he didn't already know, he could pick up, by ear, in just a few minutes.

After Glen came Marky (who had helped me collect my drums at the customs depot in Kingston) from nearby Andrew Hill who had managed to acquire a nice bass guitar and who, although he had never, ever played before, very quickly and naturally took to this instrument as if he had been playing it all his life.

Count was to become our fifth band member. Also a Compre student, he owned a small 4-octave keyboard without even a proper stand. Like Marky, he had never had any formal musical training, but his ability to play by ear was remarkable.

Finally there was Fern (another of my students) who lived at the nearby Lampard district and who was already a competent musician and rhythm guitarist at his local church.

Now that we had the basic line-up of musicians, I turned my attention to seeking one or more good vocalists. Grace, a Compre student then in Grade 9, whom I had heard singing at a school concert and who had very obvious vocal talent, fitted the bill perfectly as female lead singer.

And lastly, for male vocals, we had Prince, a young field worker with the Ministry of Agriculture, who lived at nearby Spaulding and who, to the great advantage of the band, already had his own jeep to get around in. Prince had an amazing, rich, baritone voice, as well as being a stylish guitarist, and had already written several of his own, really beautiful, gospel songs. The only band member with no direct association with Compre, he was of a similar age to myself and naturally assumed a more mature, almost paternal role in the group.

So there we were, the 'Magnificent Seven', a brand new, seven-piece, gospel band, (only three of whom were Christians - Glen, Fern and Prince) but with a wealth of talent and potential.

Now we needed a name!

At one of our first band practices (which were conveniently held in my Physics Lab), we were bouncing around various possible names. Even though I was still inwardly uncomfortable with the very concept of myself as an agnostic *leading* a gospel band, I suddenly had an idea for a name. Since our ostensible, religious aim was to 'bring people to God' through music and sound, or, as a Physicist would say, 'through the sonic medium', why not call ourselves 'Sonic Salvation'? Everyone immediately liked the suggestion and so, the name stuck. We would henceforth be known as *Sonic Salvation Gospel Band*.

* * *

Meanwhile, Third Generation was progressing from strength to strength. Apart from playing in night-clubs and bars throughout Clarendon, Manchester and other nearby parishes, with band leader Melvyn doing most of the singing, we were also earning a reputation as a competent back-up reggae band for freelance vocal artists such as Delroy Wilson, Gregory Isaacs and Dennis Brown at much larger outdoor stage-shows. By now, my hair had grown longer once again and my stage outfit generally consisted of widely flared, pink and black pants (trousers), and brightly coloured T-shirts with logos such as 'peace', 'love' and 'music' printed prominently on the front. Melvyn, a real extrovert who always stood out from the crowd, generally wore a long purple and gold robe which endowed him with an air of royal splendour, although he must have been as hot as hell when we were on stage! Clive, in complete contrast, was totally unconcerned about his appearance and was only interested in his guitar playing. Overall, the band was getting really accurate musically and tight with the timing, so much so that we were even getting requests to play as far afield as Kingston.

I will never forget one of these musical ventures, playing at a club in West Kingston. This area, I later learnt, was in an almost continuous state of violence and political turmoil and was definitely a no-go area for strangers, particularly someone white like me. Unfortunately, as far as the eye could see, I was the only white person around and while I was setting up my drum-kit, I was getting some very aggressive looks and comments from certain individuals who were unashamedly carrying machetes and even *hand-guns*, tucked in their waist-bands! This was starting to make me feel very uncomfortable and I was genuinely concerned for my safety, and wishing I had never come at all. To his credit, Melvyn, immediately picked up on my concern and discomfort and summoned together a fairly large group of the most aggressive-looking 'gangsters' and called me over.

"Yuh tink dis yah man a one *white* man? Look good, man - dat a jus white *paint* pon im skin! Him a show one love to *all* a di black bredda and sister (pointing to the 'one love' logo on the front of my T-shirt) so him is '*a white man with a black heart*'. Him name 'Skip', an him lick some *bad* reggae drum in a di band. Skip gwaan well cool, man. Now top unu foolishness an mek di man feel welcome."
[*Do you really think this is actually a 'white' man? Look closer - it's just white paint on his skin! He loves all black people like they are his brothers and sisters, so he's a white man on the outside only. His Jamaican nickname is 'Skip', and wait until you hear what a great reggae drummer he is. Skip is a cool guy, he's alright. Now stop your foolish behaviour and make him feel welcome.*]

I was immensely grateful for Melvyn's moral support and for diffusing what could have become a very dangerous situation. I was also rather touched by my new description as 'a white man with a black heart'. As for any lingering tension, it just dissipated into thin air and some of the 'gangsters' even came over to me and shook hands. When I responded to their welcoming comments in my stumbling patois, they roared with laughter;

"Tan deh! Di 'white man wid di black heart' gwaan alright, man." [*Wait a minute! This 'white man with the black heart' really is alright!*]

The band played really well and, afterwards, several of the formerly most aggressive-looking 'gangsters' came over to say thanks.

"Yuh lik di drum dem good, sah! [*You play really well!*]
"Yuh heart mussy black fi true" [*You must really be black at heart.*]

"Come back anytime man. Yuh safe ya soh. Nobady will trouble yuh." [*You can come back here any time. You'll be safe, and no one will give you any trouble.*]

On the way home later that night, I couldn't help smiling to myself at the day's events and thinking what a shame it was that there was so little intermingling of the races in the inner-city areas like where we had just played. Even those who were the most violent-looking were quite friendly once one got to know them.

* * *

As Third Generation started playing at more distant venues, so too Sonic Salvation began to broaden its horizons. After the band had been practicing and performing for several months, Brother Ira, the minister of 'my' Church of God asked if we would be willing to put on a concert at a little church he pastored in Westphalia, a small community way up in the foothills of the Blue Mountains, some 90 miles from Frankfield. Logistically, such a venture would need at least four vehicles to carry all the band members and equipment, and would involve an overnight stay because of the distances involved. Furthermore, since there was no electricity supply in the community at that time, we would need to carry our own portable electric generator. But we were assured that all our meals would be provided and also that we would have our accommodation taken care of. It sounded like a great opportunity to get to know a part of the island that I had dearly wanted to explore for some time. So once I had cleared the dates with all the band members and had permission from Mr Latty to carry with us the school's portable electric generator, we were all raring to go. Prince and myself would drive our respective vehicles, Brother Ira would drive his car and Brother Morris, one of the young assistant pastors, would also drive his vehicle to make up the quota we needed.

By this time, we had swelled our ranks to eight band members as Spenga was now playing with us on the bongos. Since Prince and myself were both band members and drivers, we therefore had a total of ten people, plus all the equipment, plus the generator, plus overnight bags, all to be squeezed into three cars and a jeep. It ended up that just about all the equipment and the generator, together with a couple of cans of petrol, were wedged into my Vogue and Prince's jeep, while most of the band members and personal bags were squeezed into the other two cars.

We just managed it, and so early one bright Saturday morning, as the sun was rising, our convoy set off. Brother Ira had decided to go on ahead along with those travelling with him, to make sure all the necessary preparations were in place in Westphalia, while Morris (who also knew the route) and his passengers would lead the other vehicles carrying all the equipment. Our intention was to get there by early afternoon to allow sufficient time to set up for the Saturday evening gospel concert. Once we had reached May Pen and were on the highway to Kingston, we made good progress, passing through Old Harbour and Spanish Town, then skirting around the north-western side of Kingston, past Kintyre (the Scout campsite) and, finally, starting the long climb up the foothills of the Blue Mountains. The higher we climbed, the more amazing the views became so, whenever we came to an appropriate point on the road where a gap in the dense foliage allowed us to look out from the mountains down towards Kingston, the airport on the Palisados Peninsula and the blue sea beyond, we made a quick stop to stretch our legs, enjoy the absolutely spectacular view and drink in the refreshingly cool air. I resolved there and then that, at some point during my stay in Jamaica, I simply *had* to hike to Blue Mountain peak, 7,402 feet above sea level, and camp out for a night there on the summit.

At about 3,000 feet above sea level the paved road we had hitherto been travelling on, became a single-width track and our rate of travel slowed significantly. At various places along the track, we had to ford small streams but the water was shallow and they presented no significant problem and so, on we drove. By now, it was late morning and, to our great disappointment, the formerly crystal clear, blue sky had completely clouded over. The clouds got ominously dark and, in a very short space of time, the air became sticky with moisture. All of a sudden, the heavens opened.

To anyone familiar with typical English drizzle, or even a so-called 'downpour', all I can say is that, until you have been in a real deluge in Jamaica's Blue Mountains, you haven't really experienced heavy rain. Rain so thick and continuous that one's windscreen wipers simply cannot cope with the volume of water. Rain delivering such immense amounts of water that in literally minutes, tiny streams previously carrying just a trickle of water, become raging torrents carrying mud, stones, logs, and any other debris that might be in the way. We stopped for a while, as much as anything because we simply couldn't see where we were going. Fortunately, the deluge lasted only a few minutes and stopped almost as quickly as it started. But the track, now saturated with water and slippery with mud, made the going more difficult and we were progressing at a snail's pace. On rounding a sharp bend, where the track widened slightly to allow vehicles travelling in opposite directions to pass, when necessary, the foliage suddenly disappeared and the track continued along a sort of shelf, cut out of the rock, halfway up the side of a deep ravine. On our left was a steep wall of shale and mud stretching skywards, while on our right was a really deep drop down into the ravine, hundreds of feet below. Not a place for a nervous driver, I thought.

Then, all of a sudden, and without even indicating, Morris who was still in the lead, came to an abrupt stop. I slithered to a halt behind him, almost running into the rear of his car. When we gingerly climbed out, noting our frightening proximity to the edge of the gorge, to find out what the problem was, we saw in dismay that about 50 yards ahead, the road was completely blocked by a huge mass of mud and stones, deposited by a tiny stream which was now gently crossing the track at that point, but which had clearly been a raging torrent during the recent downpour. Morris tut-tutted and shook his head.

> "Di road well block, man! Yuh need bulldozer fi clear dat." [*The road is completely blocked. Only a bulldozer could clear it.*]

I walked ahead to the mound of mud and stones, climbed on top of it and walked across to the other side. If we had brought half a dozen shovels with us and had a couple of hours to spare, we could probably have dug our way through. But we had neither the shovels nor the time and I was determined not to be beaten by a bit of mud in the road. I paced out the length of the blockage and estimated its height above the surface of the track. An idea was forming in my mind that could only have been dreamt up by an impulsive Physicist.

> "I reckon that if I get a good enough run at the blockage, my forward momentum will carry me across before the car sinks down into the pile of gunge. I think I can make it through."

But both Morris and Prince had serious reservations about my untested theory and neither of them were willing to be the guinea-pig for an experimental test of its validity.

> "Dat too risky, Skip! Yuh sure you know what yuh a do?"

> "I don't see that we have much choice unless we want to turn back and go home. And besides, my plan is all based on Physics!"

112

The next few minutes were spent carefully reversing the three vehicles to the widening in the track to enable me to get the Vogue into lead position and to maximise the possible run-up distance. I climbed into the driver's seat and patted the dashboard.

"Now let's see what a *real* car can do!" I said, boastfully.

I revved up the engine and slipped straight into second gear, trying to achieve the greatest speed possible over the 50 yards or so between where we had parked and the blockage. The Vogue sailed over the mound in the road for the first couple of yards, but when its weight caused the tyres to sink down into the pile of mud and stones, so that the underside of the car was dragging over the top of the heap, it came to a very sudden stop. Irrespective of what gear I tried to engage, I was firmly stuck.

Then, without warning, came the second deluge of rain. I climbed out of the driver's door, slamming it behind me, and was immediately drenched. Climbing down off the heap of mud and stones, I watched in horror as, for a second time, the gentle little stream transformed in no time at all into a raging torrent. Immediately my mind started to race; would the force of the water be enough to push the car down into the gorge and if that were to happen, could we at least save the instruments beforehand? I ran back to the other two cars where everyone else was sheltering from the rain.

"The Vogue is stuck in the mud but I'm concerned that the force of the water might push it into the gorge. I think we should at least try to save the instruments inside the car."

I didn't need to say more. With one accord, all the guys jumped out of the other two vehicles and without a murmur of 'I told you so', started helping me to drag the instruments, amplifiers, speakers and the generator out through the rear door of my poor car and pack them onto the seats of the other two cars, out of the rain. Everyone was soaked through, long before we had emptied the Vogue.

Then, somebody had an idea. A quarter of a mile back down the track, we had passed a small rural shop and seen a few men sheltering from the rain. Spenga offered to run back there, to ask if the men would be willing to come and help us rescue the car. To their credit, within a few moments, not only had the men located ropes, shovels and anything else they could find which might be useful, but ignoring the rain, they ran up to where the car was stuck, carrying everything they had collected.

For several minutes they tried frantically to shovel away at the base of the heap to see if they might be able to free the car, but to no avail. Then, attaching the rope to the rear of the car, we combined forces and heaved with all our might to see if we could pull the car back out of the mud and stones. However, whatever we tried, it soon became apparent that this was, at best, an exercise in futility. After about 10 minutes, they finally admitted defeat and apologised profusely that there was nothing more they could do. They had done their best, getting drenched in the process, so, we expressed our sincerest gratitude, and dejectedly watched them walk back down the road. Once they had left, we felt even more hopeless, especially as the rain continued unabated.

I stood there, soaked to the skin and covered in mud, bemoaning the anticipated loss of my wretched car, until Marky piped up,

"Skip, if we try and channel the water so that it flows mainly past the front and rear of the car, rather than hitting it full force on the side, we might be able to save it from being pushed into the gorge."

By now, new mud and stones had piled up to the tops of the windows so that the waves of water were flowing over the heap and actually over the *top* of the car. I was so desperate that I was going to lose the car that I didn't even notice when Marky and Fern actually *lay down* in the water, on top of the pile of mud and stones, one near the front of the car and the other at the back, to form a human wall with their bodies to try and divert the flow of water and reduce the force on the side of the car, pushing it towards the gorge. Their attempt to 'channel the water' showed complete disregard for their personal safety as the force of the water might easily have washed both of *them* over the edge and down into the gorge! But over and above that, it was an act of amazing courage and loyalty which I would never forget.

The deluge suddenly eased a little, and as I was bitterly reflecting on my ill-conceived plan, having lost all hope of saving the car, I suddenly heard the most amazing sound; the unmistakeable roar of what could only be the engine of a huge mechanical bulldozer.

Yes! It was! And, as the 'beast' rounded the corner in the track ahead of us, beyond the blockage in the road, and finally came into view, whom should we see sitting up there in the cab by the side of the driver, shouting for all he was worth and waving madly, but *Spenga*!

In all the drama and confusion, I hadn't even noticed that Spenga had had the presence of mind to try running in the opposite direction up the track to see if there was any alternative help. Apparently, only a short distance beyond the blockage, he had come across this beast of a machine parked on the side of the track. He had then located the driver who was sleeping at the time and had to be woken 'because it was an emergency' and begged for his help. Promising *great financial reward* for his services, Spenga had persuaded him to drive the bulldozer back to aid us in our desperate plight. Seeing the bulldozer, I just stood there by my half-buried Vogue with my mouth hanging open and with tears of joy and relief chasing the raindrops running down my cheeks.

115

Spenga jumped down from the bulldozer cab and we watched in awe as the 'beast' took a first huge scoop of mud and stones from the heap in front of my car and dumped it over the edge of the gorge. Then, carefully and cleverly, the huge shovel was slid into the heap of gunge, under the front wheels of the wretched Vogue, and slowly raised until the car was finally tilted at the angle I had been hoping to achieve in my futile, earlier attempt to get over the blockage. After an ominous crunch of gears as the driver selected reverse, the 'beast' was then gently inched backwards, pulling the car behind it, until it was completely clear of the remainder of the mud and stones still blocking the track.

"See if yuh can staht ee, so yuh can move ee out a di way." [*See if you can start the car, so that you can drive it out of the way.*]

I didn't need a second invitation and jumped into the driver's seat to see if the car would start. Considering the amount of water that had been flooding over the engine during the deluge, it was surely a miracle that on the very first turn of the ignition key, the engine burst into life and I was quickly able to move the car out of the way of the 'beast'. With no further obstruction to progress, the bulldozer made light work of the remainder of the blockage, shovelling the mud and stones down into the gorge, and within just five minutes, the track was clear!

Spenga, endeavouring to fulfil his promise of '*great financial reward*' for the driver, came around to each person to collect any small change that we might have to hand, but with all our personal bags having gone on ahead in Brother Ira's car, the pitiful total we managed to find between us amounted to less than *two Jamaican dollars*. The driver was clearly not best pleased, but after surveying our totally sodden, filthy state, he generously declined our offer. Nodding in resignation as we thanked him profusely, he wished us well, re-mounted the 'beast', and in a few

116

seconds disappeared from view. Then, just as quickly as it had started, the rain finally stopped completely.

These Sonic Salvation band members were certainly more than fair-weather friends! With little or no concern for their personal safety, displaying the patience of Job with my foolhardy ideas, and intelligently taking the initiative to find a solution when I had run out of steam, they had helped me to save both the instruments and the car. I also couldn't help thinking that, if there really was a God, he must surely have intervened miraculously on my behalf in this incident.

* * *

By the time we eventually reached Westphalia, the sky was once again crystal blue and the sun was just going down. We were tired, wet, cold and hungry, and to add to our misery, all the people who had been enthusiastically waiting for the concert had, by this time, mostly given up and gone home. When we explained to Brother Ira what had happened, he did his utmost to cheer us up by encouraging us to go and get washed and to put on some dry clothes, and then meet at the house where we would be staying the night to get some well-needed food and drink.

"Don't fret, Skip. Tomorrow is Sunday so, when word gets around, the people will come back for the concert which we can have in the afternoon. In fact, if we can combine the morning service and the concert into one, then we'll be sure to get a good crowd."

There were no proper showers as such, just an overhead pipe with a large brass tap which dowsed us, one at a time, with ice-cold water, causing us to clench our teeth, soap up and rinse off at break-neck speed. Even though we were only at about 4,000 feet above sea level, I was completely taken aback at how cold the water was and how chilly the air felt. But once we had washed off the mud and got into some dry clothes, we felt revived and ravenously hungry.

117

Thankfully and to our immense relief, the wonderful smell of roast chicken, rice and peas, boiled yam and sweet potato was wafting from inside the house and we needed no invitation to follow our noses;

"Unu come an si-dung yah so, mi luv. Wi mek nuff bickle fi *all* a di people dem, but now all a dem gone a dem yard, soh unu have plenty food fi eat." [*All of you, come and sit down here, my dears. We originally made enough food for everyone attending the concert, but since they've all gone home, you'll have plenty for yourselves.*]

True to their word, the two elderly Jamaican ladies heaped spoonful after spoonful of rice and yam and sweet potato onto our plates, so that when the chicken pieces were delicately balanced on top of the pile, it all looked like a miniature volcano! For a full 10 minutes, the only sound to be heard was of utensils scraping the plates and shovelling forkful after forkful of the most delicious food into our mouths. Then, one after another, hungry, tired faces began to transform into glowing pictures of contentment, and everyone started to laugh and joke and shout, as vivid memories of our afternoon's experiences came flooding back into our minds.

"Skip Vogue almos gone in a di gorge!" [*Skip's Vogue was almost lost in the gorge!*]

"If we never 'channel di water', *evry*ting would a gahn' [*If we hadn't 'channelled the water' away from the car, we'd have lost everything!*]

"Dis yah a one time dat Skip' Physics fail im, sah! [*This is one time when Skip's knowledge of Physics failed him!*]

"A did feel so embarrass when we never have nuttin fi give di poor bulldozer man." [*I felt so embarrassed when we didn't have any money to give to the poor bulldozer driver.*]

"But God is good, sah. Him save wi from di gorge!"
[*But, God is good. He saved us from the gorge!*]
The incredible memories of that afternoon were forever imprinted on our minds, and for over an hour we laughed and joked and relived everything we had gone through together. By this time, it was dark outside, except for the silver rays of a gorgeous full moon, and we were ready to turn in and get some well-earned rest. Not that I got much sleep, mind you, with three or four big guys each trying to stretch out on one of the several double beds that were available in the house. By the time we all nodded off, the combined snoring of all the men must have sounded like the engine of the 'beast' that had come to our rescue a few hours earlier!

Brother Ira was quite right about the people returning for the concert next day. By the end of the short Sunday worship service, the little church was bursting at the seams and everyone was excited, animated and eager for the concert to start. My main concern had been for the rain that might have seeped into the speaker cabinets but, however cold the Westphalia nights were, the days were gorgeously warm and, left out in the sun for a couple of hours, everything had completely dried by mid-day.

The concert couldn't have gone better; the musicians played impeccably, the singers sang beautifully, and even the old Compre generator did us proud. From the youngest children clapping their tiny hands while sitting on their parents' laps to the oldest men and women standing in the aisles and doorways, swaying to the music, everyone had a whale of a time; for them, this had been a novel and unforgettable experience. Everyone was happy, we were safe and well fed but on top of all that, I felt an inner contentment I couldn't explain. In spite of everything that had happened, Sonic Salvation Gospel Band was starting to make its mark throughout the hills and valleys of Jamaica.

Chapter 9: "Evryting A Physics!"

During the second term of my second year at Compre, the Science Department received a communication from the Association of Science Teachers in Jamaica inviting us to enter the annual Secondary Schools Science Exhibition. This was actually a science *competition*, open to all secondary schools and colleges across the island, with regional heats, followed by national finals. The heats for those parishes in the centre of the island were to be held at Church Teachers' College in Mandeville, while that year's finals would take place in Montego Bay. When the possibility of our entering the competition was floated at our fortnightly departmental meeting, it was fairly obvious that the Chemistry and Biology Departments were not particularly keen because of the anticipated volume of extra-curricular work that would be required. However, I was more than eager to participate and so it was decided that the fledgling Physics Department should go it alone.

Having never done anything of the sort before, I really had no idea what I was letting myself in for, but when one of my most able Physics students suggested we could investigate the feasibility of obtaining hydroelectric power from the Rio Minho, a seed was planted in my mind which just wouldn't stop growing. At the first opportunity, I got together all my GCE Physics students from Grades 10 and 11, so that we could plan how we might set about getting the necessary data, and decide how our results and conclusions could be presented in the most eye-catching way possible on suitable charts and displays. I also felt that it would be in our interests to make a large working model of a hydroelectric scheme to add visual impact to what was on the charts.

After stressing the amount of after-school work that would be involved, I reckoned I might get half-a-dozen students volunteering to take part but, to my amazement, ended up with almost 40! This meant splitting up into sub-groups, with the more academic students responsible for obtaining the necessary data from the river and performing all the necessary calculations from which a suitable conclusion could be drawn. In the meantime, the more artistic ones would be responsible for producing the banners and charts and posters, while the most practically inclined would undertake the task of constructing the working model in the workshops (which I envisaged would involve not a little scrounging for resources on my part).

I decided, however, to leave the difficult choice as to who would make up the student team actually presenting the project to the judges and the general public until I had had the chance to determine who would not get flustered when under pressure, expressing themselves clearly and confidently when asked challenging questions. When I pointed out to the entire group that we would probably be limited to taking a final team of about eight students, everyone involved just worked even harder in the hope of securing their place on the team. Some evenings we stayed at school as late as 7 o'clock, at which point I had to lay down the law and literally force the students to put their work on hold until the following day, to avoid walking home in the dark. I decided it was expedient to accompany all the investigative trips to the actual river just in case anyone should fall in the water, but I needn't have worried. These kids meant business!

Firstly, we had to determine the rate of flow of water, which we soon realised was not quite as simple as it might have seemed. This required a location where the water flowed smoothly between two parallel, vertical banks where accurate estimates of the width and length of the channel, together with the speed of the water could be obtained. Then we had to get estimates of the average gradient of the river-bed over the region which we felt would be the most suitable for the construction of the proposed hydroelectric scheme, and identify possible ways of diverting the water to a spot on the side of the river which would be reasonably safe in the event of a flood.

Meanwhile, the 'practical team', under the supervision of the welding and metalwork teachers, constructed an eye-catching model which included a large metal water tank that could be lifted (when empty) onto a tall, sturdy metal stand. This tank fed water to a specially designed, homemade turbine which, in turn, rotated an electric generator that I was reliably informed had been extracted from a scrapped car. The generator was connected to a series of lamps, representing a community that the proposed scheme would power.

Back in the lab, the artistic group were totally immersed in designing the most amazing charts that illustrated the principles involved and which gave concise explanations of everything that was being proposed. Everything was done in faint pencil first, before being checked meticulously for spelling mistakes and then coloured in with brightly coloured felt-tip pens. If a mistake was discovered after a particular chart was completed, we had perfected a method of cutting out the offending letter or number with a scalpel and inserting a piece of card of exactly the same colour and size, glued in place from the back, and then rewriting the correct letter or number from the front. This saved hours of work redoing the whole chart.

A couple of weeks before the heats were due to take place in Mandeville, Mr Latty had popped by one evening to see what was going on. He was clearly impressed with all the industrious preparations taking place and so, next day, I thought it was an appropriate time to pay him a visit to discuss all the necessary arrangements. From the very outset, I had felt that to travel back and forth between Frankfield and Mandeville each day over the three-day exhibition, was impractical and would involve significant transportation costs. I had already contacted the Principal of Church Teachers' College, Mr Kenneth Thaxter, about the possibility of our whole team staying over at the college for the duration of the competition and he had kindly offered us accommodation at the College as well as meals at nominal charge. So I had my pitch to Mr Latty all ready and prepared. As usual, he beat me to it!

"Good afternoon, Skip. Do have a seat."

"Good afternoon, Mr Latty. I'd like to talk with you about the forthcoming Science Exhibition, if you have a few moments."

Mr Latty nodded and smiled.

"Yes, I rather suspected you might have come to try and lever some more funds out of the school coffers."

I coughed apologetically, having already begged for significant extra resources for everything we had done thus far.

"I really appreciate your generosity so far, sir, but all the logistics of our participation point to the need for:
(a)   a minibus to take us to Mandeville on the Tuesday afternoon;
(b)   our being able to stay over at Church Teachers' College for the duration of the exhibition - the whole team, that is;
(c)   basic subsistence money for each student on the team during our stay;
(d)   a minibus to bring us back to Frankfield on Friday evening."

I had 'ticked off' all the items on my list as I was speaking and I had no idea what kind of response I should expect.

"Oh - and a bit of spare cash would be really useful in case we have to purchase any odds and ends while we are there…"

I thought I had better terminate the requests there, but then felt I should add,

> "I have already spoken to Mr Thaxter who has very kindly offered to accommodate us at Church Teachers' College at nominal cost."
> "So you don't think your salary could stretch to cover your list of expenses?"

Mr Latty laughed at his own joke, knowing full well how little I was getting for my monthly allowance from VSO.

> "I don't think it would quite stretch to that, Sir."

Mr Latty looked at his watch before replying.

> "I have a meeting I need to go to now Mr Skip. Would you be so kind as to put together a requisition to meet your needs, and specify how much liquid cash you are likely to require, and give it to the Bursar. I think the school will be able to cope with that. Oh, and please give my regards to Mr Thaxter."

Things couldn't have worked out better! The only remaining obstacle now was choosing the final team from the army of faithful workers. I decided to make up five different, possible teams of eight so that everyone would have the opportunity to try for a place, and then I asked some of my colleagues in the Science Department to come along as mock judges to give each team a good grilling. The results of the elimination process were, however, really a foregone conclusion, and we were all in full agreement on which students should represent the school. Giving that information to the students, however, was a heart-breaking task as it was clear that some were visibly upset not to have been chosen. There was little I could do but thank them all profusely for their help and to remind everyone that those who had not been selected would get first preference to go on the student day-trip that was being organised by the Science Department to visit the exhibition.

We had decided to leave straight after school on Tuesday afternoon to allow us to install ourselves for our stay at the Teachers' College and then set up our display and model in the auditorium that was hosting the exhibition. By so doing, we would be ready to commence our presentations first thing on Wednesday morning after breakfast. When everything was installed, with the 'Frankfield High School Comprehensive' banner stretching proudly across the top of our various chart-bearing display boards and our hydroelectric power station model standing in all its glory nearby, I couldn't help but feel very proud of what the students had accomplished.

The team consisted of five boys and three girls who, when we assembled for breakfast at the College early on Wednesday morning, all looked immaculate in their Compre uniforms, with beautifully ironed pleats in the girls' light blue skirts and razor-sharp creases in the boys' khaki trousers. Where they had found the time to have ironed all their clothes, polished their shoes and combed their hair styles to perfection, I could not fathom. But there was no doubt at all that, irrespective of their rural origins, my students had far greater dress-sense than I had ever had at their age.

Our decision to travel on the Tuesday and set up the evening before, undoubtedly paid real dividends. While students from the other competing schools were all scurrying around to set up their displays on the first morning of the exhibition, my team members could relax, read and re-read the contents of their charts, test each other with deliberately awkward questions and work out how they would split the verbal presentations between each pair. By midday, visitors started to arrive from around the town and waves of trainee teachers from the College came along to investigate how well the presenters 'knew their stuff'. I had decided to stand discretely to one side and not to intervene if any of the students got tongue-tied or gave any incorrect answers to the constant barrage of questions being fired at them.

But I needn't have worried; they rose to the occasion and performed flawlessly, regardless of the pressure they were under. When our bus-load of Compre students and teachers came on the Thursday afternoon, they were clearly surprised and very impressed by how confidently and eloquently everyone was performing. And by the time the judges arrived on the Friday morning, the team was operating like a well-oiled machine. Not even a single question from the judges caught the students off-guard and it was obvious how impressed they were with all aspects of the concept, the science involved, our stunning charts and the explanations given, with the demonstration of the working hydroelectric power station model being the icing on the cake.

On the Friday afternoon, when the winners were announced and we were presented with a number of trophies, including the coveted 'Best Project' award in the regional heats, the joy on the students' faces literally lit up the whole auditorium. For my part, I felt duly proud of what they had achieved and was truly happy that our efforts had borne such fruit. After the closing ceremony had finished, I assembled my team together and offered my own congratulations;

> "Well done, *all* of you; you were *fantastic*! This means, of course, that we shall now be going to the national finals in Montego Bay just before we break up for Easter. So we need to be really careful not to damage any of the charts or banners as we take them down and pack up. Does anyone fancy a stop at KFC before we leave Mandeville?"

* * *

As might have been expected, the presentations of the trophies by Mr Latty in Monday's whole-school assembly caused great excitement and tumultuous cheering. Mr Latty was beaming from ear to ear, and I knew that I would have no problem getting whatever resources we might need to attend the national finals. The days literally flew by and before we knew it, we were *en route* to Montego Bay where we were privileged to spend the next three nights in a delightful little hotel overlooking the beautiful bay of this enchanting tourist resort. Once again, we decided to travel on the Tuesday to facilitate setting up in the nearby auditorium where the finals of the competition would be held. I knew the competition would be much tougher now that we would be competing against the finalists from the top Kingston schools and colleges and tried my best to caution the students about getting their hopes up too high. I was also aware that the judges included some of the most distinguished Science Educators in the country such as the Principal of The College of Arts, Science and Technology (CAST), Dr Alfred Sangster, himself a renowned and well-respected engineer. But it was impossible to suppress the enthusiasm of my Compre team and, in the end, the only thing I could do was offer my support and encouragement in response to comments such as,

"No fret Skip. We can beat dem…jus watch an see!"
to which I could only smile.

I suppose, although hoping against hope that we might take the big prize, I was inwardly apprehensive that, particularly if the competing schools were fielding high calibre A-level students, my relatively inexperienced students from Grades 10 and 11 might have difficulty answering the more challenging questions likely to be posed by this more prestigious group of judges. Fortunately, our Montego Bay visitors on the Wednesday and Thursday were significantly more scientifically astute than the visitors had been in Mandeville, which helped our team to sharpen up their skills. By 'Judgement Day' (Friday), I could only let fate run its course and stand back and listen to the dialogue between our students and the judges. But probe as he might, Dr Sangster, in particular, could not fault the responses from my 'key players' and seemed very satisfied with everything he had heard and seen.

At the Friday afternoon presentation ceremony, my heart was beating overtime when it came to the announcement of the winning school and you could have heard a pin drop in the auditorium.

> *"And the overall winners are… Frankfield High School!"*

It was unbelievable - an almost unknown, rural secondary school, not included among those educational institutions with reputations for academic excellence, had actually beaten every school in Jamaica including all the capital city's top schools. Compre had done it! The auditorium erupted and my students just couldn't restrain themselves;

"We did it Skip; we beat them all!"

"Yes, you brilliant lot, but didn't I tell you, 'Everything is Physics'?"

"No Sah, mi tink yuh mean 'Evryting a Physics!'" [*No Sir, I think you should say in patois, 'Everything is Physics!'*]

And that was how the Compre Physics Department motto, '*Evryting a Physics!*' originated.

* * *

On our return to Frankfield, Mr Latty was ecstatic; his school might be languishing at the very bottom of the secondary schools' sports leagues, but that paled in comparison to actually winning a national competition of an *academic* nature. He decided, therefore, that it would be appropriate to invite The Hon Edwin Allen, Minister of Education and the school founder, to a special presentation ceremony in the school auditorium. For Minister Allen, our achievement was the perfect justification for his belief in what could be achieved educationally by the introduction of a *comprehensive* secondary school system. Compre was no longer 'an experiment'; it was now part of the establishment.

After presenting all seven trophies from both the regional heats and the national finals to the members of the winning team, and giving a short but obligatory political speech, he gestured in my direction, thanked me profusely for what the Physics Department had achieved, and expressed his hope that this would be my first of many such successes. My answering smile only served to conceal the inner turmoil I was, once again, experiencing in view of my proposed return to England in approximately three months' time.

The day before we broke up for the two-week Easter holiday, I decided I should go and have a serious talk with Mr Latty. I had the greatest respect for this man who had basically made it his life's purpose to put Compre on the map and steer it towards gaining recognition and status in the educational system in Jamaica. Perhaps, by this time, I saw him as rather like a father-figure from whom I could seek advice and guidance. And right now, I was really in need of guidance.

I was 23, going on 24 years old and starting to feel like I ought to be thinking of settling down; my family and particularly my parents were all looking forward to my return 'home'; I had committed myself to taking up the postgrad place at Bart's in September, was excited about the academic challenge this constituted, and was really looking forward to working under the Head of Department, Professor Rotblat; I currently had no romantic attachments in Jamaica…

And yet, everything seemed to be tugging me to stay put; I was thoroughly enjoying my job as a Physics

Teacher; I had fantastic students who actually *wanted* to learn; I had a brand new state-of-the-art Physics Lab; I had lots of musical opportunities and was enthusiastically enjoying playing in both Sonic Salvation Gospel Band and Third Generation reggae band; I was having a great time running the Scout group; and I even had a car, of sorts, to get about in. Clearly this was a decisive moment in my life; should I remain in Jamaica or should I head back to the 'motherland'? I just didn't know which way to turn.

Fortunately, I had requested a 'fairly lengthy' meeting with Mr Latty, who just sat silently and listened for the better part of 10 minutes as I poured out my concerns, before answering;

"Skip, the best advice I can give you is 'follow your heart'. There are clearly pros and cons whichever way you decide. But for a minute, perhaps we could look pragmatically at some important aspects of your future.

"Firstly, my understanding is that VSO does not generally extend its contract with a volunteer beyond two years. So, if you decided to stay, you would need to either go onto expatriate contract or continue as a local teacher. Either way, you would be earning significantly more than the allowance you are currently getting as a volunteer.

"Secondly, although I know you have enjoyed boarding at the Broomfields with your colleague Mr Lloyd, you may well be feeling that it is time to establish your independence a little more by renting your own house or, perhaps, living in one of the Teachers' Flats, where there is also off-road parking.

"Thirdly, although you were not born in our beloved Jamaica, I am very aware of the efforts you have made to get to know the local people and their culture, and even our local *patois*, more-so than any other teacher from a foreign country that I have ever known. So, in essence, you are already part-way Jamaicanised! You obviously have to make the decision for yourself, but at least I can offer two 'sweeteners' which might make the decision to stay a little easier. Our current Head of Science will be leaving in the summer and I would be only too happy to offer you that post on a permanent contract basis, and also, the member of staff currently living in the upstairs Teachers' Flat at the end of the block is off to greener pastures at the end of next term, so as a result, a flat would become available for you to occupy from the start of the summer holidays should you so wish.

"Have a think about all your options over the Easter holiday and let me know what you have decided when school resumes for the Summer Term."
With that, Mr Latty stood up and shook my hand;
"Of course, Skip, I am sure you know that I would be very happy indeed should you decide to remain here with us at Compre."
I thanked Mr Latty for all his advice and also for his generous offers. I think I already knew in my heart what I was going to do, but that still left me with two very difficult letters to write over the Easter holiday; one to Professor Rotblat and the other to my father. How on earth could I explain that, after all my promises of a year ago, I was now going to go back on my word and, instead, '*follow my heart*'?

* * *

131

The letter to the professor was probably the less difficult of the two so I decided to write that one first. On the very first day of the holiday, Andy had, once again, driven over to Westmoreland to stay with Julie, so I had no one to ask for help. On about the third attempt, I finally got the words reasonably close to my feelings, deeply thanking the Professor for his continued faith in me over the last two years and apologising profusely for choosing not to keep to my professed intentions. As best I could, I tried to explain that I was now sure that my vocation in life was to remain for the foreseeable future as a Physics teacher in Jamaica. I also expressed my sincere hope that someone else would be found to fill my place on the course.

The letter to Baba was profoundly more difficult to put together and I must have rewritten it about 10 times before I felt it was even barely appropriate, as I knew it would cause him great distress. I tried to be honest but gentle, a loving son seeking his father's blessing but one who had to be true to his own convictions and *'follow his heart'*.

When both letters were finally completed and I had hesitantly dropped them into the big, red, Frankfield postbox, I felt that a great burden had been lifted from my shoulders. I was starting a new phase of my life as an independent bachelor with my career path clearly mapped out. For the next few years, I was going to remain teaching in Jamaica at Frankfield High School Comprehensive as Head of Physics *and* Head of Science. I would inform Mr Latty that I had decided to accept the same pay and conditions as my local Jamaican teaching colleagues, rather than taking the more lucrative contract generally offered to expatriate teachers. And I would reside at the Teachers' Flats.

The only thing missing now was that 'nice Jamaican girl'.

Chapter 10: Moving On

The school year rapidly disappeared into the heat of the summer and, immediately the long holiday started, I began packing away all my odds and ends at the Broomfields, ready for the move to my new 'home'. Andy was also packing for his return flight home to England, and I think Miss Daph was quite sorry to see us both leave. Just before making my final trip carrying all my things to my new Teacher's Flat, I gave her a big hug and thanked her for all her kindness and advice over the last two years - she had been like a mother to me and I would really miss her. She wished me well and prayed for God's protection over me as she wiped a tear from her cheek. Mas' Tom, always a man of few words, simply shook my hand and, with a twinkle in his eye, expressed his hope that I would soon settle down and find that 'nice Jamaican girl' that I was looking for.

I found my parting with Andy to be quite a deep, emotional experience. We had shared lodgings together for the better part of two years and had broached almost every topic under the sun during the daily discussions that became the norm over our evening meals. I would miss our friendly banter, the opportunity to seek brotherly advice, and the convenience of always having a sounding board on which to test my opinions. After spending time with their respective families back in England, he and Julie were now planning to continue teaching on further world travels by heading for South America later in the summer. I wished him and Julie every happiness for the future and made no secret of the fact that I really envied him for how things had panned out so well for the two of them. They were ideally matched.

Apart from the fact that I wasn't awash with funds for a return flight back home, I had decided that I would spend my long summer holiday mostly in Frankfield, getting my new 'home' organised (with my drum-set taking centre stage in the apartment), doing a few mechanical jobs on the Vogue, and getting ready for the annual Scout summer camp back at Discovery Bay on the North Coast during the last week of the holiday. And I was also very excited at the prospect of becoming 'properly' independent for the first time in my life.

Living by myself at the upstairs Teacher's Flat certainly proved to be an interesting learning experience. I no longer had the distinct privilege of enjoying Miss Daph's wonderful cooking each day, and I literally didn't have a clue as to how to function in a kitchen except for my somewhat limited attempts at bush-cooking with the Scouts. I had never in my entire life washed my own clothes or bed-linen, let alone ironed them. And I had never really been responsible for cleaning my own home and generally keeping things tidy. Making my own bed was the limit of my domestic experience thus far!

Luckily for me, on the very day that I moved all my stuff from the Broomfield's to my bed-sit flat, I was approached out of the blue by a very kind church sister who offered to do all my washing, ironing and general cleaning each week for a very modest weekly payment - I don't know if word had got round that an undomesticated young teacher might need some help. I didn't need to think twice and jumped at the opportunity.

But that still left me to sort out my own cooking and so I decided it would be useful to own a few utensils and, at the same time, get some bed linen. The supermarket and a couple of the local stores proved to be very helpful and by the end of the day I had acquired two very large 'billy pots', a frying pan, a kettle, a glass jug, together with a pillow and a couple of sheets. Complimenting myself on my new-found domestication, I decided to pop down to the local bakery for a quick 'dinner' of patties and cocoa-bread, washed down with a cold ginger beer. I was pretty tired by the end of the day so decided to get a quick, soap-less shower (I had, of course, forgotten to buy any kind of soap) and have an early night.

Next morning, it suddenly dawned on me that I had also forgotten to buy any sort of food for breakfast, or crockery or cutlery to eat with. This time, I thought it would be wise to make a more scientifically organised list of things to buy, and although I was starting to feel exceptionally hungry, sat down and tried to think of all the necessary food items I could possibly need for the whole of the next week, along with crockery, cutlery and soap. Despite the fact that it was already a rather long list, I kept thinking of all sorts of additional things I might conceivably need, causing the list to get longer and longer. And throughout the process, as the pangs of hunger started to gnaw at my stomach, the only thing I could think of was the very substantial breakfast I had become accustomed to at the Broomfield's. I decided it would be expedient to drive to the supermarket as I would have quite a lot to carry back. Thank God the Vogue was still working!

I began to realise how utterly naïve I was at doing a major domestic shop and suddenly began to feel like a student having to sit an exam for which no revision or preparation had been done; full of questions but with virtually no answers to offer.

How much rice would I need for a month?
How many tins of condensed milk would I consume daily?
Was it more economical to buy a large or small jar of coffee?
How many frozen chickens should I buy?
Wasn't flour used for baking? But what kind should I buy?
Should I get powder or liquid detergent for washing dishes?

135

How long would a bar of soap be likely to last?
Should I buy fresh pineapple or tinned slices?
Would it be wise to buy a pack of candles in case of a power cut?
Would I need different towels for the bathroom and the kitchen…?

The questions went on and on, as I got hungrier and hungrier, wandering somewhat aimlessly around the supermarket. Then, almost like an angel appearing from heaven, Pauline, one of the girls from my winning Science Exhibition team appeared, walking along the supermarket aisle towards me. After a quick exchange of pleasantries, I swallowed my pride and confessed my dilemma, begging her to help me in deciding what I needed and choosing what to buy. She laughed, and rather like a mother hen shielding a helpless chick, she took my list from me, replaced half the things I had already put in my basket back on the shelves and said,

"Skip, I can't believe it! A famous Physicist like you can't manage a simple task like doing a supermarket shop? How have you managed all these years?!"

I blushed and, looking for a scapegoat, blamed my ineptitude on my (entirely innocent) mother who, I protested, hadn't taught me any basic housekeeping skills. But with Pauline's help, the shopping expedition was completed relatively quickly, and having added to my list a number of items that she thought I might find useful like toothpaste, cooking oil and bread, she bid me farewell.

On returning home and unpacking as quickly as possible, the most essential task was making breakfast. With bread, butter, sliced bacon, cooking oil, coffee, condensed milk and a frying pan now available, a large bacon sandwich and a mug of piping hot coffee was clearly the order of the day. In fact, this became my staple start to the day for the next couple of years; it was quick, easy to make and tasted wonderful; maybe not quite up to Miss Daph's standard, but it was a good start for a newly independent bachelor!

Evening meals were, however, a bit more tricky. After repeating, several times over, the same stupid error of forgetting to thaw out a frozen chicken from the evening before, and then, the next day, having to decide what on earth to do with the large, frozen mass before me, I decided it was time to adopt a radically different strategy. Firstly, I made sure to get a frozen chicken properly thawed out overnight and, immediately after my statutory bacon sandwich and coffee breakfast, cut it up into small pieces which I put in one of my very large 'billy pots'. Then I added numerous, complimentary ingredients including one whole bottle of tomato ketchup, one whole tin of pineapple slices, a dozen chopped sweet potatoes, half a dozen onions sliced up into small pieces, half a small drum of black pepper, half a jar of liquid honey, some gravy browning, some escallion and a teaspoon of salt. The pot was then topped up with water and the whole lot brought to the boil and left to simmer for three to four hours. In the other very large 'billy pot' I put some water and as much rice as possible whilst still maintaining the correct rice-to-water ratio, a table-spoon of butter and a pinch of salt, all of which was also brought to the boil and left to simmer. By the late afternoon, I had two, very large pots of the most deliciously smelling food from which I served a large helping of rice which I then smothered with copious amounts of my sweet chicken 'broth'. I must say that, for my first foray into the dark, culinary arts, it tasted (to my sweet tooth, anyway) absolutely fantastic!

By bedtime, after everything had cooled, I made space in the very large fridge (provided by the school) for the two 'billy pots', by removing some of the shelves. The next evening, all that I needed to do was to heat the (entire) contents of the two large pots to provide a second helping of my culinary masterpiece. And so it continued each evening thereafter, with the reheated contents providing substantial helpings for up to a week. Although my 'menu' was, perhaps, a little short on variety, I had resolved the problem of dying a slow death from hunger at the same time as minimising the time needed for preparation of my meals. I was sure my dear mother would have been proud of my efforts!

* * *

Once my flat was more or less shipshape, with my drum-set installed in all its glory in the open space between the front door and the bed, it was time to spend a bit of time on the Vogue. Over the next couple of weeks, having previously sorted out the generator and electrical system, I decided to give the whole engine a thorough overhaul and service. Apart from draining the horrendously dirty and smelly engine oil and refilling the sump with new, clean oil, I changed both the oil and air filters (which looked like they had not been replaced since the car was first driven), put on a new distributor cap and changed the spark plugs and leads, removed and cleaned the carburettor and checked and adjusted the timing until the engine was idling perfectly. The Vogue was now purring like a tiger waiting to pounce on its prey and I felt it was time to give it a test drive. That very afternoon, my former students, Harry and Marky had popped by to see how I was getting on in the flat, and they both jumped at the opportunity to go out for a spin in the car the following afternoon.

We decided to try a circular route via Spaulding, Mandeville, May Pen and Chapelton, a total distance of about 60 miles, which I estimated would probably take us about a couple of hours. Of course, before we left, the lads both wanted to have a try on the drums so, by the time we actually set off, it was gone 4 o'clock and when we reached

Mandeville, it was already after 5 o'clock and we were all ravenous. A stomach-filling stop-off at KFC was therefore the order of the day. We ate huge portions of chicken and chips, washed down with large paper cups of refreshing, ice-cold soda, while discussing plans for the Discovery Bay Scout camp at the end of the summer holiday. Eventually, much revived, we left to head towards May Pen along the west-east highway, a fast, straight road where I could put the Vogue through its paces. The car was running perfectly, so obviously my labours had not been in vain. At the road junction in May Pen, we turned left and headed northwards for Chapelton. By this time, it was after 9 o'clock and pitch dark, but I knew the road well and we made good progress.

At Trout Hall, about two miles before Frankfield, we came to the narrow, flat bridge which crossed a small stream feeding the Rio Minho. The bridge had two, very low walls and was only wide enough for one vehicle to cross at a time. I could see the approaching headlights of what looked like a fairly large truck, but we were already at the start of the bridge so I continued across, according to the unwritten rule of 'first to arrive, first to cross', fully expecting the oncoming vehicle to slow down and wait for me to exit. What happened next, however, was the worst of all possible nightmares.

Instead of slowing down, the truck continued to hurtle on towards the entrance to the bridge, and to avoid hitting the bridge wall to its left, swerved at last minute into the centre of the road, just as I was starting to pull over to my left on exiting. With an almighty bang, the truck hit the side of the Vogue, knocking my car rather like a cricket bat giving a glancing blow to a cricket ball. The windscreen shattered all over my face as the driver's door was sliced off the car, which was knocked sideways, veering up onto the bank on the side of the road before eventually coming to a stop. I sat there for a few seconds, dazed and in total disbelief, before quickly checking there was no glass in my eyes. Marky, who had been riding in the back suddenly called out,

"Skip! Are you OK?"

"I think so. I've still got my right arm so I must have ducked over to my left, without thinking, just before we were hit."

"Switch off di engine and mek wi get out in case di car ketch a fire!" [*Turn off the engine, and let's get out as soon as possible in case the car catches fire.*]

"Harry! You OK?"

Harry had been travelling in the front passenger seat and was picking pieces of glass out of his afro.

"Yeh man, mi good."

I breathed a sigh of relief that no one was injured. Everything had happened in the blink of an eye so I hadn't even had a chance to survey the damage to the Vogue. When I looked, I could have cried.

Apart from the driver's door which was nowhere to be seen, and the shattered windscreen, the pillar on the right hand side of the screen was twisted way out of shape, the right-hand front fender was badly crushed, the pillar between the front and rear doors was bent inwards and the right-hand rear door was severely dented. It was truly a miracle that the three of us were all unhurt.

By now a large gathering of local villagers had crowded around the car and were offering expressions of sympathy and regret.

"Di truck should a top, man." [*The truck should have stopped!*]

"What a truck-man drive bad!" [*That truck driver can't drive to save his life!*]

"Only di Lahd save unu." [*Only God saved you from dying.*]

I thanked the gathering for their kind words then, having asked Marky to stay with the Vogue, I walked back towards the bridge with Harry to see what had happened to the truck, which had come to a stop some distance beyond the bridge. To my amazement, it had suffered barely a scratch. The driver, a local man whom I knew to be from nearby Andrew Hill, absolutely stank of alcohol and, trying his best to speak coherently, offered his profuse apologies for what had happened and gave his word that he would put right (at his expense) any damage to my vehicle. Having never been in a road accident in my entire life and still probably suffering somewhat from shock, I took him at his word and arranged to meet with him at his home the following day to sort things out. But Harry was not impressed by what he had heard.

"Skip, yuh should a get di police fi come. Di man, im drunk as a bat. Mi noh trus him at all'. [*Skip, you should have called the police. That man is as drunk as a bat - I don't trust him at all.*]

But I naïvely assured him that everything would be OK and that he shouldn't worry.

Miraculously, the engine, the electrics and all four wheels of my poor car were all still functioning normally and so with some help from the villagers to push the Vogue back onto the road, we were able to continue our journey back to Frankfield. With no windscreen and no driver's door, it was a cool, breezy drive, but we managed to limp home without further mishap. As the lads left, they were as comforting as any teenage boys could be in such a situation.

"Mi really sorry, Skip."

"Noh fret, man. Evryting will work out."

I rummaged around in my flat and eventually found the large plastic bags that had helped to protect my drums from the sea air during transit and used them to cover the gaping holes where there had once been a windscreen and a driver's door in case it rained during the night. Then, reluctantly leaving the car to the mercy of the elements, I wearily climbed back up the steps to my flat, gingerly peeled off my sweaty, glass-impregnated clothes and had a well-needed shower.

I was absolutely exhausted but, that night, as the reality of what had happened really hit me, I found that I could not avoid reliving the accident over and over again in my mind and I barely slept. Whether the Vogue would ever be able to be fixed was anybody's guess, and all my labour to get it in shipshape condition appeared to have been a complete waste of time.

The next day when I wearily walked up Andrew Hill to the home of the truck driver, I discovered to my utter dismay and disbelief that Harry's intuition had been spot-on. Now that the man had sobered up, his tune had changed dramatically. Not only was he accusing *me* of having caused the accident, but also asserting that he had been advised by his lawyer that I would also have to assume responsibility for repairing the damage to *his* truck. His tone was aggressive and intimidating and I found the whole situation almost impossible to believe. It was obvious that he now had absolutely no intention of assuming any sort of liability for what had happened and was certainly not going to offer any financial assistance for any repairs to my vehicle. In view of my recent decision to remain in Frankfield for the foreseeable future, I had no desire to make any enemies at this point, so I just left him to live with his own conscience and walked off without saying a further word. He would not get a penny from me for the alleged damage to his truck but, alas, if the Vogue was going to be repaired, the onus would be entirely on me. I had learnt a very bitter lesson.

* * *

A couple of days afterwards, I had a visit at the flat from a most unusual looking rasta-man who introduced himself as 'Skinny'.

"W'appen Skip? Mi hear say yuh car did get a knock, so mi did a wonder if yuh might be needin some assistanz." [*How are you doing Skip? I've heard that you've had a car accident, so I wondered if you might need someone to help out?*]

I had no idea who 'Skinny' was, how he knew my name, where he was from, whether he could be trusted, and what skills, if any, he could bring to bear on resurrecting my ruined car. But in spite of his weird appearance and somewhat unusual manner of speaking, I was fascinated by his forthrightness and curious to know more about him.

I was just about to have my breakfast so I invited him in and offered him a bacon sandwich and a coffee.

"I-man no nyam pork but I tankyu for di bread and di drink." [*As a rasta, I don't eat pork, but thank you for the offer of bread and a drink.*]

As we both ate and drank, he pointed towards the drumset, and said,

"I see yuh is a music-man, Skip. How yuh is wid di Jamaica reggae music?" [*I see you're a musician, Skip. How are you getting on with Jamaican reggae music?*]

"Yeh man, mi a try. But di beat nice." [*Yes, I'm trying my best. I like the beat though.*]

Skinny laughed at my crude attempts at speaking the *patois*, as we sat talking for almost an hour. This was my first really close encounter with a rasta-man since the Third Generation gig in West Kingston, but I somehow felt completely at ease and immediately sensed that Skinny was someone I would get on with and, more importantly, someone I could trust. When I recounted the accident and expressed my intense disappointment from my interaction with the truck driver the following day, Skinny nodded.

"A soh it goh, Skip. Dem yah man say one ting an mean a diffren ting. Di man wuttless an good-fe-nuttin. But hear mi now, him time will cum, soh noh fret, man." [*That's how life goes sometimes, Skip. That kind of person says one thing and means another. He's worthless and good-for-nothing. But, listen to me, his time will come soon, don't worry!*]

(True to Skinny's prediction, a little while after my accident, the same driver and his truck, carrying a full truck-load of animals and agricultural produce, was involved in a serious collision resulting in irreparable damage to the truck and the loss of nearly all of the animals being carried. I can't say I felt much sympathy for him.)

I found Skinny's sentiments strangely comforting and immediately felt more at ease in discussing my desire to fix the car. Stressing that I was still living on my VSO allowance throughout the summer and was therefore a bit strapped for cash, I asked him what he thought the prospects were, and what sort of help he might be able to offer. Little did I know then that I was speaking to someone for whom using a gas welding torch to restore a car to its former glory was just as much an artistic endeavour as a famous painter's use of a brush to create a beautiful painting.

Over the next month, Skinny hammered and welded and heated and levered. More significantly, he located a scrapped Singer Vogue car by the roadside less than 10 miles away, from which he and I were able to remove the driver's door and the windscreen. With these items fixed in place, the Vogue was, at last, starting to look like its old self, although the non-matching paintwork on the replacement driver's door, and the various other welded repairs on the driver's side, reminded me of the kind of patchwork quilts that my grandmother used to sew. So, it was time for some paintwork.

Based on Skinny's advice, I decided that if we were going to repaint the 'new' door and most of the right-hand side of the car, it made sense to do a proper job of it and spray-paint the entire car. So while Skinny set about sanding down and smoothing the whole of the exterior, I procured some undercoat and a couple of tins of nice maroon red 'duco'. After removing the licence plates, we covered the bumpers, the lights, the wheels and all the windows with newspaper, held firmly in place with masking-tape. The undercoat was applied first, and after it had thoroughly dried, the maroon paint was then sprayed on using an old air compressor and spray gun, with Skinny at pains to keep the spray gun nozzle at a constant distance from the car body, as it was carefully moved back and forth. After the paint had fully dried, the newspaper coverings were gently removed and the licence plates screwed back on.

To my delight, the Vogue genuinely looked like a brand new car, gleaming in the sunshine and ready for its inaugural drive! I urged Skinny to join me, and offered to drive anywhere he fancied.

"Come Skinny, mek we go fi a spin." [*Come on, Skinny, let's go for a drive.*]

"Yuh like how im look, Skip?" [*Do you like the look of the car, Skip?*]

"It's fantastic. Better than it was before!"

With the windows all down and with Skinny's 'locks' fluttering in the breeze, we cruised up to Christiana and then into the parish of Manchester. Following his directions, we weaved along a series of back roads in an uninhabited, rural part of central Jamaica that I had never set eyes on before. Eventually, Skinny asked me to pull over and park the car. He insisted that there was something nearby that he wanted to show me and so, since I had nothing more pressing to do, we jumped out of the Vogue and set off on foot along what appeared to be a fairly infrequently used track across a couple of fields. Skinny, who had been leading the way but refusing to say where on earth we were going, then stopped and pointed to a nearby field about a couple of acres in size and covered in neat rows of a short green plant, the like of which I hadn't seen before.

"How yuh like it Skip? Dat a fi mi weed plantation."
[*How do you like that Skip? That's my personal marijuana plantation.*]

I can be pretty naïve at times but I honestly had never imagined we had been driving to some secret little plantation in the middle of nowhere, where my rasta friend was unashamedly cultivating a massive crop of marijuana, the location of which he was now happily sharing with me. I was rather surprised to have been taken into his confidence like this, but at the same time I felt extremely uncomfortable because such plantations were surely illegal and I would be in a most vulnerable position if apprehended. Visions of nightmarish Daily Gleaner headlines such as '*White English teacher and black rasta-man caught at secret marijuana plot*' started to race through my mind and so I gently requested of Skinny that we get back immediately as it was probably best that I wasn't there. Skinny obliged, but smiled and said,

"Skip, yuh tink is only mi who a grow weed soh? Mi a tell yuh, sah, nuff police and politics-man a do exacly di same ting, but since dem in autorities, dem noh ketch in a noh trouble. [*Skip, do you think I'm the only one who has secret plantations like this? I can assure you, lots of police officers and politicians do exactly the same thing, but because they're in positions of authority, they don't get into trouble.*]

I decided not to argue the point, but glancing furtively over first one shoulder, then the other, to check if we were being watched, I stumbled hastily back along the track to where we had parked the car, breathing a sigh of relief when we had driven away and got back onto more frequented roads.

Skinny had done an amazing job on my car, and I considered him to be my good friend. I was sure that it would certainly not be our last interaction, but I vowed to myself that it would be the first and last time that I would ever visit one of his 'weed plantations'. I had never in my entire life used drugs of any kind and didn't intend to start, irrespective of speculation about the activities of authority figures, and whatever my friends, rasta or otherwise, might choose to do.

Chapter 11: That 'Nice Jamaican Girl'

Time flies when you are enjoying yourself.

And I had no reason to complain and lots of opportunities to enjoy what I was doing, even though the 'nice Jamaican girl' remained elusive.

Over the next two years from 1973 to 1975, my life basically revolved around four main activities.

Academically, the Science Department, in general, and the Physics Department, in particular, continued to go from strength to strength. Although most of my Physics classes were huge (typically around 40 students, as I was still the only Physics teacher), I was enjoying the teaching immensely and now knew the GCE syllabus backwards. For almost all of my Grade 10 and 11 students, doing Physics was like riding the crest of a wave and the peer pressure to do well in the subject was extremely strong. As a result, external exam results got better and better and it was not unknown for a student to get a pass in GCE Physics while failing all the other subjects he or she had taken. On one occasion, after I berated a student for not working hard enough, I overheard a group of his peers encouraging him to work harder 'lest he spoil Skip's 100% pass rate in the Physics GCE exam!'

I was also thoroughly enjoying my new role as Head of Science and leading an expanding team of dedicated, enthusiastic, local and expatriate teachers. In the annual Science Exhibition, (where we were now both revered and feared), we continued to set the standard, both regionally and nationally. There was never a problem in attracting brilliant Compre students, such as Jeffrey, who eventually followed in my footsteps to become a Physics Teacher himself, and Clifton, who went on to further his academic studies at the University of the West Indies and become a well-known and highly-respected medical doctor. All in all, there was absolutely no doubt in my mind now that teaching was my vocation and that I had made the right decision to remain as an educator in Jamaica rather than return to England to pursue postgraduate studies in medical electronics.

Secondly, there was the Scout group which now hovered at about 50 boys, at which point I had to draw a line and put further potential entrants on a waiting list. The annual Scout camp to Discovery Bay during the school's summer holiday continued to be a favourite activity for the boys to look forward to, and separate Patrol Leaders' camps at Christmas or Easter also proved immensely popular. On one occasion I decided to try taking the leaders further west and, to our delight, we were given permission to actually camp in the grounds of the famous Rose Hall Great House near Montego Bay. I intentionally pitched our tents not far from the grave of the *White Witch of Rose Hall* and we had great fun walking by the grave late at night to see which of the boys might be scared by the possibility of meeting a 'duppy' (ghost).

During term-time, weekend bush cooking trips became a favourite activity and we often combined this with hikes to places like Bull's Head and Green River in the hills and river valleys of Clarendon. I had also received a gift of a long, thick hemp rope from one of the nearby citrus factory owners and to add a little glamour and challenge to our weekly meeting, I decided to introduce the boys to the sport of abseiling (which I was still very conversant with from my own teenage rock-climbing activities in Derbyshire's famous Peak District). Now that the Science block had a third storey with a flat roof, we had the perfect vertical wall from the rooftop down to the car park, about 60 feet below. Using ladders from the first-floor corridor to the adjacent second floor roof of the Commercial Department and from there, up to the third-floor roof of the Science block, we could safely get the boys up on the roof-top, one at a time, to have a try. I am sure that anyone who has ever abseiled, will always remember their very first attempt and the fluttering of their heart at the instant of 'going over the edge'. Although having a safety rope attached to each participant, with myself tied on at the top to hold it and control the descent as necessary, it was amazing how even the very bravest and most boastful members of the Scout group would freeze at the point of no return. Watched by huge crowds of students (particularly girls) down below, it sometimes took several minutes before they plucked up the necessary courage to go backwards over the edge and start the descent.

As far as music was concerned, my playing with Third Generation reggae band was also blossoming. We would practice most Thursday evenings and frequently gig on a Friday or Saturday. I was enjoying playing with the band and, although we were, by now, getting paid for our performances, I would have continued even if we had been doing it for free. Grace had expressed quite a lot of interest in the songs we were doing and so I took her along to one of our Thursday band practices to hear the band for herself. By this time, from singing frequently with Sonic Salvation, her voice had matured, and she was confident on stage and experienced at using a microphone, so when Melvyn asked her if she wanted to try a number, she performed like a professional and the outcome was never in question. With Grace in the reggae band, joining Melvyn in the vocal section and also playing tambourine, Third Generation was now equipped to embrace a much wider repertoire and although we continued to perform as a back-up band for various artists at stage shows and concerts, we could now comfortably put on an entire show of our own. My only regret is that we never laid down any original tracks on vinyl; maybe because, as a band, we lacked the necessary creative talent for original song-writing or possibly because studio costs were just so ridiculously extortionate. Either way, it is unfortunate, because we definitely sounded as good as, or better than, most of the other reggae bands in the island at that time.

Finally, taking up an increasing amount of my time and energy, there was my own 'baby', Sonic Salvation Gospel Band, which was now performing with increasing frequency in and around central Jamaica. One of the things I found most fascinating was the never-ending stream of musicians who always seemed to 'turn up' from out of the blue when we most needed them. Any band using student musicians is always beset by the problem of attrition, and as one after another of our original, younger members graduated from Compre to go on to further studies in Kingston and elsewhere, we were continuously wanting replacements. When Glen left to go to music college, Fairy (another musical policeman!) joined us on lead guitar; when Count left, Larry took over the keyboard; when Fern left, Phillip replaced him on rhythm guitar; and when Marky left, Fern's younger brother Zyn filled the gap on bass guitar. To the Christian band members, this was simply attributed to God being aware of and providing for our needs; for me it was merely fortuitous!

Practices were now held in my Teachers' Flat where the drums were located, thanks to the goodwill and understanding (or, perhaps, partial deafness!) of the other teachers occupying the flats to the side of and below my own. I was reliably informed that even with my louvre windows shut and the door closed, the sound of my drums and the amplified instruments and vocals could be heard all the way up to Angel Bridge, about half a mile away. But this was Jamaica and a culture where loud music was the norm, both in the secular clubs and bars as well as in the churches, so we rarely, if ever, got complaints that we were disturbing the peace.

* * *

All in all, I was active and enjoying life, with never a dull moment. Compre was also making its mark nationally in other areas besides the annual Science Exhibition and, perhaps as a result, was attracting expatriate teachers from all over the world. One such teacher was a white South African with the most unfortunate name of *John Crow*! As Jamaican readers will know, a john-crow is a large black vulture, common in Jamaica, and frequently seen pecking at dead animals in the road. To call a *person* a 'john-crow' is considered a serious insult, which might even lead to a fight!

So, one must feel sympathy for this unfortunate teacher, whose sojourn in Jamaica must have been made hell from the taunts and ridicule he suffered through no fault of his own. And although I have already noted that most Jamaican students were respectful, well behaved and eager to learn, there are, of course, exceptions to every rule. The name 'John Crow' was a particular challenge for some Compre students who found it both puzzling and difficult to believe that any parent could be so cruel as to give their offspring such a derogatory name. It was not unusual therefore, for him to hear low echoes of his name from well-concealed provocateurs, or to see students tittering and flapping their arms like wings as he made his way around the campus.

One day, a cheeky boy in Grade 9, unable to curb his mischievous instincts, must have made a comment about black vultures in one of John's classes. Unfortunately for the boy, this jibe was the straw that broke the camel's back and, realising he had gone just a little too far on that occasion and seeing the murderous expression on the teacher's face, the boy decided that a hasty exit from the class was probably in his best interests. My involvement in the whole matter started at this point when, looking through the louvre windows of the Physics Lab, I saw flying through the door of the third-floor English classroom on the opposite side of the quadrangle, a very frightened-looking boy with his school bag in tow, followed by an extremely angry Mr Crow in turn followed by the entire class of students!

The boy vaulted down the two flights of steps to the ground floor where, for an instant, he appeared to think he was safely out of harm's way. On turning round, however, the boy was clearly horrified to see that, far from giving up the chase, 'the flying Crow' had every intention of exacting revenge and had already reached the bottom of the steps himself. By this time the commotion had incited a near riot and class after class of curious students, hearing the growing furore, were all running out of their own classrooms to find out what was happening.

I immediately became concerned that the boy might well end up being mauled and so, feeling it was necessary to intervene, I myself ran down the Science block stairs to the quadrangle and joined the swarm of students who, by now, formed a moving mass, snaking towards the car park entrance in front of the workshops, with the boy marginally in the lead, closely followed by the enraged teacher. Things weren't looking good, so I sprinted past most of the students only to see the boy with his pursuer hot on his heels now running at full pelt down the long school drive towards the main road!

On this occasion, my stern admonishments to the swathes of students to get back to their classes, and bellowed warnings about the dangers of traffic on the road, were totally ignored; everyone wanted to witness the revenge of 'the flying Crow'. On reaching the road, the unfortunate boy glanced round, surely expecting at this stage that the chase would go no further. But clearly his assailant was in no mood to give up, so the boy, quite oblivious to all vehicles, shot off - straight down the *middle* of the road! - in the direction of Frankfield.

In those days, I was quite fit and healthy and so I had been gaining on 'the flying Crow', but my shouts for him to stop were either unheard or ignored. What had started as an in-house incident had now become a public spectacle and I was starting to have serious concerns that I might be about to witness the unfortunate demise of a cheeky student at the hands of a crazed teacher or even a major traffic accident. The boy was now running for all he was worth, past the rum-bar (still pounding out "Cherry oh Baby"), the Church of God and the Teachers' Flats, then down the incline towards Long Wall.

By now, about half a mile from the school, the boy had a lead of about 20 yards on John, with me following close behind. At this point, he decided to cut his losses, dashed his school-bag down in the middle of the road, and leapt over the wall, dropping *almost 15 feet* into the Rio Minho below, before splashing through the water and disappearing into the thick bush and foliage on the far bank!

'The flying Crow' had to concede defeat; he could not, on this occasion, catch his prey. Instead, puffing and blowing, his face scarlet with rage or exertion or both, he picked up the boy's school-bag, threw the contents on the ground and then proceeded to furiously rip the boy's English book to shreds, flinging the pieces all across the road, in full view of the massive crowd of students who had followed *en masse*, and were completely blocking the road.

"John…! …It's OK. Take it easy, man. Don't worry about the boy."

He was literally shaking with rage and I put my arm around his shoulder to offer a little comfort (and to try and protect the remainder of the boy's books). Then it was my turn to get mad and I yelled with all my might at the massive crowd of students who had gathered round to witness the massacre.

"Right! Get back to school, all of you. It's over - there's nothing more to see. And keep off the road! *Unu move - NOW!*"

By this time, one or two other members of staff had arrived and the students sheepishly dispersed and headed back up the road. I stayed to try and console John as best I could and to help pick up the un-torn books and collect the remnants of the English book. By now he had calmed down and his eyes were flooding with tears; he realised he had completely lost his cool and had gone way too far.

"It's OK, John. Let's head back to school and get things sorted."

I left him at the door of Mr Latty's office and wished him well. In the end, I learned that he actually apologised to the boy for what had happened and even paid for a new English book to replace the one that he had destroyed. As a member of staff, he undoubtedly got his 'knuckles rapped' by Mr Latty for how he had responded to the incident but, as for the boy, Mr Latty was going to have no behaviour of that sort from any student at 'his' school and, as was the norm in the 1970s, the unfortunate boy received a caning that he would never, ever forget.

* * *

By the start of 1975, word of my 'legendary' skills as a Physics teacher had spread far and wide, and I was getting numerous requests to give private lessons to students doing A-level Physics at other schools and even to students taking Physics modules at the University of the West Indies (UWI). Although it was a bit of a struggle to fit these classes into my already hectic schedule, I enjoyed the private A-level and university tutoring as it represented a well-needed academic challenge over and above teaching only O 'levels.

One such university student, originally from the Frankfield area, who was doing a Natural Sciences degree at UWI, used to come by my flat fairly regularly, one evening per week. Rico, as he was known, and myself became firm friends and after our Physics lesson, we would frequently talk late into the night about girls and our respective plans for the future. Since it wasn't the wisest thing for him to travel back to the Mona campus of UWI in Kingston so late at night, he usually stayed over at my flat and travelled back to the university early the next morning. During the previous two years, I had dated one or two very eligible, Jamaican young ladies who were intelligent, good-looking and keen but, for one reason or another, none of these relationships had quite worked out.

When I bemoaned this fact to Rico, he encouraged me to cast my net wider afield and maybe survey the scene at the university where, according to him, there were 'lots of really eligible girls', who were apparently 'just waiting for husbands'! This description rather amused me but, given that none of my attempts so far had worked and deciding to adopt the motto 'nothing tried, nothing gained', I accepted his invitation to join him at a small birthday party the following week. This would take place at the university hall of residence where he resided during term-time, and I could stay over in his room for the night and return to Frankfield the next day. After Rico had volunteered various bits of brotherly advice about how to maximise one's chances of attracting these 'really eligible girls', we left it at that and I said I was looking forward to seeing him in a few days' time.

The 'party' was not quite what I was expecting but there was a really good selection of tasty food which I certainly took full advantage of (before most of the guests arrived). Fortunately, I just had time to go and clean my teeth after eating. True to Rico's predictions, the young ladies who came were all outstanding in their dress, hairstyles and general demeanour. Those were the days of big afros and short mini-skirts and I was fascinated at how beautifully and precisely cut the girls' hairstyles were and how really attractive their long, elegant legs looked.

Rico was a really good host and introduced me as 'Skip' to each of the girls individually, before disappearing and leaving me to my own devices. I was particularly attracted to a small group of girls who were obviously Christians, discussing how difficult it was to find a truly faithful man who had the potential to be a really good, Christian husband. I listened silently to the discourse for a while and then, out of the blue, and not really having considered beforehand what I was going to say, I suddenly blurted out,

"Likewise, I suppose it must be really nice for a young man to find a truly faithful woman with the potential to become a really good, Christian wife."

The three girls looked at me in disbelief and I sensed a certain amount of derision directed towards my contribution to their conversation. The shorter one of the three, whom I found particularly attractive, smiled and asked,

"So, I take it you are a Christian believer then?"

My impulsiveness and my big mouth had now got me into dangerous territory and, racking my brain as to how best to answer the question honestly, I hesitated before saying,

"Well, to be honest, I would say that at this time I am probably best described as an agnostic."

"And do you attend church or do anything else to help you to come to a conclusion about the validity of the Christian faith?"

"Yes, I'm in church most Sundays and I also have my own Gospel Band."

"So, you are a musician then? Where are you from and how come you are here in Jamaica?"

This gave me the opening I had been looking for and the opportunity to get to know the three girls better, particularly the slightly shorter one with the really pretty afro. Just before I could get started however, I heard Rico's voice behind me,

"Skip - I want you to meet another of my friends."

157

So my conversation with the three girls unfortunately came to an abrupt end.

My drive back to Frankfield from Rico's party in the Singer Vogue early the next morning was uneventful but, as dawn broke over the winding road from May Pen to Frankfield, with delicate pink fluffs of cloud hovering in a crystal blue sky, I couldn't help thinking that maybe Rico was right. Even though, on this occasion, I had failed abysmally in not acquiring even the *name* of the young lady with the 'really pretty afro', perhaps this *was* the place to come to find that 'nice Jamaican girl'.

* * *

On my return home, I was immediately immersed in preparations for that year's Science Exhibition. We had decided to investigate the effect of using different roofing materials on keeping a house cool in the hot, summer months. Our project, relatively simple in both design and execution, was not only topical but also proved to be very illuminating in its conclusions, namely that a bamboo roof was a better insulator than one made from tiles or any other roofing material currently in use. The judges loved it and were further impressed by yet another excellent set of Compre students whom I had selected to communicate our findings. Once again, to Mr Latty's delight, we ended up both regional and national winners, further establishing Compre's academic credentials and its ability to compete successfully against Jamaica's long-established top secondary schools.

Then, after the Easter holidays, we were straight into revision sessions and preparations for that year's GCE's, which included my procuring all the necessary materials to construct the apparatus required for the Physics practical exam (which, in those days, was compulsory).

As soon as the long summer holiday started, my friend and colleague, George, and myself, had decided to take the opportunity to hike up into the Blue Mountains and to camp for a night on the summit. George was one of the first graduates from Compre, who had gone on to the College of Arts, Science and Technology (CAST) to gain a degree in Engineering and was now back at his *alma mater* teaching Technical Drawing and Mathematics. He was lean and fit and as enthusiastic about the expedition as I was; but it went without saying that scaling a 7,000-foot mountain on foot was no mean feat and it was fortunate for us that we had our pick of all the Compre Scout equipment, including the tent, rucksacks and bush-cooking items that we would need. Our map suggested that a good starting point would be Westphalia, which I was already familiar with from my previous trip with Sonic Salvation, and where we could safely leave my car. However, in all our fervent enthusiasm, what we didn't realise from studying the map was that, starting from this vantage point at about 4,000 feet, we would first have to *descend* about 2,000 feet to cross the river (which ran between Westphalia and the mountain's summit) way down in the valley below, before actually starting our 'real' ascent to the peak.

Leaving Frankfield in the middle of the night so as to set off from Westphalia by early morning, we reckoned we could reach the peak by late afternoon. The journey there was fairly uneventful and the weather looked really promising. Then, as expected, getting from Westphalia down to the river bed, way below us, was a breeze, with the weight of our rucksacks literally pushing us down the steep path to the valley bottom. There, we removed our boots and socks to wade across the river, glad for the feel of the refreshingly cool water on our legs. Now we only had a further 5,000 feet to climb!

The path snaking up the slope on the far side of the river was, however, horrendously steep so that, by the time we had climbed back to an elevation roughly level with Westphalia, which still looked tantalisingly close on the other side of the valley, we were drenched with sweat and already tired from the exertion. After a brief stop to catch our breath and have some water and a couple of 'bulla-cakes' to replenish our fluids and energy, we set off again, following the fairly well-trodden path upward through the thick vegetation. Every now and again, a gap in the foliage afforded a glimpse of an ever-diminishing Kingston, way down below us, but we hastened on, with our rucksacks seemingly getting heavier at every step. The strange thing about climbing the last 2,000 feet to Blue Mountain Peak is that, although the summit seems to be so comfortingly close, a further hour's hiking seems to bring you no closer. Also unexpected was that, although we were still walking in the full heat of the mid-afternoon sun, the air was becoming surprisingly chilly.

By 5 o'clock, our feet were sore, our leg-muscles were aching, our shoulders were tender from being constantly rubbed by the rucksack straps, and we were both ravenous. Only an act of supreme will-power enabled us to reach our destination which catches one somewhat off-guard as the path finally curves around a small mound, with the undergrowth on either side of the path suddenly replaced by deep blue sky, stretching out in every direction. We had made it! And there, shimmering gently in the distance way down below us, was a miniature Kingston, a tiny airport, and then only the deep blue sea, reaching out to the distant horizon. It was outstandingly beautiful and all our aches and pains were forgotten as we gazed at the unforgettable view and celebrated the success of our mission.

Our next task was to pitch the tent and get a small fire going. Before long, we had a pot of rice simmering on the flames and a pot of boiling water to make coffee. We had decided to bring along some pre-cooked, roast pieces

160

of chicken so, within less than an hour, we were sitting by the tent eating copious helpings of chicken and rice while dreamily watching the sun go down over the cockpit country to the west of the mountain. As night fell, the beautiful, twinkling lights of the city took on an almost magical aura and I couldn't help thinking that maybe this was a foretaste of heaven, if such a place actually existed.

I have no idea if George snored that night; I was so tired that almost the moment I hit the sack, I was asleep like a log. When I awoke, it was bright sunlight outside and George had already got the fire going again to make some breakfast. It was still quite chilly even in the direct sunshine and more hot coffee was definitely the order of the day, together with egg and fried dumpling and some beautifully sweet, fried plantain. We were in no hurry to leave; the return journey to Westphalia would all be downhill except for climbing back up from the riverbed, and our rucksacks would be significantly lighter now that the food we had carried had all been conveniently transferred to our bellies.

After packing away the tent, extinguishing the fire and clearing up our campsite, we reluctantly said farewell to that majestic location. We had hiked up one of the highest peaks in the Caribbean and we both sensed that our expedition would remain an unforgettable memory in the years to come. Retracing our steps back down the track, sometimes walking, sometimes even running in our new-found exuberance, we made it to the river in the valley below Westphalia in less than two hours. Once again drenched with sweat, we stripped off our sodden clothes for a 'skinny dip' in the refreshing cold water, only emerging bashfully to cover up, on suddenly noticing a rather attractive young lady just about to cross the river from the Westphalia side where we were headed! By early afternoon, we were back at the car and getting ready for the long drive back to Frankfield. Our trip had been perfect. Even though we had only climbed to 7,000 feet, the beauty at the summit was breath-taking, and perhaps this was a taste of how Tenzing and Hillary must have felt on conquering Mount Everest.

* * *

Most of the rest of the summer holiday was spent relaxing, playing music and getting ready for another summer Scout camp at Puerto Seco in Discovery Bay. I couldn't wait to get back to the beach and swimming in the warm, crystal blue sea, and playing dominoes with the lads. Meanwhile, my close friend, teaching colleague and very accommodating neighbour, Venice, was clearing out her flat, adjacent to my own, to leave Compre to marry her long-time boyfriend and fiancé. She had tried her very best to teach me how to cook, with little success, but I had learnt a great deal about Jamaican culture and history during the two years we had been neighbours, which I was sure would serve me well in the future. By the time I was ready to leave for Scout camp at the end of the summer, she had vacated her flat and I had no clue as to who my new neighbour might be. Hopefully, it would be someone just as nice.

Chapter 12: "Hi! Who Are You?"

Joan, the second of six children raised by her parents, Felicita and Linden, in Grange Hill, Westmoreland, Jamaica in the early 1950s, was a happy, intelligent child, affectionately known as 'Cherry' to all her family. She possessed a vivid memory, enabling her to learn, by heart, all sorts of poems which she delighted in reciting whenever the opportunity arose. Despite having forfeited some of her own primary education to help at home with her younger siblings, she nonetheless gained a partial scholarship to attend Montego Bay High School for Girls and so, at age 11, went to live with her Aunt Ella in Montego Bay. Enjoying everything that secondary school had to offer, she continued into 6th Form, gained A-levels in History, Economics and Geography, and was delighted to be one of a handful of students nationally who were awarded a prestigious scholarship to attend the University of the West Indies. She decided to pursue an undergraduate degree in History and Economics, but to help finance her further studies, she deferred her university course for a year, working as a pre-trained teacher of History, Geography and Commerce at Mannings High School in Savannah La Mar in Westmoreland.

During her third year of undergraduate studies, she began to give serious consideration to the idea of teaching as a career and wrote to enquire about possible vacancies at a number of secondary schools and colleges - including Frankfield High School (Comprehensive). Waiting for replies to her enquiries, she busied herself with her studies for final examinations, while continuing her involvement with as many church activities as her spare time allowed. As a sincere, practicing Christian, she pursued numerous social activities related to her faith, including being Christian Union Hall Representative. This involved both 'local' pursuits, such as leading Bible studies, as well as representing the University of the West Indies further afield at the Universities and Colleges Christian Fellowship (UCCF) inter-regional conference in Barbados.

She was also an active member of the drama group, and along with her small circle of close, Christian girl-friends, enjoyed refined, social activities. So, when she was invited by Rico, one of her male, university friends, to attend his birthday party, she happily accepted the invitation.

After sampling some of the food that was provided and listening to some recent Jamaican songs in the background, she was making small talk with a few of her girl-friends when Rico walked towards them with a young, unknown white man in tow, whom he introduced as his friend, 'Skip'. Rico then just walked away, leaving 'Skip' with Joan and the other girls.

Joan looked at this young man with some degree of curiosity. His black hair, though silky, was scruffy and far too long. She wondered when he had last had it cut; maybe he was a white rasta! And his attire, though neat, was somewhat garish; he obviously needed guidance in this area. He was, however, tall and muscular. She wondered how he and Rico had met, and why he was at the party.

The girls were talking about the lack of good, available, Christian men, and basically ignoring 'Skip's' presence completely. He had been listening politely with a faint smile on his face and not interrupting but, suddenly, and without invitation, he interjected with the following comment,

"Likewise, I suppose it would be really nice for a young man to find a good Christian wife."

There was a momentary silence as Joan and her two friends digested what had been said and immediately prepared for their offensive. Joan began with,

"So, I presume *you* are a Christian?"

to which Skip, after a moment's hesitation, responded,

"Not exactly... I think I would describe myself as an agnostic."

Joan laughed and wondered, with some degree of incredulity and disapproval, why this stranger thought it was appropriate to be making such uninvited and audacious declarations. Before the conversation could really get to the heart of the matter, however, Skip was dragged away to meet more of Rico's friends. The three girls looked at each other and then burst out laughing before Joan aptly summarised the encounter with,

"What a brash, presumptuous man!"

* * *

The following week, Joan started to receive some replies from the schools she had written to. Westfield School for Girls in Trelawny looked promising, but offered no teacher accommodation. A letter from a 'Mr Latty' offered exactly the job she was looking for, but Frankfield was located in the God-forsaken 'bush' of rural Clarendon and was also without any available teacher accommodation. Some of the other schools were only offering positions to teach related subjects which were not in her area of specialisation. She decided to defer her decision until she had had a little more time to consider her options. Out of Westfield and Frankfield, the former was probably the more attractive, so after some reflection, Joan wrote back to Mr Latty thanking him for his kind offer but declining because of the lack of accommodation. She had never really warmed to the idea of going to Frankfield anyway; it was just too rural and remote. The very next day after posting her response, a further letter arrived from Mr Latty:

Dear Joan,

I trust you are in good health and that your preparations for your final examinations at the University are going well.

Further to my previous letter, I am very happy to inform you that I can now also offer you accommodation, which has recently become available in the form of an attractive apartment in our Teacher's Flats, close to the school.

Should you now wish to accept my offer of a permanent post as full-time Teacher of History and Geography at Frankfield High School (Comprehensive), commencing September 1975, please be so kind as to reply in the affirmative as soon as possible.

Yours sincerely

F C Latty
Principal

The two letters had clearly crossed in the post! Things were not working out as she had anticipated but considering all the pros and cons of both offers, it was clearly the Frankfield post that was now the best option. Joan immediately wrote a second reply thanking Mr Latty for his offer of accommodation and asking that, if the post was still available, her earlier response be ignored. She would be happy to accept both the teaching position and the accommodation. Then she said a quiet prayer that, if it were God's will for her to teach at Frankfield, Mr Latty would receive her second reply before offering the job to someone else.

* * *

When we left for Scout Camp towards the end of August, I still had no idea who would be occupying the vacant Teacher's Flat adjacent to my own on the upstairs floor but, in any case, my focus was now on other things, one of which was to purchase all the food items necessary for the camp. To satisfy the ravenous appetite of the Scouts for a whole week, I had to buy a vast amount of bulla-cake, and on asking for 20 dozen bulla, the Frankfield shop-keeper clearly missed hearing the word 'dozen' and brought a bag with 20 freshly baked bulla in it. When I pointed out that this was not what I had asked for, he was unsure what I meant, so I repeated 'No, no; I need 20 *DOZEN* bulla please'. His facial expression was an absolute picture;

"Mr Skip, if yuh nyam all a dem bulla, yuh mus tun bulla!" [*Skip, if you eat that many bulla cakes, you'll turn into one!*]

He had never before experienced anyone buying such a large quantity of bulla, but then, he had also never seen how my Scouts could eat when they were hungry!

In order to transport all the boys who wanted to go on the camp, I had to drive my own car, as well as hire a minibus to get us there, and to return a week later to bring us all back. With over 20 lads and a ton of gear, plus a huge quantity of foodstuffs, both vehicles were laden to the point where the tyres were barely clearing the wheel arches!

The camp went like a dream. The boys, some of whom had never had the chance to visit the North Coast, and many of whom had never even been outside rural Frankfield, behaved impeccably. We ate like kings, played dominoes until we fell asleep at the picnic tables, swam in the beautifully warm water like fishes, and slept like logs. Fortunately, by then I had my own, small, leader's tent,

167

which I made sure to lace up tightly each night when turning in, lest I should become the recipient of 'flouring' or 'tooth-pasting' by a 'ghost-Scout' in the night-hours while fast asleep. Our presence caused quite a stir whenever a bus-load of local day-trippers from a school or church arrived at the beach, with friendly rivalry between the older Scouts who were always vying to chat up the most attractive girls amongst the visiting group. Those who were successfully wooed would often join us for freshly cooked dumplings and fried fish, or whatever other bush-cooked delicacy was on offer.

We also went on a number of hikes up into the hills overlooking Discovery Bay, where the four, intensely competitive patrols would undertake a variety of orienteering tasks to determine which was the best at map-reading and compass-use. It therefore did not come as any surprise to me when, several years after leaving Compre, some of those same boys reached high-ranking positions in both the Jamaica Defence Force and the Jamaica Constabulary.

Alas, the week soon came to an end and our minibus arrived to take us home. There was no need to carry a vast quantity of food on the return journey, so it was not quite the squash it had been on the outward trip. By the time we arrived back at Frankfield on the Sunday night, the day before school reopened for the new school year, it was already dark, and after all the camping gear had been safely stowed away in our Scout storeroom up at the school, it must have been after 11 o'clock, and I was absolutely exhausted.

The apartment next to my own was in darkness and I wasn't even sure if it was now occupied so, postponing any possible introduction to my new neighbour until the following day, I headed for the shower and after a quick wash to try and remove the worst of the grime, wearily dropped into bed and was soon sound asleep.

Next morning, the start of the new school year, I woke very late and barely had time to make my breakfast of the statutory bacon sandwich and coffee. Hastily dressing, locking up my flat and rushing down the steps, I decided to make up for lost time by heading straight across the playfield. I was quite proud of my reputation for being *on time*, and it wouldn't look good to be late, especially on the first day! However, just as I got to the corner of the building, I heard a gentle female voice call from the path behind me;

"Hi Skip."

I was so startled that I almost dropped the books I was carrying and pivoting on one leg, turned around to see the most beautiful sight I had seen for a long time.

"Hi! Who are you?"

Now it must be said that this illustrious reply was probably *not* my most endearing introduction of all time! Although the young lady looked somehow familiar, and I had a strong suspicion we had met at some point in the past, I honestly didn't have a clue whom I was facing. As I had been told on a number of occasions by various people, 'Skip, unless it's Physics or Maths, you never remember *anything*!' And now, true to fashion, with this wonderful, angelic-looking young woman before me, my mind was drawing a complete blank.

She had a smooth, dark brown complexion, brown eyes and a cute, gently curved nose. Her hair was combed in an absolutely perfect afro, which I found irresistibly attractive. She was smartly attired, with her ample bosom modestly hidden by a light-blue, short-sleeved blouse, neatly tucked into an alluring, red mini-skirt which would have caught any man's eye. Each time she smiled, her teeth shone white in the bright morning sun and I noticed that her lips had on the faintest hint of pink lipstick. Although she was not very tall, the mini-skirt accentuated the length of her smooth, dark brown legs, while her feet were adorned in a pair of smart new sandals.

I stood there, spellbound, no doubt with my mouth hanging open, but totally lost for words. I wondered if I might possibly be dreaming, but this was no dream. Finally, and no doubt sympathising with my obvious forgetfulness, the angel took pity on me;

"I'm Joan. Don't you remember? We met just a few weeks ago, before the summer holiday, at Rico's party. I'm your new, next-door neighbour."

Her speech sounded clear and refined, her words delicately spoken in perfect 'Queen's English' - quite unlike the 40 Scouts I had become accustomed to hearing over the last week.

"My new next-door neighbour...? Wow! You caught me by surprise. So sorry I forgot who you were - typical of my memory. Welcome to Compre. Are you going up to school? We'd better hurry or we'll be late!"

As we walked across the newly cut playfield and up the school drive together, I couldn't help but wonder if this might be that 'nice Jamaican girl' I had been waiting for. My heart was beating overtime as we chatted amicably, smiling back and forth on our first walk together up the Compre school drive.

Later that day, I called in at Mr Latty's office to appraise him of our most enjoyable Scout camp and to put his mind at rest by playfully assuring him we had not lost any of the boys while we were away.

"Very glad to hear that, Skip. Thank you for giving up some of your summer holiday to take the boys camping."

And then, with a slight hint of mischief in his smile, he went on,

"I presume you have met your new, next-door neighbour? She seems very pleasant and refined, so I am sure you will get on."

170

I nodded in the affirmative, wondering to myself if Mr Latty was intentionally trying to do a bit of match-making.

"Oh, and Skip, many congratulations on another set of excellent GCE results."

* * *

A couple of weeks after the term started, I met Joan's mother, Felicita, and her younger sisters, Ava and Mara. Following a recent promotion, Felicita was, at that time, working as the Superintendent of Poor Relief in Spanish Town, just over an hour's drive from Frankfield, while Ava and Mara were cheerful, young teenagers, in the middle of their GCE's at secondary school. On a typical monthly visit, Felicita would invariably bring with her massive pieces of meat and other food for her precious daughter, Cherry, 'marooned' as a teacher in the wilds of Clarendon, and to generally check on her health and welfare. Felicita and I immediately 'hit it off' and she seemed happy that I was her daughter's immediate neighbour and that Joan and myself got on so well. Although a little shy at first, Ava and Mara gradually learnt to appreciate my eccentric sense of humour and, before long, we also became great friends.

After a few such visits, Felicita suggested that on Cherry's next trip to the family home in Westmoreland, I would be most welcome to accompany her and to stay over for a couple of days, so as to have the opportunity to sample the beautiful 7-mile-long Negril Beach at the western end of the island. I sensed that Joan felt a little uncomfortable with this proposal as we were relatively new acquaintances, but I was more than glad for the opportunity and looked forward to meeting the rest of her family and visiting the famous beach.

In the meantime, I took every opportunity to get better acquainted with my very attractive new neighbour and, whenever invited, to sample some of her incredible cooking. I think Joan must have inherited her mother's (and possibly her grandmother's) abilities in the kitchen because, on the heaven-sent occasions when I was invited round to her immaculately neat apartment for Sunday dinner after church, I felt like I was being entertained in a terribly 'posh' restaurant, being served a plethora of delicacies, all of which tasted absolutely fantastic. Perhaps Joan was hoping I might pick up a few culinary tricks of the trade but, having politely sampled my chicken broth 'creation' on repeated occasions, she realised my limitations in the kitchen and took pity on me, given my obvious inability to vary my menu.

* * *

About halfway through the Christmas Term, I commenced a new and massive, personal project. An opportunity had arisen for me to purchase an old MGB open-top sports car and, as a young man in his mid-twenties who fancied the James Bond, fast-car experience (with an attractive girl in the passenger seat, of course), I couldn't let the chance pass me by. With a fold-back open top and quick-change, spoke wheels, the car would be the ideal means to get around for romantic dates as long as one was not needing to carry large quantities of luggage - there were no rear seats, as such, and the boot was small. Additionally, the car itself was not overly expensive and, in my unbridled enthusiasm to emulate my film idol, I estimated that it would require a minimum of work to get it into good shape. Before too long I might be the owner of a really classy-looking, high performance sports-car.

Or so I thought!

I decided to commence with renovating the engine, after which the body-work could be rapidly sorted out. But as I began to dismantle the 'top half' of the engine block, I soon realised that what was going to be involved, was many, many times more onerous than I had anticipated. In fact, it became obvious that I would either need to get the heavily worn engine block re-bored and re-fit oversize pistons or, alternatively, buy an entirely new block. Since a completely new block would work out significantly more expensive, I decided this option wasn't economically feasible. I would therefore need to remove the entire engine and gearbox assembly from the car and dissemble it completely in order to carry the existing block to Kingston to get it re-bored. This, in turn, meant relocating the drums back to the Physics prep-lab, while my new Teachers Flat became, once again, my temporary auto-repair centre. Within a short space of time, a multitude of parts from the engine dismantling process, including literally hundreds of nuts and bolts in appropriately labelled glass jars, occupied the bulk of the available floor space in my flat, with just a narrow walkway from the kitchen area to my bed at the far side of the room.

During my various mechanical jobs on the Vogue, I had happened to meet a very skilled engineer in Kingston who had been trained in England before relocating to Jamaica. When I presented him with my engine block for re-boring, he strongly advised me to simultaneously re-grind the crankshaft and install new under-size bearings during the reassembly. This brilliant man (whose name I have unfortunately forgotten) was someone for whom I had the greatest scientific respect, and I wasn't going to argue. So, now somewhat less affluent than when the job started, with one re-bored engine block, four new oversize pistons and rings, a re-ground crankshaft with new, undersize crankshaft bearings and a new clutch for good measure, I began the exciting task of reassembly. The bottom half of the engine would now be almost like new. Fortunately, the four-speed gearbox, the cylinder head and the twin Weber carburettors were still in good shape and only needed a good clean, except for the cylinder head valves which needed re-grinding - but I could do that for myself. Although the expenses were steadily mounting, I had gone too far to turn back now.

But then I also discovered that the entire exhaust system was rusted out and needed renewing, along with all four spoke-wheels (which I realised on closer examination, had numerous broken spokes), and all four tyres and inner-tubes.

At this point, I decided to contact my old rasta friend, Skinny, about the bodywork, which also had some seriously rusted areas including the entire region under the driver's feet! When we discussed doing a complete welding job, Skinny was quick to point out that this would also mean a complete paint job afterwards. Feeling, by now, somewhat demoralised (and seriously wondering if it would have been cheaper to have bought a brand-new car), I agreed. However, I trusted him to do a good job and was a little happier when he said,

"Noh fret, Skip, When I-man done wid di car, dem will all tun dem ed an marvel at what dem will see. Truss me." [*Don't worry, Skip, when I'm finished fixing the car, it will be a real head-turner, an absolute marvel! Trust me.*]

I left the bodywork in his capable hands, helping when I was needed but, meanwhile, focused my attention on the mechanical work, such as installing new brake-pads, new front disks, and new wheel bearings front and back. By the time Skinny had finished, the car was unbelievably transformed. With sparkling blue metallic paint as the base colour over the entire body, and with reflecting silver stripes front and back, the car now looked like a racing car ready for the Le Mans circuit! In fact, when the new wheels and tyres, the bumpers and the lights were all installed, the car looked so terrific that I decided to fork out and change practically the only thing that had *not* yet been replaced; the

174

folding, black, flexible top. With the new top in place, it was literally a brand-new car - and as Skinny had predicted, a real head-turner.

Word had obviously got around to all the mechanics in the area, and on the inaugural day for putting the car through its paces, quite a large group of guys had all assembled to see if all my mechanical work had been to any avail (or was just fanciful talk). It was a beautiful autumn morning when I finally connected the leads to the battery and rechecked (for the 50th time) all the wires and fuel lines for anything I might have missed. I was perspiring profusely and felt terribly nervous. If the car failed to start now, I would look like a real idiot with a shiny but non-functional toy! Joan was kindly standing by to give me some well-needed moral support and Skinny encouraged me with,

"Go deh Skip. Mek dem all see how a car fi run good." [*Go on, Skip - let them all see how well the car runs.*]

I gingerly climbed into the driver's seat and with a silent prayer to an unknown God, turned the ignition key. The engine roared into life on the very first turn, with a wonderful throaty sound from the exhaust - and without a trace of smoke! The watching crowd clapped and cheered before all ambling over to the rum-bar to quench their thirst; I had sat their exam and passed with flying colours.

In view of his major contribution to the success of the venture, I felt it only appropriate to let Skinny accompany me on my inaugural drive, so I called him over to climb in beside me. We moved gingerly forward through the gateway to the Teachers' Flats and then, with an exhilarating acceleration that I had never experienced in the Vogue and an enormous roar from the exhaust, we literally *shot* up the road towards Angel Bridge. We were both ecstatic; the MGB was on the road! Now I had a vehicle truly fit for purpose, ready and waiting for when Joan and myself would make our first trip to the family home in Westmoreland.

* * *

As it turned out, however, I would have another 'amorously-perceived' adventure in the MGB, before I ever got the opportunity to show off my new automobile to Joan (ideally on a long, romantic drive).

Just a few days after getting the MGB on the road, I needed to pick up a few things from Frankfield during the lunch break so, to save time, I had driven the car from the Teachers' Flats up to school in the morning. It was a gorgeous day so, as soon as I had finished teaching my last morning lesson, I jumped in the car, folded back the top, and set off towards Frankfield. Halfway down the school drive I saw a rather strangely-dressed lady, probably in her late thirties, walking in the same direction. She was holding a colourful umbrella to shield her face and head from the hot, midday sun, yet was wearing an ankle-length skirt and a woollen cardigan, both of which must have been unbearably hot. Although having never set eyes on the lady before, I screeched to a halt, feeling especially chivalrous in my new automobile, and enquired of her if she would like a lift to Frankfield. She gladly accepted and speaking in rather 'posh' Queen's English, climbed into the passenger seat and folded up her umbrella. The journey took less than a minute in the car, but it was just enough time for me to introduce myself as Skip and to learn that her name was Miss Hall. Once I had dropped her in the town centre, I thought no more about the lady, collected what I needed, and shot off back to school to try and squeeze in a bit of lunch before afternoon lessons started.

I later found out that she had recently arrived from London, having been jilted by her lover, and that the whole affair had affected her mental stability. Totally unaware of the predicament I was now in, I had been conversing with 'the mad woman from England', as she was locally known!

My rendezvous with Miss Hall having completely disappeared from my typically unreliable memory, however, it was with complete astonishment that, on a trip to the supermarket later in the week, I was asked by the cashier at the check-out whether, in future, I was intending to pay for Miss Hall's groceries! I had absolutely no idea what or whom the cashier was referring to, and asked her what on earth she was talking about. She informed me that the said Miss Hall had visited the supermarket earlier that morning, claiming that *I* would be paying for *her* groceries as well as for the items she needed for Paul, *our* child…!

I confess that the story seemed so ridiculous that I started to laugh, but soon realised that the cashier was not joking and was actually quite concerned. Fortunately, the supermarket supervisor had insisted Miss Hall put her shopping basket items back on the shelves, at which the lady had apparently stormed out of the building, vowing to 'have words with Mr Skip!' That same afternoon, when I was chatting amicably with Joan on the balcony outside our two flats, I did indeed receive the promised visit from Miss Hall, who to my embarrassment, began lambasting me very loudly for failing to provide for 'our' child and herself. She was clearly very angry that I had dared to talk with any lady other than herself, at which point, I advised Joan to go inside her flat and leave me to deal with the problem. But try as I might, Miss Hall could not be consoled, at which point I went into my flat and shut the door. After hanging around for a while and striking the door of Joan's flat several times with her umbrella, she stormed off, accusing me of having an affair with my neighbour, while failing to provide for 'our' child.

Whilst I found the entire incident highly amusing, Joan was extremely frightened at the possible consequences for herself, fearing that she might be

177

attacked one evening when I wasn't around. When the encounter was repeated several times afterwards, I eventually started to take it all rather more seriously and threatened Miss Hall that I would report her to the local police if she didn't stop harassing myself and making physical threats against Joan. The last time she came by happened to be when Skinny had dropped by to see me. When he witnessed her hostilities for himself, he didn't take kindly to it at all and informed her in no uncertain terms that if he ever saw her at the Teachers' Flats again, she would have 'a rasta man and his cutlass' to deal with! She must have taken him at his word for we never saw her again.

* * *

Our first weekend trip to Joan's family home in Grange Hill, Westmoreland near the end of the Christmas Term, was an unforgettable experience. We set off after school on the Friday afternoon and the MGB drove impeccably. With virtually no traffic on the road, the top of the car folded back and the warm breeze whistling over our heads, it was pure joy for 'James Bond and his lady-friend' as we continued westwards on the four-hour drive via Mandeville, down Spur Tree Hill, along Bamboo Avenue and past Bluefields Beach and Sav la Mar, into the beautiful setting sun.

That weekend, having been warmly welcomed by Joan's father and mother, and her brothers and sisters, I was treated as if I were just another family member. On the Saturday afternoon, myself and Joan (accompanied by Mara and Ava, squeezed into the back of the MG), made the short drive to Negril where we spent the whole afternoon enjoying one of the most idyllic, and unforgettable, experiences of my life. Negril Beach, at that time, was an almost endless, uninhabited and undeveloped stretch of soft *pink* sand, with perfectly warm, crystal clear, turquoise water, coconut trees gently waving in the breeze, and a perfect canopy of blue sky above. But, wonderful as our beach visit was, on the Saturday evening, my heart's real desire was to take Joan out by myself, so I offered to treat her to a meal at a fancy restaurant not far from Negril. I can still remember how she looked that night - absolutely radiant in a long-sleeved, light blue sweater and a pleated, tartan-patterned skirt - and with her perfect afro and beautiful smile, I couldn't have wanted for anything.

Maybe I was already falling in love as I couldn't help myself feeling that this young lady was much, *so much* more, than just a 'nice Jamaican girl'.

Chapter 13: Let Battle Commence

The remainder of the 1975-76 school year simply flew by. Most evenings I would pop round to Joan's apartment for a chat, or she would wander round to my apartment if I didn't. So, each of us had every opportunity to get to know the other really well, to discuss our views on important issues, to share our individual aspirations for the future, and to observe countless little details about each other's lifestyles and preferences.

We weren't exactly dating at that point, although everyone quite reasonably thought we were, since we invariably walked together to and from school each day, attended the same Frankfield Church of God most Sundays, went on long drives together (including to Joan's family home in Westmoreland), shared our meals together several times a week, and were, according to the rumour-mill '*obviously* having a physically intimate relationship' - a totally incorrect assumption! We were both frequently asked by our students if we were boyfriend and girlfriend, whether we were 'in love' and when we were going to get married, to which we invariably answered,

"Right now, we're just very good friends."
Similarly, the staff at Compre delighted in exchanging knowing glances whenever they saw us together and clearly thought it was simply a matter of time before they would see the engagement ring on Joan's finger.

The fact that Joan was black and I was white, was never really an issue; after all, my own mother and father were in a mixed-race marriage which had stood the test of time, and black-white relationships in Jamaica, with its national motto, '*Out of many, one people*', were hardly uncommon. For Joan, the one, major, unresolved issue was my reluctance to embrace her deep Christian faith; as for me, there was no desire to hasten things to a premature conclusion and I was quite happy to let the relationship take its unrushed, natural course.

However, I was absolutely certain in my own mind that I was now madly in love, and had every intention of asking Joan to be my wife as soon as I thought the time was right. As far as I was aware, she had no other amorous attachments.

In view of the strength of my convictions, and the fact that these feelings continued to increase the more I got to know her, I felt it was time to organise a trip back to England in the summer of 1976. This would give me the opportunity to inform my parents and brother and sisters of our impending marriage, which I had, by then, decided to plan for the summer of 1977 - despite having made absolutely no mention of my intentions to Joan.

Furthermore, in summer, 1976, both my brother, Aydin, and my sister Janet would be getting married and I had been asked to be Best Man at Aydin's wedding. Suzan had, by then, already been married for several years to her childhood sweetheart, Paul, the bass guitarist in my first 'pop' band, *The Jandas*. So, basically, by the end of summer 1976, I would be the only one of the four children still remaining unmarried.

I knew they would all be ecstatic at my news.

* * *

However, before I was able to book tickets for my journey, about half way through the 1976 Summer Term and right before the start of GCE exams, with Jamaica's 'wet season' in full swing, the Rio Minho started to swell as tiny tributaries became voluminous streams, the ground having already been saturated by the frequent rainfall. After several days of this inclement weather, the stepping stones over the river to Cow Pen were not even visible and in order to get from Frankfield to their homes, the Cow Pen residents had to trek on a circuitous route via Lampard. But, when the rain had been falling continuously for over a week, things really started to become serious.

The first victim of the deluge was the low bridge over the Rio Minho tributary between Grantham and Frankfield, which disappeared overnight, leaving in its stead a gaping chasm which completely prevented any vehicular passage from Frankfield, via Grantham and Sanguinetti, to Spaulding. This was a particular problem for the older Compre students from the Sanguinetti area who were just about to start their GCE exams. A number of students who were unable to get back home after their first exam were forced to remain at the school, and had to be accommodated temporarily at the homes of kind Compre teachers. Naturally, Joan was one of the first members of staff to offer this hospitality to two of her female GCE History students.

It soon became obvious that those people whose houses were close to the river banks could be in imminent danger, and a group of able-bodied male teachers at Compre, including myself, thought we ought to check whether any residents near the river needed assistance. I became acutely aware of the value of this endeavour, when I was walking into town and saw an elderly couple waving frantically and calling out for help from their riverside cottage. The river was, by then, swirling dangerously around their home, located not too far from the Teachers' Flats, and I had to wade through the dirty, fast-flowing, knee-deep water to rescue them, as they were unable to escape unaided. With no alternative, I was forced to carry them, one at a time, in my arms from their house to the safety of the nearby road!

Having done my civic duty, I continued my journey along the road towards Frankfield, which provided the opportunity for a systematic investigation into the extent of the flooding further downstream. To my amazement, the water in the Rio Minho was almost up to the top of Long Wall with the odd wave even splashing over onto the road. Then, upon reaching the main bridge on the Chapelton road into Frankfield (the single-vehicle width structure with its massive steel girders which I used to traverse on my daily walk from the Broomfield's up to Compre), I stopped in complete astonishment. The river, which was normally 20 feet *below* the bridge's paved road, was now actually lapping over the *top* of the road! Uprooted trees, and various other floating objects were being tossed around like matchsticks by the torrent of water, and I decided, in the interests of my safety and self-preservation, not to even set foot on this structure, lest the force of the water and debris should also wash away even this bridge - and me with it! - as had already happened to the tributary bridge near Grantham.

Compre's very first Science Exhibition suddenly came to mind. We had investigated the potential of the Rio Minho as a source of hydroelectric power for the local community but, clearly, with floods of this magnitude, any such scheme would be in danger of being totally washed away in prolonged wet weather. The gap in the road near Grantham was eventually repaired by the Jamaica Defence Force, but until then, vehicles wishing to travel the seven miles between Frankfield and Spaulding had no choice but to drive the long way round via James Hill and Cave Valley, an *extra* distance of about eight miles.

Once the rainy weather had subsided, I was then able to book my air tickets for the three-week 'wedding announcement' trip to England, and to focus on exams and all the other, usual end-of-term activities, as normal. I would be leaving immediately after school broke up, while Joan had decided to remain at her Teacher's Flat in Frankfield for most of the summer holiday.

* * *

Before I knew it, I was on the huge British Airways plane to London and settled down to plan how I was going to break the news of my intended marriage to the members of my family when I got to my former home in Derbyshire. I had deliberately endeavoured to travel as light as possible so that I could easily get from Heathrow to St Pancras Station in central London and then catch the train up to Sheffield, rather than expecting anyone to drive all the way down to London to pick me up at the airport. A brief walk from the railway station in Sheffield got me to Pond Street Bus Station, where I took the first available bus that would pass through Grindleford. The bus stop in the village was conveniently right outside the family home.

It would be an understatement to say that my parents were overjoyed to see me. Mum was still looking quite young and sprightly but 'Baba' had aged significantly and was, by then, almost totally bald. They hugged me and wept and then hugged me some more, before ushering me into the dining room where Mum and my twin sisters, Suzan and Janet, had prepared a literal feast to celebrate my arrival. With my brother, Aydin, also present to complete the family reunion, it almost felt like I had never been away, even though it was fully two years since my last visit, and five years since I had emigrated from England.

After we had devoured all the wonderful culinary delicacies, the whole family went to relax in the sitting room where I thought it was as good a time as any to make my announcement.

"By the way, I've got some rather exciting news to share, while we are all here together."

Everyone stopped talking simultaneously and there was an awkward silence, which made me feel a little nervous.

"I'm getting married next summer!"

Then there was absolute pandemonium, with everyone talking at once, laughing and questioning until I beckoned for silence, and continued,

184

"Her name is Joan. She's a graduate History teacher, two years younger than me, and teaching at the same school I'm at. I'm sure you'll all love her. I'm thinking of Grindleford Church, with you, Aydin, as Best Man, and Sue, Jan and Tara, (Aydin's fiancée) as bridesmaids."

Baba immediately got up to get a bottle of homemade wine while Mum fetched some wine glasses for a toast.

"What's she like?"

"Is she Jamaican?"

"When did you get engaged?"

We were now getting into deep water and this was going to be a bit more tricky.

"Well... she's a Christian, very beautiful with a fantastic afro hairstyle, born and raised in Jamaica, has five brothers and sisters, got her degree from the University of the West Indies, and... oh yes, we're not *exactly* engaged yet; in fact, she doesn't even know we're going to be getting married because... because, I haven't actually asked her yet."

There was a stunned silence, immediately followed by further pandemonium with even more questions and shouting:

"Hang on; she doesn't even know you're getting married!?"

"How do you know she'll say 'yes'?"

"How can you plan to get married when you're not even engaged?"

"Is she black?"

I nodded in the affirmative.

"Will she be able to cope, teaching over here if you decide to come back to England?"

"Have you thought of the many problems often experienced by children of black-white, mixed race marriages over here?"

185

"Why on earth haven't you asked her?"

"Do you *really* love her?"

"Why haven't you got engaged?"

As the questions and repeated questions continued unabated, Mum and Baba had said very little, but started to pass round the glasses of homemade wine. Then, beckoning for silence, Baba, acknowledged as the family patriarch spoke, slowly and deliberately, in the language he was still trying to master after having lived in England for 30 years,

> "Deniz, oğlum [*my son*], we will support you whatever you decide. Mummy and I are married 30 years, and we have four *beauty* children. I came England, and still here. As long as you love her, and she love you same, you have my blessing. Now, I offer toast to Deniz and Joan."

Baba raised his glass along with everyone else. I was very touched by what he had said because I knew only too well of the prejudice he himself had suffered when he had come to England from Turkey to marry the woman he loved many years before. I felt sad that, while my own father living in England was still referred to as an 'immigrant', I was usually referred to by the more highly-regarded descriptor, 'expatriate', during the time that I was resident in Jamaica. Maybe this was a consequence of the Jamaican ethic, as summarised in the motto *'Out of many, one people'*.

> Suzan and Janet came up to me afterwards with a word of loving reassurance,

> "Everything will work out OK, bruv. We're sure she is a lovely girl. Just let us know what you want doing over here for your wedding and we'll get everything organised."

* * *

186

Having got all that behind me, I now wanted to really enjoy the rest of the holiday. The two weddings went perfectly and my only regret was that Joan was not by my side to share in these joyous occasions. After Suzan had left to go home with her husband, Paul, and Aydin and Jan had departed with their new spouses on their respective honeymoons, I wanted to spend as much time as possible with my parents, and to renew acquaintances with some of my old school-friends. I had already hand-written and posted a couple of letters to Joan, whom I was missing terribly, but whether they would actually be received before I returned, was anyone's guess. Then, after what seemed like far too brief a visit to my former home, I was once again getting ready to depart for Jamaica and Mummy was tearfully urging me to 'come home before I got too old to find a good job in the British education system'.

On the return flight to Jamaica, I was determined not to miss the view of the Blue Mountains this time round and made sure I kept wide awake. As we approached the airport on the descent towards Kingston, and looked down on the mystical blue peak towering above the capital, I felt strangely 'at home', happy to be back in 'my' Caribbean Island of Jamaica. But, most of all, I couldn't wait to return to my Teacher's Flat in Frankfield to see the woman of my dreams and to find the perfect opportunity to 'pop the question'!

* * *

As soon as I got home, and had taken a quick shower and freshened up, I immediately skipped next door to see Joan. While over in England I had bought her a lovely, light blue cashmere sweater which I knew she would appreciate as the temperature started to fall in a couple of months' time. With my gift in hand and without knocking, so I could surprise her, I quietly opened the door and crept in

187

to find her standing in her kitchenette with Rico by her side. Of course, I knew that Rico was her good friend from UWI and that his family home was not too far away, so it was perfectly normal that he had dropped by to see her while his university classes were suspended for the long summer break.

But something wasn't right.

I immediately sensed in my spirit that something had changed in the three weeks since I had left. I couldn't lay my finger on what it was at that moment, but something was definitely *different*. Anyway, irrespective of any misgivings I might have had, which I brushed aside as probably just the result of jet lag, I gave Joan a huge bear-hug, presented her with my gift, and shook Rico by the hand. She smiled and thanked me for the gift, which she proceeded to unwrap while Rico and I made small talk about my trip.

> "Oh, Skip, this sweater is beautiful! Thank you so much. How are your family back in England? Did you have a good time?"

We talked for a while about my family, the joy of once again seeing my beloved Derbyshire countryside, and the weddings of my brother and sister, but while we were talking, I couldn't help noticing that her dining table had just two places set for dinner.

> "Rico and I were just about to eat; I had no idea when you would be getting back."

My letters clearly hadn't yet reached her but, even so, this response was somewhat out of place, coming from the Joan I knew. At any other time, she would have quickly set out a third place at the table and shared out the food to cater for an unexpected guest. After a slightly awkward pause, I replied,

> "Oh, that's fine. I'm sure there's food in my fridge that I can heat up. You two go ahead and we can talk later."

As I returned to my flat to retrieve my big billy-pots of chicken broth and rice which had been in the fridge for over three weeks, to heat them up for the thousandth time, my head had started to ache and my mind was running in all sorts of directions. My first thought was that maybe I had picked up a dose of the flu from the changes in temperature between the cold, air-conditioned interior of the aeroplane and the intense heat of Kingston. But it had never affected me before and, in any case, I hardly ever got sick anyway. Possibly I was merely exhausted from the long journey and the effect of jet lag. But a good night's sleep ought to solve that.

Eventually, as I sat down at my table to eat, another thought suddenly struck me. Maybe I was just jealous that Rico was the guest at one of Joan's sumptuous meals while I was all alone, languishing with my wretched chicken broth and rice. But then, Joan and myself weren't even officially dating at that point and, after all, I certainly hadn't yet taken the obvious initiative of promoting the idea of us being in a *proper* boyfriend-girlfriend relationship. Maybe Joan saw our friendship as just being good friends, but nothing more. Maybe she thought that was how *I* perceived the relationship! I silently cursed myself for having been so casual and slow on the uptake. What if Rico had taken the initiative and made *his* move while I was out of the picture? He had also known Joan for some time but, unlike myself, he was a Christian - so could it be that he had now filled the role of the Christian suitor whom Joan was seeking, while I had been away? I tried to dismiss such an idea as an illogical consequence of my obvious jealousy.

A couple of unhappy hours later, just as I was thinking of popping back round to see the woman I was in love with, there was a knock on my door and I opened it to find Rico, with what I perceived as a slightly sheepish look on his face, and I tried to jokingly lighten the mood:

"Come in, man. I'd offer you some of my chicken broth and rice, but I doubt it would taste very good in comparison with what you've just eaten."

Rico sat down and then, without any warning, he blurted out,

"Skip, I just wanted to let you know that Joan and I are now a couple. I asked her to be my girlfriend while you were away. But now that you're back, I didn't think it was fair not to let you know."

My heart must have missed about a dozen beats as I tried to digest what I had just heard and my head, heavy like lead, slouched down so that my chin was almost resting on my chest. This was surely the worst moment of my entire life to date. No wonder I had sensed something wasn't quite right when I had arrived a few hours before. But my mind was now racing and I was horrified, devastated, indignant, and furious, all at the same time. I raised my head and looked Rico straight in the eye, before responding.

"So, Joan is *your* girlfriend?"

He nodded in the affirmative.

"Since when?"

"A couple of weeks, I suppose."

"You know I love her?

"Well, I suspected that, but 'all's fair in love and war', as they say."

"I find it hard to believe that someone whom I *thought* was my good friend, would go behind my back and do *that*, in the full knowledge that I loved her."

"Sorry, Skip. It just seemed a natural step for me. I wasn't trying to cause any problems."

"Well, Rico, hear this,"

and I paused to ensure that what I was about to say fully communicated my absolute resolve and determination,

"I shall fight you for her, with everything that I'm worth. And no holds barred!"

We both knew that I was not talking about fighting *physically*. But apart from a physical confrontation, I was deadly serious, and I had absolutely no intention of losing. Rico smiled, before responding,

"Well Skip, I don't fancy your chances in that contest."

"We'll see. May the best man win!"

As Rico left, I shook his hand firmly with what I hoped was a resolute expression on my face. I still considered him my friend and felt no evil towards him, but until my dying breath, I would put my heart and soul into seeing that I would win the battle for Joan.

* * *

From the start, I felt there were a number of factors in my favour. Firstly, despite my brief absence abroad, during the university term-time, it was actually Rico who would be living almost a hundred miles away on the UWI campus, which meant that, at most, he might get to see Joan once a week. I was living literally a foot away, on the other side of the dividing wall between our two apartments, and I had every intention of making the most of this proximity by seeing her daily.

Then, I had already met and got to know almost her entire family, who seemed to already think of me as another family member, so I was confident that her mother, Felicita, as well as her younger sisters, would all be fighting in my corner of the ring.

Thirdly, I was already working, had a good job and a secure salary, while Rico was still a student, in a much weaker financial position.

Fourthly, I owned a very attractive MGB sports car which was at my disposal any time I needed it; Rico had neither his own vehicle nor the means of running one.

Fifthly, my mind was already made up; I loved Joan with all my heart and my intentions were for a permanent relationship as man and wife. However, I sincerely doubted whether Rico's very recently initiated boyfriend-girlfriend relationship was based on anywhere near the same depth of feeling.

What really concerned me, however, was my lack of religious belief. In this area, Rico, as a practicing Christian for as long as I had known him, had the upper hand. In spite of this, however, I had no intention of making a false declaration of faith to try and swing things in my favour. I had been fully aware from the very start of our friendship how much her Christian faith meant to Joan, and how important she felt it was for her future husband to share that faith. This was a problem, and at that point in time I could see no solution other than my getting more involved in a wider variety of Christian activities. As a good Physicist, I thought this would enable me to conduct a more thorough investigation of Christianity. Despite my lifelong agnosticism to date, I was prepared to do whatever was necessary for the sake of winning the woman I loved.

The other thing I needed to tackle - immediately - was to make Joan fully aware of the depth of my feelings for her and my fervent hope for the two of us to make our future together as husband and wife. Perhaps she would never have started dating Rico if only I had let her know how I felt!

* * *

A couple of evenings later, Joan and I were talking in my flat and, throwing all caution to the wind, I looked her straight in the eye and said,

"Joan, I want you to know just how much I love you. In fact, I think I probably loved you from the very first time I set eyes on you, but didn't realise it at the

192

time. I know you are currently in a relationship with Rico, but he will *never* love you like I do. My entire future here depends on your response to my love. I need you more than anyone I have ever needed. I may as well just go back to England if we can't be together in a mutually loving relationship. I know your heart's desire is for a genuine Christian husband and so I'm asking you to give me time to sort out my current lack of faith. Please pray for me in this regard, if you think it will help. And please believe that everything I have just said is true because it is coming straight from my heart."

Joan looked at me in return.

"I do believe you, Skip, but why didn't you ever say this to me before? You must know that I like you very much, but I thought we were just good friends, almost like brother and sister. Anyway, thank you for telling me, so that I know now where we stand. I promise that I'll pray about our relationship and also about Rico and myself. If it's God's will for you and I to be together, nothing can come between us. Oh... and don't even consider going back to England!"

My heart was beating overtime, and considering the current circumstances, I suppose I couldn't have hoped for a much better response to my declaration of love.

* * *

So, without further ado, it was imperative for me to begin my rather more serious study of Christianity. If our relationship hinged on my theological position, I would do everything necessary to deepen my understanding of the Christian faith and learn more about its 'God'.

For the remainder of the school holiday, I made sure to spend some time with Joan every day, or even twice a day if possible. I tried to make romantic gestures such as taking her pretty bunches of flowers, and whenever the opportunity arose, I would organise trips in the MGB to one of the theatres in Kingston, as I knew she enjoyed going to see professional productions and Frankfield offered little or no entertainment of this calibre. Joan also liked eating out at the 'posh' restaurants located in Mandeville, and so we patronised these venues whenever possible.

I also made a point of being round at her flat whenever I knew Rico would be visiting (and taking as much time as I politely could before leaving).

Whenever Joan's mother, Felicita, visited, I left her in no doubt about my feelings for her daughter and my desire to ask her to become my wife; likewise dropping similar, obvious hints to her younger sisters, if they were around. I felt that 'mobilising the infantry' in that way was a sound battle strategy and I was confident that they would forcefully petition in my favour.

As far as my faith was concerned, I actually retrieved the Bible that Joan had given me as a gift soon after we first met, from under a pile of other books and Physics magazines, and read the entire thing from cover to cover - very thoroughly - for the very first time. To my surprise, parts of it were more exciting than I had imagined, especially some of the Old Testament stories like David and Goliath, Jonah and the whale, and Elijah and the prophets of Baal. But I found the story of Jesus' life and ministry and subsequent crucifixion more thought-provoking and difficult to reconcile with my existing views, and had so many questions that I had to start writing them down in case I might forget them.

I tried to pay closer attention in the services at church each Sunday, with a determined effort to avoid falling asleep during the sermon. I even started attending the interdenominational Bible study group that Joan had initiated and hosted in her flat each Thursday evening. It was regularly attended by several local church leaders, and

I literally dominated the discussions each week with my growing list of questions. But I was still some distance away from accepting Christianity as my *own* faith; as a Physicist, I needed more evidence, proof that it applied to me *personally* and was more than just a fairy tale.

* * *

It was around this time that I was approached by some of the members of 'my' church about their need for a new church choir conductor. The minister previously in charge of the choir (and responsible for their traditional Easter and Christmas cantatas) had recently left, so, without beating around the bush, they asked me if I would take over. Flattered as I was to have been asked, there were two major obstacles to my accepting this illustrious role. Firstly, my knowledge of reading printed music was, at best, limited, apart from which I had never conducted anything or anybody in my entire life. Secondly, such an endeavour would need a really competent pianist who would need to be an excellent sight-reader of choral scores, and I was not aware of the availability of any suitable pianist in the area. Not being in any way eager to take on yet another role to add to my already hectic schedule, I thought, naïvely, that in view of these two major obstacles, I would be able to easily wriggle out of this proposed venture.

To my surprise, the very next day one of the music teachers at school paid me an unexpected visit. Ernesto, originally from Guatemala and fluent in both English and Spanish, duly informed me that he had been asked to speak with me about 'the church choir that *I* was in the process of creating', and to offer his services as the pianist. Clearly, plans were already being made that I was unaware of! Not really having had the opportunity for any interaction with Ernesto since his recent arrival at the school, I had no idea of his capabilities in accompanying choral music, but as soon as I heard him play, it was immediately obvious that he had considerably more than the necessary skills needed for the task. And trying to convince the aspiring choir members that I lacked the musical skills needed was quite simply a non-starter. After all, I *was* the leader of a now well-known, local Gospel band!

A week or so later, the choir had its first practice, and I was happy to welcome Joan as one of the sopranos! In order to be more confident in what I was doing, I had made sure to go through the musical scores I intended to use with Ernesto in detail beforehand. As I suspected from my knowledge of the vocal talent available at 'my' local church, we had plenty of sopranos and basses, but were sadly short of altos and tenors. Then someone made the suggestion that we could easily balance the sections of the choir if we looked a bit further afield and expanded to become an *inter-denominational* choir. This proposal was unanimously accepted and within a very short time we had swelled our numbers to about 30 members and were practicing on a regular basis. Although I had been almost terrified at the thought of taking charge of a musical activity about which I knew next to nothing, I could not back out now. So, with Ernesto's help and a considerable time input on my part, I was determined to master the mysterious art of reading a score with four vocal parts and piano accompaniment. And to my surprise, I was really enjoying this new challenge!

Before long, the choir was being asked to perform in churches throughout Clarendon and even further afield. The members were serious about learning their individual parts and the ladies even took it upon themselves to design and make a proper uniform for them to wear at our concerts. About the same time, I procured a bright red jacket to look the part of conductor and managed to find a proper conducting stick to use instead of an extended finger. It became a really enjoyable activity that not only brought people of different backgrounds and musical ability together, but also served to bring the different churches in the Frankfield community closer together as well.

After we had been working together for a few months and made significant musical progress, I felt it was time to attempt what is surely one of the most well-known and popular of all choral works, Handel's *Messiah*. It was an outstanding success and I couldn't wait to inform my family back in England of my most amazing musical achievement to date - especially my Father, who loved listening to Classical music, and my brother, Aydin, who was a professional classical pianist.

* * *

Meanwhile the days were ticking by, the long summer holiday had come to an end and the 1976 Christmas Term was in full swing. The time I had left to plan my proposed wedding for summer 1977 was diminishing daily and despite all my efforts (plus those of my army of soldiers and supporters), Joan and Rico were still an item. I was aware that close friends such as Spenga, before he left for America, and Harry (who were both, ironically, also good friends with Rico), had frequently petitioned Joan on my behalf, singing my praises and encouraging her to lean in my direction but, for now at least, their advice seemed to be falling on deaf ears.

My praying for help didn't seem to make much sense either, since I didn't really know who or what I should pray to. However, I did know that there was a group of elderly, Christian ladies at church who, I was reliably informed, prayed for me daily. So, casting aside my pride and my general tendency to try to do everything for myself, I shared with them my dual dilemma of lack of faith and lack of a mutually loving relationship with Joan, and begged them to pray on my behalf. At least God, if he existed, might hear *their* prayers, even if he wasn't hearing *mine*.

But by the end of November, nothing had changed and I was becoming more and more desperate. Joan and Rico were still dating, despite her receiving frequent admonitions from her mother and sisters to rethink what she was doing. Although I was still attending the weekly Bible study and slowly getting a better understanding of what Christianity was all about, the prayers of the elderly group of sisters at church were clearly not working; it seemed that God, if he *was* 'up there', was, perhaps, hard of hearing. On the other hand, if he *was* actually listening, it looked as though he was either disinterested or unwilling to intervene on my behalf.

* * *

On the last weekend of the month, both Joan and myself had reason to make a trip into Kingston. On the Saturday night, she had been invited with Rico to the birthday party of one of her girlfriends, whom she planned to stay with overnight and during the following day. I needed to buy a few things which I couldn't get locally, and also wanted to catch up with several of my former students, intending to stay over with Peter, a Physics-teaching colleague whom I had got to know over the last couple of years and hadn't seen in a while. Seeing an opportunity, I reasoned that it made sense for us to go to Kingston and return together, and dutifully suggested that Joan was welcome to travel with me in the MGB. I reckoned that, if nothing else, at least we would get a few hours' journey time together when we could talk. As it happened, however, on the drive there, I was so upset that it was Rico taking her to the party instead of me, that I found it hard to make useful, congenial conversation.

We had arranged for me to pick up Joan for the trip home at about 7 o'clock on the Sunday evening, near the home of her girlfriend. The proposed meeting place was not too far from the bridge at Six Miles which crossed over the main east-west highway just outside town. Frustrated with the lack of progress in my romantic circumstances, without even realising it I arrived at our rendezvous point with a couple of hours to spare, so I just sat there in the car, parked on a slip-road off the highway, and listened to the most cheerful music I could find on the radio. My trip had been useful in that I had managed to get all the things I had wanted to buy, rendezvoused successfully with my former students, all of whom were progressing really well, and had also had an enjoyable time getting reacquainted with my friend, Peter. Unfortunately, however, the excursion had not helped me to gain much ground in my continuing battle for the woman I was in love with. Although it was a particularly beautiful evening, I was hardly aware of the world around me, being focused only on the extent of my sorrows and my apparent powerlessness to change the status quo. As afternoon turned to evening, my head sank back onto the top of the car seat and I was soon fast asleep.

Chapter 14: The Agreement

After I awakened from my 50 winks, I found that I still had an hour to kill, so I decided to drive back onto the highway, take the slip-way leading to the minor road passing over the top of Six Miles bridge, and park on top of the bridge to watch the sunset. It was obviously going to be a spectacular affair, with fluffy wisps of pink cloud arcing across the blue-purple sky from Blue Mountain peak in the north, to the ocean way beyond the airport in the south. I sat there in the MGB with the top folded back, watching the huge, beautiful, red fireball sinking gradually lower and lower towards the horizon, thinking to myself that those Physicists who asserted that such a beautiful world all came about entirely by chance, rather than by intelligent design, clearly couldn't see the wood for the trees! The creation theory just seemed such an obvious explanation; there must be a higher power behind everything, who had planned it all in minute detail. If people wanted to refer to that 'higher power' as 'God', then so be it; I had no problem with that.

But then, I reasoned, if I accepted that 'God' had the power to create the entire *physical* world, surely he must also have the power to sort out *people's* problems. Maybe, *just maybe*, if I were to put my trust in this almighty power and acknowledge him for whom the Bible claimed him to be, he might just show me a little of his infinite greatness and mercy and help solve my particular problem of being irrevocably and deeply in love with a woman who didn't love me back in the same way.

As I continued these theological reflections, without warning, I felt a strange, unusual tingling sweep through my body when I asked myself what I would have to lose by casting aside my reluctance to believe in God? After all, as a Physicist, I couldn't deny that many of the things I implicitly believed in already, such as the universality of the laws of Physics throughout the universe, were just as much an act of faith on my part as believing in an unseen God. If I really believed such all-encompassing theories to be true, what was stopping me putting my faith in an all-creating, invisible God in the same way? Was it just stubbornness on my part? If so, was there actually any *genuine* obstacle to my embracing the Christian faith? Was my current agnostic state really any more justifiable than believing in a *real* God?

For some reason, my mind suddenly focused on the crucifixion of Jesus which I had been reading about recently in my ongoing, personal Bible study. From all my research, the evidence definitely pointed to Jesus' death as a factual, historical event. So if, as the Bible would have me believe, he did that *for me*, as the means by which I (or anyone else) could retrieve the intimate relationship with God that I *should* have, why shouldn't I accept it? In fact, it would make less sense *not* to believe.

In any case, *what did I have to lose*?

With embarrassing tears running down my cheeks, I bowed my head and prayed - as best I knew how - unsure whether it should be God or Jesus that I should be praying to:

"Thank you Jesus for dying that awful death by crucifixion to allow God to forgive me for all the 'bad things' I have ever done."

(I was afraid to use the word 'sin', which would have made me feel like I was admitting to being a really wicked criminal.)

"Please help me to believe in you and to accept God's forgiveness for all those wrongs."

(...and come to think of it, there *were* quite a few)

"And please help me to start a new life as a Christian 'believer'. Oh, and one more thing, Jesus; if you would be so kind as to intervene on my behalf in my

201

relationship with Joan, so that she starts to love me as much as I love her, *then, in return, I promise I shall serve you faithfully in every area of my life from now on."*

That seemed like a pretty fair bargain, in view of all the things I would probably need to give up.

"Thanks, Jesus, for listening to my prayer. Talk again soon."

(Finishing my prayer with 'Amen' sounded just a bit too pious for me at that particular point in time. Much later in my spiritual walk, I shuddered to think that I could have been so audacious and cocky as to try and *bargain* with God in my conversion prayer, to reach an agreement where I would give lifelong service to Him in exchange for receiving Joan's love. God really must have an outstandingly merciful nature and an even more amazing sense of humour!)

I felt a wave of relief pass through me, rather like I used to feel as a small child when, after being found out for having done something really bad, I had, with sorrowfully bowed head, owned up to my father for my misdemeanours. Instead of being scolded or spanked, however, as I no doubt deserved, I had been willingly forgiven and was gently lifted up into his arms to demonstrate that I was still loved, irrespective of whatever I had done. I felt as if my life up to this point was like having been trapped in a cold, filthy mud-hole, into which I had fallen, but now I had been rescued, washed clean, and was warm and dry again.

My whole being was inexplicably tingling with a sense of joy and *spiritual* exhilaration that I had never experienced before.

* * *

When I looked at my watch, it was almost 7 o'clock, so without delay, I raced down from the top of the bridge in the MGB, back onto the highway towards Kingston, and over to the home where I was supposed to pick up Joan. She must have perceived something different in my facial expression compared to my demeanour when driving into Kingston, because the first thing she asked me was,

"Skip, you look different. Has something happened?"
I found it impossible to conceal my excitement;

"Yes - something wonderful has happened! I have decided to become a Christian. Just now, while I was waiting to come and pick you up. I asked God to forgive me for all the wrongs I have committed and I accepted Jesus' death on the cross as the means by which I have been forgiven by God for all those wrongs!"

(I was still avoiding words like 'sin' and 'righteousness'.)
Joan looked at me in amazement, and with a radiance on her face which I hadn't seen before, replied,

"Skip, I'm so glad for you. Truly, I am. This is the most wonderful news!"

The drive back to Frankfield was in complete contrast to the one travelling into Kingston. I was really animated, exuberant and happy. We talked openly about my experience on the top of Six Miles bridge, except for one detail; I said nothing of my 'Agreement' with God - there were various things I had to do first.

* * *

Although my playing with Third Generation band had been a lot of fun, enabling me to learn a great deal about reggae and other Caribbean rhythms, there were also negative aspects to the experience which I had always felt uncomfortable with. Some of the places we performed at were really sleazy, or even downright immoral, such as

203

strip-clubs, and nightclubs where the smell of marijuana was so strong, I could hardly breathe. In spite of any musical enjoyment and fun I might have had, there was no way I could continue with this lifestyle, and at the same time, claim to be a Christian believer. Undoubtedly, I would miss the music and the fellowship with the guys in the reggae band, which was just at the point of moving on to bigger things, but whatever the fallout, it was now imperative that my time with Third Generation come to an end. From this point onwards, my entire musical focus would be on evangelism through the ministry of Sonic Salvation Gospel Band.

On the Thursday evening after we returned from Kingston, I drove up to our Third-Generation band practice, just as I had done every week for the last few years, but this time *without* my drum-kit. I felt decidedly nervous about informing the band members about my decision to leave, but I knew in my heart that I had no choice; I was determined to keep to my side of the 'Agreement' I had made with God.

Melvyn was the first to comment:

"W'appen to di drums, Skip? Dem mash up? [*What's happened to your drums, Skip? Are they broken?*]

"No, man, but mi come fi tell unu dat mi haffi leave unu an di band. Mi sorry, man, but it jus no fit wid mi new Christian fait." [*No, but I've come to tell you that I've got to leave the band. I'm sorry, but it just doesn't fit any more with my new Christian faith.*]

Melvyn was not happy at all, and made his feelings very clear with a sarcastic,

"So yuh tun Christian? Mi is a Christian but it nah tap me play in a di ban." [*So, you've become a Christian, have you? Well, I'm (also) a Christian, but it's never stopped me playing in the band.*]

"Mi sorry bad. Mi really luv fi lik di drum dem in a di band, an unu ah mi bredda an good frens, but me kyahn gwaan." [*I'm truly sorry. I really do love playing drums in the band, and I think of you all as my brothers and good friends, but I just can't continue in the band anymore.*]

But, I felt I couldn't leave without saying a proper individual farewell to each band member, and giving them a big hug or a handshake. This was a deeply emotional parting. It had been my first test as a new Christian, and it had been an excruciating, distressing experience which I found really, really hard!

Hopefully, my 'new' life was not going to be like this all the time.

As I drove back down to Frankfield, I felt relieved but sad, both at the same time. I would miss the guys and the band, but once I had decided upon that particular course of action, I was going to stick to it. I was determined to live up to my side of the 'Agreement' with God.

On my arrival at the Teachers' Flats, it so happened that I crossed paths with Rico who was just walking out through the gate. He did not look happy at all, and when he saw me, came over as I parked. I wasn't sure what was troubling him, but when I got out of the car, he held out his hand to shake my own, and said,

"Skip, Joan and myself have broken up. I won't get in your way any more. I wish you well."

I could hardly believe my ears. Could God be answering my prayer so soon? I wasn't sure what to say but still firmly shook his hand and responded,

"As *you* said to me a while ago, Rico, 'all's fair in love and war!' ", but then I paused and added,

"No hard feelings, man - wi still frens."

He managed to force a wry smile before, somewhat dejectedly, walking away.

* * *

In the days that followed, my relationship with Joan now seemed to take on a very different perspective. She was more relaxed, more responsive and much happier when with me. A few weeks after her break-up with Rico, we were together one evening in her flat having dinner together; it was a wonderful meal, especially after the last few months of my wretched chicken broth and rice. When we had finished eating, I looked into her eyes and, for the thousandth time, told her how much I loved her. She smiled happily and replied in a gentle, sincere voice,

"Thank you, Skip. I'm much happier now for us to be more than just friends."

This was the first time she had ever said anything like *that* and I was overjoyed! My mind raced back again to my experience on Six Miles bridge and the 'Agreement' I had made with God. Perhaps He really was going to grant my heart's desire, that I might be loved, deeply and completely, by the woman with whom I wanted to spend the rest of my life.

I took Joan in my arms, held her close, and for the first time ever… felt her soft lips meet my own! My heart was beating furiously; surely, this was a foretaste of heaven! We were now, officially, boyfriend and girlfriend and I was absolutely determined that, from here onwards, there would be no going back on my side of the 'bargain' with God; the rest of my life was *definitely* going to be spent serving Him.

Over the next week or two, I was literally walking on air and could barely concentrate, even in my beloved Physics lessons. Now that Joan and I were finally dating, I was keen to move things on quickly and get engaged. We already knew each other really well, and there had been absolutely no doubt about my own feelings for quite some time, but I also wanted my marriage proposal to be a magical moment in our lives, something that we would always remember - so it had to be at the right place and at

206

the right time. Maybe it was still possible to get married in the summer of 1977 after all - as I had presumptuously announced to my family on my last visit to England!

Soon afterwards, Joan got word of a Christian weekend retreat for young adults, which was going to be held at the start of the Easter holidays. This was to take place at Moorlands Christian Centre, located in a somewhat isolated but beautiful spot at the top of Spur Tree Hill, a few miles out of Mandeville. While Joan had expressed a keen interest that we attend this retreat together mainly for its spiritual benefit, I thought it might also be just the ideal place and time for that 'magical moment' I had been searching for. We sent off an application form for two persons, and a few days later received a reply confirming that we had secured the last two places.

I could hardly wait for the retreat and to drive to Moorlands with Joan in the MGB. On this occasion, I felt it imperative that the car should look immaculate, so gave it a good wash, clean and polish. We left immediately after school on the last day of the Easter Term, having already packed our weekend bags the previous evening. On our arrival, we were allocated our individual rooms and after freshening up, joined the rest of the group in the dining area for our evening meal. Joan was delighted to reconnect with some of her old girlfriends from UWI, and I was elated to be introduced as her *boyfriend*, Skip.

A number of well-known Christian speakers had been booked to lead the various sessions, which I found really interesting and inspiring. I was definitely benefitting from the teaching sessions, my faith appeared to be getting stronger on a daily basis, and I was overjoyed to be with the woman I loved. On the Saturday evening, we were free to do our own thing and although it was a bit misty outside, I asked Joan if she would like to accompany me on a short walk to stretch our legs and get some fresh air.

I thought it would be a nice, romantic walk to follow the track which ran from the Moorlands centre up to the top of the hill. It wasn't far so we made it in about 30 minutes. Joan was feeling a bit chilly, however, so I took my right arm out of the sleeve of my over-sized anorak, put my arm around her waist, and pulled the coat over her shoulders so that, now squeezed close together, we could both keep warm. The mist was swirling all around us, reducing visibility to just a few yards. Instead of immediately returning from the top of the hill, however, we paused for a minute and lovingly embraced.

Her cheek was cold against my own while her lips were tender and moist; it was that 'magical moment'! In my heart, I knew that this was exactly what I had been waiting for, and gently released my embrace. Then, I got down on one knee before her, holding her hands in mine.

"Joan, my darling, my love; would you do me the honour of becoming my wife? Will you marry me?"

She had a wonderfully happy expression on her face, and responded without hesitation,

"Yes Skip! What a wonderful surprise - I thought we were just going for a walk! I honestly didn't know you were planning this!"

As I stood up, all of a sudden, an amazing scene unfolded before us as the mist completely cleared. There, almost 2,000 feet below in the valley, appeared a magical array of thousands upon thousands of tiny, twinkling lights, like a reflection of the majestic canopy of stars now visible above us in the clear, black sky. It was the bright lights of the huge bauxite works at the bottom of Spur Tree Hill. This breath-taking scene was one of the most beautiful sights I had ever seen, and was so unexpected and amazing, that neither of us could speak for a moment. In our hearts, we knew this was no 'chance occurrence'; it was a sign from God. It was his seal of approval for our engagement.

Joan was now my fiancée! We were going to get married! We literally *ran* back down the track, laughing, crying, stumbling, embracing. And I thanked God with all my heart. What more could I have asked for?

Although we had not yet acquired an engagement ring (which I was well aware all new fiancées liked to show off on their finger!), we had nonetheless decided to announce our engagement to all the participants at the retreat, and this was greeted with wild enthusiasm. I suppose we should have expected no less!

On arriving back in Frankfield on the Sunday evening, we decided on the spur of the moment to take a trip into Kingston the following day to try and find an engagement ring. Although not a person who, by nature, revelled in shopping expeditions, I was more than willing on this occasion to spend an afternoon with my fiancée, happily wandering around from one jeweller shop to another in the New Kingston area, until we found exactly what Joan was looking for.

It was a very unusual ring, featuring a single diamond elevated just above the centre of a protecting gold hemisphere. The diamond sparkled and glittered with a radiance matched only by her smile when she slipped the ring on her finger. Now we had the *visible* symbol of our intention to become man and wife.

* * *

We then thought it only appropriate to pay a visit to Joan's family home in Grange Hill to formally announce our engagement and for me to ask her father for her hand in marriage, even though this was, by then, a somewhat belated request. So, a few days later, we packed our bags once again for a slightly longer trip, this time to Westmoreland. The weather was perfect, with just a hint of a breeze and a beautiful clear blue sky.

Ava was the first to spot the ring and ran into the house shrieking,

"Cherry's engaged! Cherry and Skip are engaged!"

That evening, we all shared a feast fit for a king. The whole family, including Joan's grandparents, were really happy - they had all been aware of my intentions to ask Joan to be my wife for some time, and fully supported the idea of our marriage. Mara even joked, with her usual outspokenness,

"Cherry, ow come yuh keep Skip waitin soh long?"

Over the next few days, we visited the beautiful beaches at Negril and Bluefields to swim and frolic around in the exquisitely warm water, and had a wonderful time celebrating our recent engagement and starting to feel the excitement of our forthcoming wedding. The days simply flew by and, before we knew it, it was time for our return journey to Frankfield.

Once we had unpacked and had had a bite to eat after the long drive, I thought it would be appropriate to inform Mr Latty, so Joan and myself took a walk up to his home just by the top of the school drive. I was sure I detected a twinkle in his eye just before I broke the news;

"Hello Mr Latty. I thought you might like to know that Joan and I are engaged to be married."

While Mrs Latty and Joan excitedly examined the engagement ring, Mr Latty poured four glasses of wine for a toast.

"To Skip and Joan. May you both be blessed with good health and happiness as future husband and wife! Didn't I tell you, Skip, that you would eventually find that 'nice Jamaican girl'?"

At the first opportunity, we also made a formal announcement to the congregation at our local church. Everyone was very happy, and the group of elderly ladies who I had asked to pray on my behalf even danced around singing,

"Thank you Lord! Thank you, Jesus! God has answered our prayers!"
Yes, God had certainly answered their prayers *and* mine! And I was immediately reminded of a Bible verse that I had learnt recently, from James, chapter 5, verse 16: 'The effectual fervent prayer of a righteous man availeth much'. I presumed that the verse applied equally to 'righteous women'.

* * *

I had already written to Mummy, Baba, Aydin and the twins in England to inform them of our good news and to confirm that our wedding would indeed take place that very summer - now less than three months away! When I discussed the wedding with Joan, however, she expressed concern that if we were to get married in England, most of *her* side of the family would be unable to attend. I immediately pointed out that if we were to marry in Jamaica, most of *my* family would similarly be excluded. We appeared to have reached an impasse, when I suddenly had an idea:
"I've got a brilliant solution! Let's have *two* weddings, one in Jamaica and the other in England!"
And that is exactly what we decided to do! Two weddings, two receptions, and two lots of presents! The first celebration would be in Jamaica, our beautiful 'Island in the Sun', and the second would be in my beloved, Derbyshire Peak District in England.
If we were going to get married, we were going to do it in style!

* * *

The 1979 Summer Term at school whistled by like an express train. There was so much to get organised.

211

Without all the help we had from our friends, like Sissil, who kindly offered to design and sew a beautiful, white, hand-embroidered wedding dress for Joan, we could never have got everything done in time. Meanwhile, I located a nearby tailor who made me an eye-catching light blue suit with dark blue, velvet lapels, and a dark blue bow tie to match, along with appropriate garments for the Best Man and ushers.

After much soul-searching, we chose not to hold the marriage service at our local Church of God in Frankfield which was just too small, but instead to use one of the larger churches in Mandeville which was close to the hotel where we planned to hold the reception after the service. We had booked two rooms in the hotel for the day of the wedding, one in which Joan and the bridesmaids, Bev, Mara and Ava, would get ready and the other for myself, the Best Man, Harry, and ushers, Spenga and Fern. The arrangement was for the wedding car to firstly pick up myself and the male party from the hotel, drop us off at the church, and then return for Joan and the bridesmaids afterwards. As a Physicist, I was at pains to emphasise to Joan to be ready ON TIME, as I still found it difficult to understand why she always seemed to take longer than me when getting ready to go out.

As it happened, on the day of the wedding, we all got to the hotel in Mandeville nice and early, so that we could dress at a leisurely pace without getting too hot or flustered in the Jamaican summer heat. But, just as the other men and I were putting the finishing touches to our attire and hairstyles before proceeding to where the wedding car would pick us up, I realised something was wrong. Terribly, *terribly* wrong!

I had forgotten my elegant, dark blue, velvet bow tie back in Frankfield - at *least* an hour's drive away! I was panic-stricken and at a loss to know what to do; and none of the other guys had anything that they could offer as a substitute which would look even remotely appropriate with

212

my light blue suit. Going to my wedding in a casual looking, open-necked shirt just wasn't an option! In desperation, we rushed out of the hotel in all our finery, and ran for all we were worth towards the centre of the town, in search of a suitable replacement. After having rummaged through every bow tie we could find in numerous men's clothes shops, with me praying fervently that God would urgently help me in my present distress, we eventually found a similar bow tie to the one I had left behind in Frankfield. Jubilantly thanking God for his infinite mercy, back we ran to the hotel, perspiring profusely, and just caught the driver of the wedding car, who presumably thought we had made other arrangements and was about to leave.

By now, we were nearly an *hour* behind schedule and I couldn't imagine what Joan, her bridesmaids and the congregation might be thinking; after all, didn't Skip always claim to be ON TIME? Had he had an accident? Even worse, had he suddenly got cold feet and done a runner? Mopping our brows, we finally got to the packed church, to the relief of the two ministers who were patiently waiting to start the service. The car could then finally return to the hotel to pick up Joan and her bridesmaids (who, on this occasion had, in fact, been ready *early*). To the relief of everyone, the bridal party arrived at the church shortly thereafter, and what followed was a perfect marriage service.

As I later discovered, my bride-to-be had actually had every confidence in my good intentions, and simply thought there must have been a good reason for my delay. But I was not allowed to forget that, the night before the wedding, Joan had actually advised me to make a list of all the clothing items I would need to take with us for the ceremony which, of course, I had ignored in my usual blasé fashion. This episode, however, turned out not to be the only salutary lesson I would learn about *listening* to my future wife and taking on board her well-meant advice. But from that time onwards, I did at least try my best to avoid making assumptions and doing *everything* my way, even if I didn't always succeed! I suppose it was inevitable that this incident made me the butt of many jokes for years afterwards, and I never quite lived it down.

After the expected hundreds of photographs, with Joan looking absolutely radiant in her stunning wedding dress and perfect afro hairstyle, everyone headed back to the hotel for the reception, where, after a sumptuous meal, my friend George, the MC for the occasion, quickly got the programme into full swing. The delayed start to the wedding was soon forgotten. Sonic Salvation provided brilliant musical entertainment and the speeches and jokes from Harry, Spenga, George and others had everyone in fits of laughter. It was everything a reception should be. When I gave my concluding speech, I thanked everyone from the bottom of my heart for helping to make our marriage such a magical occasion.

Unfortunately, however, after the reception, we still had to load up all the Sonic Salvation equipment into the Vogue, drive it back to Frankfield and unload it, before returning to the hotel. Then, at long last, Joan and myself could retire to the hotel room we had booked, and finally share our first night together, 'to have and to hold', as husband and wife.

* * *

After our return to Frankfield and having caught our breath from all the excitement of our 'first' wedding, I insisted that we travel to Joan's family home in Westmoreland for a few days to have a well-earned rest and a refreshing swim over at Negril beach before we left for our second wedding in England. Joan, for no reason I could discern, just wasn't enthralled with the idea, but I put it down to her anxiety to get everything together for our imminent trip and persuaded her that we had plenty of time to get ready and so, not to worry.

The drive to the western end of the island in the MGB was truly beautiful, especially as it was now James Bond *and his wife* travelling together! The exquisite sea bath at Negril, on an almost deserted 7-mile beach, was just what I needed, apart from my getting the odd mosquito bite while lying on the beach after my swim; that is to say, 'just what I needed' except that Joan, to my dismay, refused point blank to even set a foot out of the car for the *entire* beach trip, claiming that there were far too many mosquitos around after the recent rains. In spite of my teasing her that she was too 'nesh', my pleas for her to join me in the water were to no avail and eventually I decided not to press the issue further.

That night, however, in the huge bed dominating the family guest room at Joan's former home, I found it hard to sleep. Along with a splitting headache, I had started to perspire and, as the night progressed, so did my degree of sweating. By the next morning the bed and my nightclothes were drenched through and I was shivering and felt terrible. Given some government warnings on the news at that time about mosquito-borne sicknesses in coastal areas, Joan insisted on measuring my temperature, and discovered, to her horror, that it was hovering at around 103° F and she began to fear she might suffer a bereavement within days of our marriage. When I was examined by a nursing friend of Mama's, I was immediately diagnosed with dengue fever (a malaria-type sickness), no doubt resulting from the mosquito bites received after ignoring my wife's warnings at the beach. By now semi-delirious, I was just able to hear the lady add,

"He will ha di feeva fi couple days, but mek him res in bed an lik di tempature dung wid a cole bath if him wusen." [*He will have the temperature for a couple of days, but make him rest in bed and keep his*

215

temperature down by giving him a cold bath if he worsens.]

But, resting in bed 'for a few days' would mean missing the flight to London at the end of the week for our 'second' wedding in England! So, by an extreme act of self-will on my part, I managed (with great effort) to get up, have an ice-cold shower, pull on some clothes and convince a sceptical Mama and the rest of the family that I was feeling much better although, in fact, I had never felt worse in my life! At this point, Joan had not yet learnt to drive, so I knew it would be me who would have to undertake the four-hour return drive to Frankfield. With a steady stream of prayers from Joan's family to prevent my imminent demise and with God helping me with holding the steering wheel and using the brakes, we made it back in one piece.

* * *

Back home, the next day, poor Joan had to unwrap all the Jamaican wedding presents herself, showing each one to me in turn while I languished on the bed, bathed in perspiration, barely coherent and almost unable to move. Joan also had to pack all our things for the trip to England, including our wedding attire, while I slept solidly, as she periodically wiped my fiery forehead with a cold, damp cloth. Fortunately, I had already arranged for one of the ex-pat teachers to transport us to Kingston airport the next day, as it would not have been wise to drive myself - and I must have slept soundly, since I remember absolutely nothing of that journey.

For the first time we were now travelling as Mr and Mrs. Önaç, with our marriage certificate carefully placed in Joan's light blue Jamaican passport, which was still in her maiden name. Despite having lost over 10 pounds from my illness, I made a concerted effort to look healthy and happy, accompanied as I was by my beautiful new wife, and, after faking a cheery smile at the nice lady at the British Airways check-in desk, we finally boarded the huge plane for London. Once on the plane, I settled down in the (mercifully) rather comfortable seat and slept solidly for the *entire* flight, even missing the sumptuous evening meal provided, as well as breakfast, just before landing in London in the early hours of the morning of the following day.

On arrival at London Heathrow and after collecting our suitcases, we were picked up by my brother, Aydin, who, by that time, was living permanently in the city. Our intention had been to spend a few days with him and his wife, Tara, enjoying some of the sights of London, before we all travelled with our wedding finery up from London to my Derbyshire family home.

The morning after our arrival, I was feeling slightly better, but there wasn't much improvement in my still uncomfortably high temperature or symptoms. When Aydin and Tara mentioned that there was a local doctor's clinic less than five minutes' walk away, I decided that I would pay the doctor a visit, and insisted on going alone despite Joan's objections and the concern of my brother and his wife. I wanted to get out of the house and once again enjoy the freedom of the city in which I had studied years before.

The rather young, male doctor, who looked like he was fresh out of medical college, gave me a very brief examination, turned pale when he took my temperature and even paler when I told him I probably had dengue fever (which he had never even heard of!). No doubt terrified that I might have brought a deadly new disease into the country, the poor young man spent the next half an hour frantically telephoning every medical colleague he knew, to try and get advice about malaria-like infections. Eventually, having been duly reassured that dengue fever could only be transmitted from a mosquito to a person and not from person to person, he breathed a long sigh of relief and sent me on my way, armed with a week's supply of tablets which, hopefully, would help reduce my temperature. After a couple of days recuperating, I felt well enough for us to set off on the long drive up to Derbyshire and felt it was now nigh time to say a silent prayer of thanks that I hadn't died.

I had, on this occasion, learnt a *second* salutary lesson to pay more heed to Joan's advice in future; I certainly would not want to repeat my interaction with mosquitos carrying dengue fever ever again!

* * *

As we motored steadily northwards, Joan was understandably nervous as she would be meeting all the members of my family for the very first time. But she needn't have worried; on our arrival, everyone was really welcoming and excitedly showered us with questions about how our first wedding in Jamaica had gone, and complimented Joan on her fabulous afro hair. Mummy was a bit perplexed about my wish to share the same bed as Joan prior to our forthcoming (second) wedding and I had to keep reminding her that we were actually *already* officially married before she finally relented.

After a long sleep with a good lie-in, and a very substantial *English* breakfast - a new experience for Joan - we headed out to meet David, the minister who would be conducting the marriage service for our English wedding. He pointed out that although he would endeavour to tailor the service as closely as possible to a normal wedding ceremony, he would, in fact, not be able to issue a formal marriage certificate as we were, in fact, already joined in marriage. We assured him that that would be fine and, as it turned out, hardly anyone at the wedding, except for my immediate family, was aware that we were not getting married for the first time.

This time round, the invitees were mainly members of my side of the family, together with as many of my former school friends as my brother and sisters had been able to contact. It was another beautiful service and we were also blessed with perfect weather which enabled us to get a second set of lovely wedding photos. The male party consisted of myself, my brother Aydin as Best Man, and my two brothers-in-law, Paul and Richard, as ushers, while the bridal party comprised Joan, with my two sisters, Suzan and Janet, and Aydin's wife, Tara, as bridesmaids. They all looked terrific in their wedding suits and bridesmaids' dresses. The reception, immediately after the church ceremony, was held at a historic old hall tucked away under Stannage Edge where I used to go rock climbing. In my final groom's speech, I endeavoured to convey just how appreciative I was for everything my family had done in our absence, to enable the wedding to go ahead and be such a wonderful celebration. When we all got home after the reception, I also thanked each one of them individually for what they had arranged on our behalf; I would never be able to repay them.

* * *

Then, at last, it was our official honeymoon! We would still have a week left after the honeymoon to explore together some of the beautiful Derbyshire countryside before our return to Jamaica, so we had decided to have our honeymoon in Paris, as Joan would then have the opportunity to enjoy as wide a variety of experiences as possible on the European side of the Atlantic.

Now fully recovered from my bout with dengue fever, I, too, was able to enjoy the honeymoon package. This included the boat trip on the ferry across the English Channel, visits to Notre Dame Cathedral, the Arc de Triumph, the Palace of Versailles, climbing to the top of the

219

Eiffel Tower to see the spectacular view of the city, and a lovely boat trip on the River Seine. Also included was a classy Champagne Dinner for two at one of Paris's top restaurants in the Notre Dame area, where we sat talking for almost four hours. And then, while walking hand in hand along one of the quaint Paris streets, we were beckoned by an amazingly talented street artist who painted our picture to keep as a memento of our trip. It was a magical time together to celebrate our union and our love, and I couldn't help but think how blessed I was to have this beautiful princess as my bride.

After our time in Paris had come to an end and we returned to London, we just had time to visit a few more famous tourist attractions, including the National Art Gallery in Trafalgar Square, before taking the train back to Sheffield and travelling from there to the beautiful hills, valleys and rivers of the Derbyshire countryside.

Over the next week, we did a lot of walking along the gritstone edges above Hathersage, Curbar and Froggatt, and to scenic hilltops like Mam Tor, overlooking the villages of Castleton and Edale. We drove to see the picturesque Ladybower and Derwent dams and then up the twisting moorland road to the Cat and Fiddle, one of the highest pubs in England. We also spent an awesome day touring the interior of Chatsworth House with its wonderful paintings, statues and furniture, and then wandered outside to stroll over its beautiful, manicured lawns by the lake and fountain. I wanted Joan to really understand why I loved this beautiful area of England where I had been so fortunate to spend the first 18 years of my life.

She had read books such as Jayne Eyre and Wuthering Heights, and had participated in numerous Shakespearean plays while in high school, and was fascinated to explore the country from which this literature had originated. She was also delighted by how many aspects of the Derbyshire countryside mirrored the descriptions she had read, including its topography, herds of sheep, moorland heather, 'stiles' and 'kissing gates'.

Finally, during our last week in Derbyshire, I had the good fortune to see a local advertisement for an old, red, Ford Transit six-wheel minibus. Although it looked a bit tatty, it drove well, was cheap, and I thought it would be the ideal vehicle for Sonic Salvation Gospel Band to move around in and to carry our increasing amount of musical equipment. I had just enough time before we left to purchase this minibus, drive it to Liverpool and have it loaded into a big container for it to be shipped to Jamaica on the first available vessel.

With the shipping of the Transit successfully accomplished, our wedding holiday was at an end and, after thanking my family profusely for their hospitality and generosity during our stay, we once again took the train to London. Soon, we were back on the huge jet bound for our Caribbean island of Jamaica. It had been an unforgettable trip and surely one of the happiest times of my entire life to date.

Chapter 15: Adventures with The Chariot

As soon as we were back in Frankfield and had unpacked from our trip to England, we immediately had to start packing again for the move to our new home. A quaint, detached, wooden cottage had become available to rent, very near the school gate and snugly nestled between the rum-bar and Rev Alexander's Church of God. My good friend, Mas' John, the school watchman, lived on the same plot of land but in his own small, wooden house situated a few yards behind the cottage. Our home was therefore protected at the rear and also visible from the road, so it offered a safe environment for my growing collection of musical instruments and equipment. The garden was a delight, with our own lime and orange trees, an Otaheite apple tree, and a huge jackfruit tree. With the two citrus trees we would never be short of refreshing, homemade drinks, while the jackfruit tree provided me with exquisite fruit segments which I could freeze and eat with ice cream whenever one of the massive jackfruits fell off the tree (and if one of those ever fell on your head, woe betide you!). On the road-facing side of the cottage was a pleasant little veranda, adorned with a variety of beautiful flowers which Joan enjoyed using for floral arrangements throughout our home.

Inside the cottage were two bedrooms, a lounge, a small dining room, and two spare rooms. One of these I immediately 'captured' for the drums and my other musical equipment, and the other became mine and Joan's shared library for our teaching resources. At the rear of the cottage, a lean-to addition to the building provided a small kitchen, a small bathroom and a back porch. It was picturesque, more than adequate for our immediate needs, and the rent was cheap. God had, yet again, provided exactly what we required.

Once we had packed all the personal belongings from our two Teachers' Flats and ferried these, load by load to the cottage in my Singer Vogue, it was just a case of deciding what went where in our new home. Within a couple of days we were installed and enjoying our quaint cottage as a newly married couple.

My only reservation was that neither the Vogue nor the MGB had anywhere to park *inside* the property boundary and so had to be left, temporarily, outside the Teachers' Flats further down the road. My intention, however, was to sell the Vogue as soon as the Transit arrived, after which I planned to dig out a parking area for both the Transit and the MGB, just inside the gate leading into the front garden of our new cottage.

* * *

Towards the end of the 1977 summer holiday and just as I was starting to get impatient for the arrival of the Transit, the shipping and customs documents arrived in the post. I thought it might be expedient for Joan to accompany me to the docks, although we would have to go by public transport to Kingston and get a taxi to the docks in order to travel back to Frankfield together in the Transit (assuming we could successfully clear it through customs).

On our arrival at the docks, we were shunted back and forth from one department to another before eventually coming face to face with the officer who would assess the vehicle for import duty. He was a pleasant young man who seemed quite surprised when we told him we were married and both teaching at Compre. He immediately asked if we knew Mr Latty, as he was a former student of the school who had left the year before I arrived. Once our mutual connections had been established, things became much easier.

"So how long since you at Compre?"

"Mi come in seventy-one as a volunteer teacha, but mi enjoy tings plenty plenty soh mi stay on an tief one o yuh Jamaican princess fi married." [*I came to Jamaica in 1971 as a volunteer teacher, but since I enjoyed things so much, I decided to stay, and have even married one of your 'nice Jamaican girls.'*]

The young man looked at Joan, who smiled demurely, and then he said,

"So your wife has been trying to teach you some of the dialect?"

To which Joan replied, in her 'posh' Queen's English voice,

"*Me*? Certainly not! His students have done all the teaching!"

The man laughed heartily:

"What a ting, sah! Di white man from foreign a tahk lak a Jamaican, an im black wife from Jamaica tahk lak she come from Englahn. Unu a mek joke wid me!" [*What a remarkable thing! The white man from abroad talks like a Jamaican, and his black wife from Jamaica talks like she is from England! Surely you're playing a joke on me!*]

By that time, we had reached the container in which the Transit was hiding, so the customs officer released the padlocks on the massive steel door and asked me to drive the vehicle out, down some long metal ramps. After looking it over, he asked,

"Soh yuh a go lef teachin an tun bus-drivah now?" [*So, are you leaving teaching now to become a bus driver?*]

To which I replied,

"No Sah! Di van a fi me Gospel Ban - fi carry di musician dem an all di equipmen." [*Definitely not! The van is actually for my Gospel Band, and will be used to transport all the musicians and equipment.*]

"Soh yuh is a church bredda?" [*So, you're a church-goer, are you?*]

"Yes man, me serve di Lawd wid music. Yu mus come a one a di concert dem." [*Absolutely, and I'm glad to serve God through music. Why don't you come to one of our concerts sometime?*]

The young man scribbled something on the customs form and gave it to me.

"Give dis to di man at di gate. An yuh betta memba fi gi mi a free pass if mi come a one o yuh concert!" [*OK, give this form to the man at the gate, and you'd better remember me and give me a free pass if I come to one of your concerts!*]

I suddenly realised that this pleasant, young customs officer was actually waving us through without any customs levy. I was flabbergasted and got down from the driver's seat to shake his hand.

"Tank yuh man, tank yuh plenty plenty. God bless yuh."

He laughed some more and, as he walked away, called after us,

"An keep goin wid di patois. Dem will soon tink yuh is a Jamaican!" [*And keep working on your patois - everyone will soon think you're Jamaican-born.*]

As we drove back home, I couldn't help thinking how, once again, my attempts to speak the local dialect had come to my rescue. On our way out of the city, we stopped in one of the plazas to get a bite to eat. I was feeling very happy and chatted excitedly with my 'Jamaican princess' about the newly acquired vehicle, oblivious to the many passers-by who stopped to stare at us through the window of the restaurant.

Sonic Salvation now had a 'Chariot' to get around in!

* * *

225

In spite of my elation on getting the 'new' vehicle, however, when we got back to Frankfield, I somehow just felt uncomfortable about leaving all three vehicles down by the Teachers' Flats. Not that they were in anyone's way; it was more an issue of security, especially at weekends when most of the ex-pat teachers who lived in the flats headed off to the North Coast, leaving most of the building empty and the car park deserted. For now, however, I could do little more than live in faith and rely on God's protection for my new acquisition.

Selling the Vogue was no problem. It was still in good shape mechanically and it was soon snapped up by a man from a nearby village who wanted to use it as a local taxi. But that still left the Transit and the MGB vulnerable, especially the MGB with its soft top. So I started right away on digging out the short driveway just inside the gate to the garden of our new cottage, and preparing the hard standing area where I was intending to park the two vehicles as soon as I could possibly get the job completed.

It happened the weekend just before school was due to reopen. I had made sure both vehicles were securely locked when I left them on the Friday night assuming, naturally, that they would still be where I had left them when I returned next morning. But when I strolled from our cottage down to the Teachers' Flats the following day, what did I see but a solitary MGB!

The Transit was gone!!

In utter disbelief and horror, I recalled the traumatic experience of my very first car being stolen in London when I was a student at UCL. On that occasion, I was so shocked that I wondered if I had forgotten exactly where I had parked the car and must have walked several miles, looking for it, before finally accepting that it was, indeed, no more. Now, suddenly awakening to the absence of my new minibus outside the Teachers' Flats, I racked my brains to try and determine if I could possibly have left it up at school, parked by the Science block where I often worked on my vehicles. I was so flustered and confused that, in total denial, I actually ran across the playfield and up the school drive to check. Alas, it was nowhere to be seen. Then I finally accepted the reality of the situation; the Transit had been stolen!

Devastated, and with a sickly feeling in my stomach, I walked dejectedly back to our cottage to inform Joan, and then Mas' John. Joan was equally devastated, while Mas' John, muttering under his breath, proceeded to sharpen his cutlass. We had had possession of the Transit for less than a week and I hadn't even had chance to give it a proper inaugural drive. How could God have allowed it to have been stolen when its sole purpose was to assist with my gospel band's musical ministry?

Trying to be as composed as I possibly could, I climbed into the MGB and drove into town to report the theft at the local police station, located across the bridge over the river, beyond the post office. The burly officer at the desk took all the relevant information in laborious detail but, although very sympathetic, offered little encouragement that the vehicle would be recovered. Apparently, minibuses were in high demand, as using them to provide communal transport was a lucrative source of income, and thieves took full advantage of this fact.

Then I circled back into town to see if any of the minibus drivers, lined up in the town centre to ferry people to May Pen or Kingston, had any relevant information, but their responses were even more discouraging. Some of them even seemed to find my dilemma quite amusing, which I found particularly disappointing and hurtful. With little else I could do, I returned home, dejected, frustrated and disillusioned with God. The Christian life just didn't seem fair.

Whether or not it was a complete waste of time or an exercise in futility, I decided to continue with digging out the

227

entrance through the gate into the garden and levelling the hard standing area beyond, covering the exposed soil with a thin layer of marl. I had just completed the job when, around midday, a man I didn't know came running up to the gate.

"Skip, dem find a red bus on a track jus before yuh reach Trout Hall. Dem say is *your* bus." [*Skip, someone has spotted a red minibus on a track off the road just before Trout Hall - they're saying it's yours.*]

I ran up to the cottage to tell Joan then jumped into the MGB, briefly stopping in Frankfield to ask Tookuma (who was, by then, playing tambourine in the band and assisting us as a roadie) if he would come with me, and raced down towards Trout Hall on the Chapelton road. It didn't take long to locate where the bus had been abandoned by the thieves, as there was a crowd of people already standing by the roadside at the start of the track. With my heart pounding, we bumped along the dirt track, with the MGB's exhaust scraping the ground, and there, just around a slight bend which hid it from the road, was the Chariot. Or at least, what was left of it!

My heart sank as I surveyed the current state of my wretched minibus. The front passenger door was gone, together with the bonnet, front grill, and the radiator; but worse than the loss of any of those items, the *entire engine* had been extracted, *including the clutch and gearbox*. The criminals who had done the job must have been truly amazing mechanics, fully able to make an honest living from vehicle repair work had they so desired, to have removed all those items from the vehicle in the pitch dark. It could only have been the morning sun and the likelihood of them being seen by locals walking along the track, that saved my wheels, the seats, the lights, the windows and the cabin.

Alas, what was left of my beloved Chariot was just a shell, although, 'out of the kindness of their hearts', the thieves had left the steering and braking systems intact to enable the shell to be safely towed away. Devastated and incredulous, I asked Tookuma to stay with the shell while I drove back to Compre to pick up the long abseiling rope from the Scout store-room. Then I hurried back into the town to see if Mas' Tom, my former landlord, could possibly give me a tow with his truck. Fortunately, he was at home and only too willing to help.

But there was no way that I was going to leave the Chariot, shell or not, for another night at the Teachers' Flats. So, after towing it back to Frankfield, we carried on a short distance up the road to our new cottage, where I had already decided that, by hook or by crook, I was going to get what was left of the vehicle inside the property and onto the parking area I had just created.

This aspiration was, however, rather more difficult in practice than I had imagined, as the driveway through the gate was quite steep and the poor Chariot was now engine-less and so had no power of its own to help. Fortunately, I had acquired a literal army of helpers by this time, who were more than willing to provide assistance. First I engineered the rope so that it stretched from where I had tied it at the front of the Chariot, (which was temporarily parked on the road in front of the house), through the gateway, around a very large tree higher up in the garden, back through a gap in the hedge bordering the road, and finally to where it was attached at the rear of Mas' Tom's truck, which by then had moved a little further up the road.

With the truck pulling the front of the bus and my small army of helpers pushing the rear, as I sat in the driver's seat and steered it through the rather narrow gateway, we managed to get it inside the garden and onto the level parking area where it could stand freely with no danger of it running back onto the road. After profusely thanking everyone involved and supplying them with a crate full of very much appreciated cold beers from the rum-bar, I then drove the MGB up through the gate and onto the standing area inside, behind the transit. Now illuminated by the lights of the cottage when it got dark, and with a solid padlock on the gate, the two vehicles were as safe as they could possibly be. The real tragedy was that I hadn't done this just a couple of days earlier, but I couldn't turn back the clock; sadly, that omission on my part would have to be considered water under the bridge.

* * *

Now, all that remained to be done was the 'small' task of rebuilding the Chariot. The 'easy' option would have been simply to order all the replacement parts from England - a prohibitively expensive procedure, particularly for a young couple just after a wedding! The only alternative was to scour the surrounding area for cheap, second-hand parts and thereby resurrect the vehicle a little bit at a time. Given that we didn't have any money set aside for a proverbial rainy day like this, Joan's mother very kindly stepped in to support us, even making trips to our cottage once a month to supply us with a wide variety of food items. We hadn't asked for her help, but she must have sensed, with a mothers' instinct, that we were in dire straits.

Over the next three months, I made numerous weekend trips hunting for what was required. The immediate need was a door to keep the inside of the vehicle dry. Having got that sorted, I turned my attention to the drive-train. Having gradually got to know most, if not all, of the second-hand car dealers in Clarendon and Manchester (many of whom were Jamaicans who had been living in England and had since returned to their homeland), I had built up a network of sources who, if they couldn't supply my immediate needs, could refer me to someone else who might be able to do so. I was blessed with help from both my Sonic bass-guitarist, Zyn, as well as Tookuma. The three of us spent many long hours, often carrying on as late as 4 o'clock in the morning, cleaning old engine parts, grinding-in new valves on a reclaimed cylinder head, and conducting the bit-by-bit reassembly of the second-hand engine, which mainly took place in the living room of the cottage on a carpet of old newspapers, spread out over the floor. In spite of all the mess and the oily smell drifting into the bedroom, and the very real danger of petrol (being used to clean all the parts) setting our wooden cottage on fire, Joan was very tolerant and accommodating and graciously kept us supplied with food and drink throughout our labours.

By the time we eventually 'dropped' our synthesized engine and gearbox into the shell of the Chariot, I knew every conceivable aspect of the workings of a Ford Transit 2-litre V-4 petrol engine that one could possibly want to know. By the Christmas of 1977, the mechanical part of the work was largely done. However, having not been driven for almost four months, the Chariot had succumbed to quite extensive bodywork rusting and clearly needed rescuing in that department. Skinny was no longer in the area, so I asked Willi, the auto mechanics teacher, if he had any promising students who might be interested in doing a bit of welding for me. As a result, we were joined in our endeavours by Compre student, George, who did a fantastic job patching up and strengthening the structure of the entire vehicle, using metal pieces cut out of old oil drums (and who subsequently joined the band as a second 'roadie').

The Chariot was now purring like a happy cat, although looking like a patchwork quilt, so I felt that, having gone this far, it would be worth getting a complete, new paint job. I therefore commissioned a church brother I knew in May Pen to take on the task. At this point in time the political situation in Jamaica was becoming quite tense, with Edward Seaga's JLP party and its green banners and Michael Manley's PNP party and its orange banners, fighting it out for the election of the next government. I decided, therefore to request that the paint job be completed imaginatively in *both* orange and green, to avoid any possibility of the band being associated with either of the political parties when travelling to and from concerts. The result was outstanding and the Chariot now looked quite unlike any of the public minibuses elsewhere in the island. The final touch was to get a very talented, local artist to superimpose the 'Sonic Salvation Gospel Band' logo, blazoned in silver paint, on both sides of the vehicle over the top of the green and orange body paint.

The Sonic Chariot was now, at last, ready for business!

* * *

By the start of 1978, the band had acquired a mass of equipment, all of which needed to be carried to concerts along with the musicians and vocalists. I therefore reorganised the seating inside the Chariot so that myself as driver, plus 10 other band members, could all be seated reasonably comfortably, if a little squashed, towards the front of the vehicle, with the remaining area in the rear, which was retained for all the equipment, appropriately partitioned off.

Prince, with his unique, baritone voice, was still our main lead singer and was, by then, writing quite a lot of his own, excellent material.

Floyd, who had joined Sonic in 1975, was now 'fronting' the band at concerts, making the most of his excellent communication skills with all kinds of audiences. Having significantly developed his musical skills by this time, he was also doing extensive, contemporary song-writing, while simultaneously juggling his teacher training at Church Teacher's College in Mandeville. He and I developed a really close, brotherly relationship and I soon realised that he was particularly gifted at composing really catchy melodies set to Caribbean styles such as reggae and calypso. We therefore spent many a long evening collaborating on new songs for the band to perform at future concerts.

Spenga, after successfully completing his A-levels at nearby Knox College, had left in the summer to further his studies in America while Grace had departed to go and live in Kingston in the hope of furthering a career in the music world. Howie had recently joined us on lead guitar, while Zyn continued on bass guitar. Dainty had also joined us on keyboard to replace Larry, who had moved to Kingston to continue further studies to become a teacher. I was still playing drums, ably assisted by Tookuma on tambourine.

Sonic was replete with instrumentalists and male singers, but we were now in desperate need of one or more female singers to provide lead and backing vocals.

While at Church Teachers' College, Floyd was also singing in a small, independent gospel group which included himself and four young ladies who were also studying there. When I mentioned to him my concern about the current lack of female singers in Sonic Salvation Gospel Band, he suggested that we invite the ladies in his group at the college to the next band practice to see if they would be interested in singing with Sonic. This sounded like a brilliant idea, although it proved to be quite a squeeze, fitting four more people in the same tiny practice room along with all the equipment.

The rest, as they say, is history. As soon as I heard the natural ability of the girls to harmonise (especially to *original* Sonic songs that they were hearing for the first time!) I knew we had found what the band was so desperately in need of. Sheila, Sonia, Sharon and Beulah, all sincere Christians, were the well-needed final touches to the new, enlarged, Sonic Salvation Gospel Band.

Furthermore, Sheila was also writing *her* own original, Christian songs, which meant the band was now blessed with three talented songwriters, Floyd, Prince and Sheila. Our concerts now took on a new, enhanced dimension with a much greater variety of material and more original songs, performed with beautiful backing vocal harmonies. While other well-known Jamaican gospel groups stuck mainly to the traditional gospel repertoire, I wanted Sonic Salvation to be *different* and to have a distinctive Caribbean flavour, while still fulfilling our primary objective of spreading the Christian message through our songs and witnessing.

And our audiences loved it!

We started to get invitations to play in churches and at concerts as far afield as Montego Bay in the west and Port Antonio in the east. Almost every weekend, we were either practicing or performing at a concert. If the concert was at a distant venue, by the time we had performed, packed away the equipment and loaded the Chariot, driven back to Frankfield, dropping band members off at Mandeville and May Pen as necessary, and then unloaded all the gear and put it away in the cottage, it was often after 3 o'clock in the morning. If it was a Sunday concert, that meant just two or three hours' sleep before we had to get up for school, but we were all young, strong and full of vigour and enthusiasm. Joan, who always travelled with us, whilst not performing on stage with the rest of us, was perceived as the 'mother of the band', and together, we were just like one big family.

We deliberately didn't charge a fee for our performances as our primary aim as a band was *'to bring the gospel message to people through music'*. However, I tried to ensure that *all* band members including Prince (if he needed to drive his jeep to a concert) and myself (with the

Chariot) were always reimbursed for travelling expenses, and I always insisted that our concert hosts provided the whole band with a proper meal at the venue before we performed. Christian evangelism and entertainment were Sonic Salvation's *raison d'etre* and I was determined to fulfil my side of the 'Agreement' with God that I had made a year before.

Although using the Chariot primarily for Sonic Salvation activities, I did, occasionally, drive it to Scout camps, the annual Science Exhibition and the odd trip to the beach during school holidays. But two memorable experiences in the vehicle which didn't involve Sonic Salvation will, for ever, remain in my memory.

* * *

The first of these was the driving test. At that time, if you were driving any type of vehicle using a foreign driving licence you were required to obtain the corresponding Jamaican driving licence within one year of acquiring the vehicle. Since I had imported the Chariot in the summer of 1977, and had been driving on my lifelong British driving licence since that time, I knew I would be required to take the necessary Jamaican test before summer 1978. I had also been made aware that the licence needed for minibuses required the passing of a different driving test to that used for cars, and that this test was deliberately designed to be as demanding and difficult as possible, to 'keep the roads safer'!

Undeterred and buoyant as usual, one bright sunny morning during the Whitsuntide half-term holiday, I drove the Chariot down to the test centre in May Pen for the examiner to make a judgement on whether or not I was capable of driving safely. The first surprise was that I was also required to take a multiple-choice theory paper, which I had to sit prior to the practical part of the test. Most of it was pretty basic, but amongst the few questions on the mechanical workings of a petrol engine, was one which contained an error which I was 100% sure made it an invalid question. When I pointed this out to the young lady in the reception office, she was neither pleased nor helpful and after I tried to explain to her the reason for the question's invalidity, she merely responded

"Well, dis a whah we use, soh yuh betta raise dat wid di examiner." [*Well, that's what we use, so you'd better raise it with the examiner.*]

before continuing with her marking of the rest of my theory paper. Clearly, that wasn't the best of starts to my driving test, so I decided to be less argumentative and as compliant as possible for the remainder of what I had left to do.

The first part of the practical test was to go out on the road with me behind the wheel and the examiner in the passenger seat. Apart from giving me the odd instruction about which road to follow, he appeared decidedly more interested in some documents he was looking at, rather than in whether I was or wasn't driving safely. When we got back to the test centre, I then had to demonstrate my ability to park the vehicle, which I did with ease, followed by a reversing manoeuvre around a curved, narrow circuit. This was obviously the crux of the test, and so, as I might have expected, I had an intimidating group of onlookers, sitting on a nearby wall, just waiting to see if I would fail. They were clearly hoping that I might clip the curb with one of the Chariot's wheels.

The problem was, it was impossible to see the intentionally short, guiding posts along the curb on the blind side of the vehicle, because of the height of the bottom of the window in the passenger door. When I respectfully pointed this out to the examiner, he was unsympathetic and merely told me to 'mek haste', as he was already late for his next candidate. The only solution was for me to *stand* immediately in front of the driving seat, with my left heel on the floor and left toe on the clutch pedal, and my right heel on the floor with my right toe on the accelerator. In this very awkward driving position, I was just able to lean over towards the passenger door sufficiently to see the tops of the guiding posts, while still keeping both hands on the steering wheel as the Chariot slowly inched backwards.

To say I was nervous would be a gross understatement, as I knew the derision and ridicule that I would get from the observers on the wall if I failed. By the end of the exercise, I was drenched in sweat but, thank God, I made it. That was surely one of the hardest tests I had ever done. When the examiner had given me the duly signed pass certificate, he asked me why I had omitted to answer one of the questions on my theory paper, which he was holding in his hand. I told him that as far as I could determine, there was no correct answer provided, so I had just left it blank. After a brief scrutiny of the question, he laughed and shook my hand;

> "Yuh right, man. Whoever write dis ya question his a *idiot!*" [*You're dead right, man! Whoever wrote this question is an idiot!*]

With a cheery wave to the men on the wall, I drove off breathing a sigh of relief, with the coveted pass certificate on the seat beside me.

* * *

The second memory was of a far more serious encounter. During the 1978-79 school year, myself, Joan and our Compre teaching colleague, Marj, had decided to pursue our postgraduate In-Service Diploma in Education, which required trips to the University of the West Indies in Kingston each Friday (on day-release from Compre) as well as selected Saturdays for intensive lectures, and longer sessions during the school holidays. It made sense to

237

travel together, and since the MGB was really just a two-seater, I had little option but to use the Chariot. Our usual drive to Kingston passed along the valley to Chapelton, down to May Pen, then eastwards along the east-west dual carriageway through Old Harbour and Spanish Town, and for the last few miles before Six Miles bridge, continued through extensive sugar cane plantations on both sides of the road.

On one of these journeys to UWI, having set off immediately after school on the Thursday afternoon, just after passing the Ferries Police Station, I started to hear an ominous knocking noise coming from the engine. From my extensive work rebuilding the Chariot's engine, I knew right away that one (or more) of the big-end bearings had gone and I slowed down immediately so that we were just coasting along. I was hoping we might be able to reach Six Miles, where we could safely pull off the road to consider possible sources of help, before the bearing broke down completely. However, with a final clang, my worst fear was realised as the engine seized up and we ground to a halt, right in the middle of the cane fields.

Thinking that the best thing to do was for me to hitch a ride into town to get help, I suggested that Joan and Marj remain with the Chariot while I stood on the edge of the road to flag down a passing vehicle. While I was waiting, however, I turned around to see Joan and Marj waving madly and calling me to come back as they ran towards me. They both looked really frightened and said they had seen what they thought was a man, lurking in the cane stalks. In typical blasé fashion, I told them they must be imagining things and to go back to the vehicle, but they would have none of it.

Rather than leave the Chariot completely unattended while all three of us hitched into town, I therefore suggested that, instead, I would stay with the vehicle while the two of them went into town to seek assistance, since we had several mutual friends there. They were much happier with that idea and soon acquired a lift with a passing car. First of all, I had a good look round in the cane field for any sign of life but, apart from a couple of small rodents, could see nothing. It was around 5 o'clock in the afternoon and the sun was still brightly shining, so it didn't unduly concern me that I was by myself. Furthermore, the Chariot was in full view of literally hundreds of cars and trucks that were hurtling by on the highway every minute, so the situation could hardly be described as vulnerable. Thinking that it might be a while before the two ladies found someone who could give us a tow, I settled down in the driver's seat, locked both doors just in case, and lowered the tops of the windows in the two front doors just enough to allow sufficient air into the vehicle to prevent it getting unbearably hot. By 7 o'clock, there was still no sign of Joan or Marj and I was getting sleepy. The sun was starting to set and I knew it would be dark soon, so I thought I might as well get 40 winks while there was still at least some light left.

All of a sudden I was startled out of my slumber by a *massive* bang on the passenger side of the vehicle. Immediately wide awake, I lurched round to face the passenger window where, by the lights of the passing cars, I could see the face of a man peering through the glass. I must have been asleep for a considerable time as it was, by now, quite dark. However, as the lights of each passing car illuminated the Chariot, I saw again and again the most ugly, evil-looking face that I had ever had the misfortune to see. The man had very dark, almost black skin and wildly unkempt, knotty hair splayed in all directions; he was missing several teeth and had a large scar on one side of his face and as he stared menacingly at me through the front passenger window, his demeanour was also exceedingly vicious and threatening. In his raised hand, he had a large stone which had obviously caused the loud, wakening bang when he had used it to strike the window.

239

Now, at that time, I was in peak physical condition; all the Scout hikes and digging out my car parking area had seen to that! Furthermore, I still had all the self-defence and judo skills that I had internalised from the 4th dan British Judo Champion who was my instructor during my three years at UCL. In a one-to-one combat, all things being equal, I reckoned I would have stood a good chance of coming out on top. But here in the dark, in the middle of nowhere, with not even a penknife to defend myself, and not knowing if the man had accomplices working with him, or whether he was armed, things didn't look too promising. Thank God that Joan and Marj had insisted they not be left alone with the vehicle to come face-to-face with this monstrosity!

"OPEN UP!"
bellowed the vile monster, and for the second time he *slammed* the stone on the window glass. How it didn't shatter, I shall never know.

"OK... OK... I'm coming. Give me a second."
I would not try to deny that I was scared stiff, but was now desperately playing for time. I swivelled round to try and see if he had any accomplices peering in through the other side windows, but could see no one. If it were one-to-one, at least the odds were a bit better. But when I turned back round to face the passenger window, I found myself in an even more desperate situation. Pointing straight at my head on the other side of the glass window was a double-barrelled, sawn-off shot-gun!! I knew that if he were to fire that weapon at such point-blank range, I was a goner! All my judo skills and self-defence knowledge would be to no avail at all.

It is strange how the rate at which time passes can change in an emergency. I probably had but seconds to live, yet all sorts of images and thoughts were racing through my mind. I wondered how Joan would cope if my headless body was discovered in the Chariot on her return.

I wondered how my mother would take the news that her first-born son had been murdered in Jamaica. And I wondered how God could allow my life to be snuffed out in this ignominious way, before I had barely started to fulfil my side of our 'Agreement'.

Then suddenly, I was back to the immediate reality of the dire predicament I was in. If the monstrosity *did* fire the gun, he would immediately expose himself to the passing cars, but then he might not have the sense to realise that. My best chance was to *escape*. Still *thinking as a Physicist*, even in this desperate scenario, I calculated that, in the time he might take to get from outside the passenger-side window and to circle round the front of the van to my driver's side which was facing the road, I should be able to duck down, unlock and fling open the driver's door, and RUN. I didn't think twice, now that I had formulated my plan. Without even a backward glance, I ducked down, catapulted out through the driver's door and, casting fate to the wind, continued my flight straight across all four lanes of the highway as tyres screeched and cars swerved to avoid this white madman running across the road.

Once on the far side of the highway, I knew I was relatively safe as the monstrosity would hardly be likely to follow me across the road, but taking no chances, I ran for all I was worth back towards Ferries Police Station. Not even Usain Bolt could have caught me on that occasion! To my relief, a kindly taxi driver screeched to a halt beside me and asked me if I needed a lift. Though utterly breathless and with my heart pumping at well over twice the normal rate, I managed to describe what had happened. In a few seconds, we had reached Ferries Police Station, where he dropped me off as I thanked him profusely for his help. Once inside the station, I could breathe once more and just as I had started to give a statement to the officers, who should run in but Joan and Marj and a male friend who had brought them in his pickup truck. Joan was actually in tears and hung on to me, unwilling to let me go. When they had got back to the Chariot to find the driver's door wide open, my travel bag missing from the back of the vehicle and me nowhere to be seen, she had feared the worst, and was afraid she might never see me alive again.

The officers were very helpful, however, and drove us all back to the site of the hold-up with their guns loaded and at the ready. Apparently my experience was one of several similar incidents in the area that they were currently dealing with and they desperately wanted to catch the villain. However, despite their intense searchlights which they used to peer into the dense cane field, and walking back and forth along the side of the road to the front and rear of the Chariot, the monstrosity was nowhere to be seen; he had made his exit from the scene with just the small bag that I had left behind in my escape from the Chariot, and was long gone.

Just as the police were about to leave, one of the more friendly minibus drivers from Frankfield who was on his way back home from Kingston, drew up on the far side of the highway. He had seen the Chariot with the fancy logo on the side, and the police cars, and realised something was wrong. We had decided that there was no option but to somehow get the Chariot back to Frankfield. Thankfully, without waiting to be asked, the minibus driver offered to tow me and the Chariot all the way back, which I thought was exceptionally kind of him, considering that the distance involved was nearly 90 miles. Meanwhile, Joan and Marj had been offered a lift by Marj's friend, and continued to the university campus in Kingston, where the accommodation for the postgraduate course was already booked.

Eventually, well after midnight, the minibus driver and I finally arrived back in Frankfield and, once again, I used my long abseiling rope and the tree in the garden to help get the Chariot (pulled this time by the minibus that had towed me all the way back to Frankfield) back onto its parking space inside the property. In spite of my persistence, the kindly driver refused, point-blank, to take a cent for everything he had done. His incredible generosity helped to make up for the unforgettable, terrifying experience I had endured, just a few hours before.

That frightening encounter was clearly 'one of my nine lives' gone. I was still alive to tell the tale, thank God, but that still didn't stop me reliving my encounter with the monstrosity in vivid nightmares, for a considerable time afterwards.

Chapter 16: 'If Music Be the Food of Love...'

After a cursory examination of the Chariot's engine, it was obvious that remedying the problem of the damaged big-end bearing was not something I was going to be able to solve with the engine *in situ*. So with the assistance of my faithful helpers, Zyn and Tooku, we completely removed the engine from the vehicle and carried it back up to the cottage which, once again, was to become my temporary automotive workshop.

Unfortunately, the damage was rather more extensive than I could possibly have imagined. As a result of the disintegration of the bearing, the corresponding con-rod had become totally detached from the crankshaft and, flailing around like a freshly caught fish, it had hit the inside of the thick, steel block and actually *cracked* it! Quite apart from any other undetected damage, the lower part of the engine block, even with a brilliant bit of bronze welding, would now almost certainly leak oil or water or both if it were not replaced.

I sat there in my dirty overalls, cursing myself for not having turned off the engine completely, immediately upon hearing the tell-tale knocking sound, and wondering out loud why I was being made to suffer in this painful fashion. On top of the trauma of my being held up at gun point, we would now have to find the money for yet more parts and repairs. Why was God making my life so difficult? It just didn't seem fair!

Joan was as consoling and supportive as possible, and suggested that instead of wasting time going on another trawl of the second-hand shops, we should just bite the bullet and buy brand new replacement parts for whatever the engine now required. There was a degree of wisdom in this, in that it would be more likely to prevent further repairs becoming necessary should any other damage be subsequently discovered. For my part, I smiled and pledged to try and save money by living on bread and water for the next month but, inwardly, thanked God for providing me with such an understanding wife.

So, without further deliberation, I accepted the inevitable and the next day, headed into Kingston in the MGB to buy a brand new, sparkling 'bottom half' for the engine. This 'package' included the block, the crankshaft, the four pistons and con-rods, and all the crankshaft and conrod bearings. In one swift blow, however, the purchase completely obliterated both our teaching salaries for that month, but there was nothing else to be done. A compulsory diet for me would clearly be inevitable! The positive side of things was that the Chariot would then have half a brand new engine and, hopefully, would be most unlikely to present any further mechanical problems for the foreseeable future. I prayed earnestly that God might help me not to feel so bitter and left it at that.

While I was in Kingston, I thought it might be useful to pay a visit to the island's well-known recording studio, Dynamic Sounds. After passing through the massive security gate and being interrogated by the armed guards on duty, I eventually got inside the extensive complex to meet the people in charge and was given a leisurely, guided tour of the studios, the mastering room and the vinyl-disk pressing plant. I stood awestruck in front of the huge mixing console with equally huge monitor speakers in the control room, looking through the thick glass window into the recording room, and badgered the sound engineers with a stream of questions about all the processes involved in recording an album. I had been toying with the idea of recording a Sonic Salvation gospel album for some time now, so this was all extremely relevant information.

When we got to the financial side of things, however, I almost couldn't believe my ears. With studio time, mastering, and pressing the disks, as well as supplying labels and album jackets, we were talking several *thousands* of dollars! There was no way that Sonic Salvation, as a non-profit making enterprise, could ever come up with that sort of money, and after the recent fiasco with the Chariot, myself and Joan didn't exactly have any surplus funds. But the tour around the studios and my talking with the engineers had sown a fascinating seed in my mind. I had a good pair of ears and a significant amount of technical knowledge about sound engineering already. If we couldn't afford a commercial recording, why couldn't we do it for ourselves? My brain started to work overtime as I impulsively started planning what I would need, equipment-wise, and the trip to England that I would have to make to procure it, as usual having forgotten the immediate financial predicament.

Before taking any trip to obtain recording equipment, however, the Chariot repair needed to be completed. After having completely emptied our bank account at the local Ford dealers in Kingston to get the necessary parts, I spent the next couple of weeks reassembling the engine with Zyn and Tookuma's unstinting help, before getting everything installed back into the vehicle. I was overjoyed when the job was finally completed and I, once again, had the Chariot available for Sonic Salvation concerts. Now I could focus my attention on the equipment-procuring trip that was needed to enable the band to get some of our songs on vinyl.

* * *

Once our financial situation had recovered somewhat, Joan and myself took what we had decided should be a fairly short trip to England, during the 1978

246

summer holiday. We would spend the first week in and around London, so I could hunt down the audio gear needed for the Sonic Salvation recording project, and the second week with my parents up in Derbyshire. After all the trauma with my hold-up and with disruption at our cottage while the various engine repairs were taking place, we both felt ready for a complete break. Before we left, I ensured that both the Chariot and the MGB were securely chained and padlocked, as well as the gate into the property. Mas' John promised to be on guard throughout each night, with his cutlass at the ready, so the vehicles were, hopefully, as safe as they could be anywhere.

By the summer, I knew exactly what I wanted. In the preceding weeks, I had spent countless hours poring over various audio magazines and studying any book I could get hold of on audio recording, as there was no such thing as the internet in those days! The Beatles had recently recorded their 'Sergeant Pepper's Lonely Hearts Club Band' album using a new 4-track simul-synch technology, where individual tracks could be laid whenever you wanted, one at a time, while still achieving perfect synchronisation of all the recorded tracks. Prior to that ground-breaking audio-technological milestone, any recording of a group of musicians and singers was generally done with everyone playing and singing at the same time to achieve the necessary synchronisation. To my great delight, a very reasonably priced, 4-track, simul-synch, quarter-inch, reel-to-reel tape recorder had recently been released by Teac, and this would be my essential multi-track recording device - as I write this story, over 40 years later, this very tape machine is still in my possession, still works, and serves an essential purpose in my home studio!

Once the tracks had been laid, they would need to be mixed down to 2-track stereo, so I would also need a good mixing console, for which I chose a Studiomaster 16-2 desk. And, finally, a top-of-the-line 2-track tape machine was needed for recording the 2-track master, and for this task, I selected a 2-track, quarter-inch Ferrograph. Once armed with these three essential core items, I reckoned I could compete fairly successfully against the big Kingston studios and save Sonic Salvation at least the thousands of dollars we would otherwise need for studio time.

We stayed with my brother and his wife again, while I visited just about every professional audio outlet in London to hunt down what I intended to purchase and, within just a few days, I found the three major items that I was looking for. Having had them suitably packaged in large, sealed boxes, and delivered to the airfreight terminal to be transported out to Jamaica, we headed up to Derbyshire to spend a lovely, relaxing week with Mummy and Baba at the family home in Grindleford.

When we returned to our 'island in the sun', the items I had purchased were already at customs, waiting to be collected. This time, however, despite all my attempts at speaking in the local dialect, I wasn't able to clear the three, massive packages through customs without incurring significant duty, since they were obviously brand new items of electronic equipment. But, everything had arrived undamaged, so I couldn't really complain, and furthermore, both the Chariot and the MGB were there waiting at our cottage, safe and sound, thanks, I am sure, to Mas' John's vigilance.

Initially, all the equipment was set up, crammed into our ever-shrinking practice room at the cottage but although this allowed rough versions of our future recordings to be made, I had other ideas for where and when we would lay down the proper tracks for Sonic Salvation's first gospel album. As 1978 whistled by, Floyd and myself spent many hours, often going late into the night, modifying and honing the songs he had written and getting rough versions on tape. At regular band practices, we also recorded 'first takes' of Prince's and Sheila's songs, working diligently on the musical arrangements and vocal harmonies. At the same time, I was familiarising myself with all my new 'toys' and learning about audio tape splicing, the equalisation required for different microphones, and all the other ins and outs of studio-quality, audio recording.

* * *

Towards the latter part of 1978, I received a long letter from Spenga who had, by then, been living and pursuing his university studies in the USA for almost three years since leaving Jamaica. The content of the letter, though it came as a wonderful surprise, was not unexpected. He and Gracie, whom he had met at one of the annual Church of God Youth Camps, were to be married that December in Jamaica and I was being asked to serve as Best Man at the wedding. It was fabulous news, particularly since I had been present at the same Youth Camp where they first met and had, therefore, known Gracie since the very start of their relationship. There was absolutely no doubt in my mind that they would make a great couple. I started work on my speech right away as I wanted to really do justice to one of my closest friends who, by the end of 1978, would have known me for over seven years. It had to be sincere but amusing, anecdotal and uplifting. Spenga and myself had shared many adventures and had had lots of fun together, both through Scouting and with Sonic Salvation. And, unusually for someone like myself who tended to shy away from writing letters, we had kept up our friendship through a frequent correspondence across the miles while he was doing his undergraduate degree in America.

The wedding ceremony and reception had both been arranged to take place in Kingston, on Boxing Day, with the honeymoon at Runaway Bay Golf and Country Club on the North Coast, not far from where we had our Scout camps at

Puerto Seco in Discovery Bay. Spenga had booked a flight from the USA to Montego Bay where he had arranged to pick up a rent-a-car to drive via Frankfield to Kingston. The plan was for him to leave the car in Kingston before the church ceremony and for a friend, who would be at the wedding, to carry him and Gracie to the hotel in Runaway Bay for their honeymoon after the reception. However, as the bow tie incident at my own wedding proved, even the most meticulously planned wedding arrangements do not always work out quite as planned! Exhausted from all the hectic preparations prior to his flight, Spenga was travelling alone and late at night along the North Coast road from Montego Bay when he must have dozed off for an instant, allowing the rent-a-car to swerve off the road and career down a rocky slope towards the sea! Thankfully, his guardian angel must have been in the car with him, to bring it to a merciful stop just before it reached the ocean, and he was able to clamber out of the tangled wreckage without a single broken bone or cut to his body. The outcome was all the more remarkable considering that the car was a total write-off!

When he eventually reached Frankfield, shaken and dazed but alive, we could hardly believe what had happened and immediately offered to carry him and his suitcase to Kingston with us in the MG on the following day. It was a bit of a squeeze in a car made for carrying only two people, especially since Joan and myself were also carrying all our wedding attire with us, but having folded down the top and praying earnestly that we would have a rain-free journey, we managed to make it without any further problem.

Although Gracie was fraught with concern that Spenga might suffer some unexpected after-effects from the crash, the actual marriage ceremony and reception proceeded without a hitch and, overall, it was a wonderful, memorable day. My Best Man's speech, having been duly modified to include appropriate references to Spenga's flawless driving skills, was well received and heartily applauded.

And then came problem number two! The 'friend' who had previously promised to carry Spenga and Gracie to their honeymoon hotel after the reception, informed us at the last minute that he would be unable to fulfil his promise because he had some other (vague) commitment in Kingston early the next day. I was not impressed at all and made my feelings very clear but, in the final analysis, since I was Spenga's Best Man, I considered it my duty to find a solution to the problem. I therefore took it upon myself, as a Physicist, to organise the squeezing of four adults (Spenga and I being of not insignificant size), and two appreciably large suitcases, into a sports car which was really designed for just two people. And any member of our party who thought the ride *into* Kingston was a tight squeeze, was now in no doubt at all about the meaning of the phrase 'tight squeeze'.

With no choice as to our having to travel 'open top', we again prayed that we might be spared a downpour, and also, for this journey, that the springs, wheel bearings and brakes would all prove to be fit for purpose. Probably for the first time since I had built the car, I deliberately made a conscious effort *not* to put the MG through its paces. Mercifully, the car, its occupants and the other various items being carried, all made it to the intended destination in one piece and we were able to leave Spenga and his new bride at Runaway Bay for a well-earned honeymoon holiday. Of course, had I known in advance that we would need to drive to the honeymoon destination after the wedding with *four people* in the vehicle, I would have driven the Chariot instead of MG!

When Joan and myself eventually made it back to Frankfield, we both felt like we could do with another honeymoon ourselves! Thankfully, we had the remainder of the Christmas holiday in which to relax and get some well-needed rest before school reopened in January 1979 and we were, once again, plunged back into the whirlwind of activities that we were both involved with. My thoughts gradually refocused on various forthcoming events like the 1979 Science Exhibition and several up-coming Sonic Salvation concerts. And then there was all the planning involved for the Sonic Salvation album we were hoping to record in the forthcoming summer holiday.

By Easter of 1979, we had initial versions of 10, really good, original songs, ready and waiting to include on our first gospel album. I wanted this album to be really distinct from what was then being commonly recorded in Jamaica by other well-known gospel artists and groups. Not only were our songs totally original but they also reflected a wide variety of different musical styles currently in fashion, including reggae, calypso, rock, folk and ballad. Nothing like that had ever been done in the island before; Sonic Salvation Gospel Band was going to chart a new course in the history of Jamaican gospel music.

* * *

Towards the summer of 1979, I heard that Stevie Wonder would be one of the guest artists at that year's Reggae Sunsplash music festival in Montego Bay (Mo' Bay). I was immediately determined to get to see and hear this blind, musical genius, whose songs I had been playing on the drums since I was a young teenager in secondary school. Having secured a three-day package deal for two at one of the 'posh' north-coast hotels, which included entry tickets to the festival, Joan and myself drove to the hotel in the MGB, parked in the security of the hotel car park, and then took a taxi to the large playing field in Mo' Bay where the festival was being held. The sheer scale of the show, with its beautiful, multicolour lighting and huge stacks of

252

speakers and high-frequency horns on either side of the stage, was absolutely spectacular. And standing right by the sound desk, where I enjoyed chatting with the two sound engineers, we had a perfect view of the stage and could hear the sound of each band or artist performing in vivid detail.

After a number of introductory acts, the Jamaican reggae band 'Third World' came on stage and delivered a brilliant set of songs, affirming, in my humble opinion, their unrivalled position as the best reggae band I had ever heard. Not far from midnight, and with Third World still on stage, a hush descended on the crowd as the MC introduced none other but my musical idol, Stevie Wonder. As he was led by one of his assistants to the microphone at the front of the stage, the crowd erupted and the cheering and whistling was deafening. To my amazement, Third World served as his backing band for the entire performance, demonstrating their unbelievable musical skills by playing all his songs exactly like they sounded on his albums. When the show concluded with a perfect rendition of 'Happy Birthday' (to Martin Luther King), one of my favourite Stevie Wonder songs, I was spellbound and speechless. This had been a truly magical night.

The next day, back at the hotel, after a very lazy morning and a gorgeous swim in the crystal blue sea, Joan and myself were walking through the hotel lobby when I spotted someone being led by the arm over to the lifts on the opposite side of the room. He looked surprisingly familiar, so I asked one of the hotel staff who it was. To my astonishment, I received the reply,

"Hey man, that's Stevie Wonder. He's staying here at the hotel while Sunsplash is on. He's in the Master-suite on the top floor." I looked at Joan and tugged at her arm;

"Come on, honey, we're going to meet Stevie Wonder!"

Joan thought I had gone completely mad and, in the lift going up to the top floor, even I began to have doubts about the sanity of such an unarranged rendezvous with such a famous artist. What if he had guards to protect him from intruders, or simply didn't want to be bothered by nosey individuals like us? When we got to the top floor, with its panoramic views of the bay where we had been bathing earlier, and I knocked on the only door I could see, my doubts were realised when the door was opened by a physically massive guard, who had a very straight-faced, no-nonsense demeanour. Trying to be as friendly as possible, I introduced myself and Joan, and asked,

> "Good afternoon sir. I wonder if there is any possibility of my having a word with Stevie. I'm a local musician and sound engineer."

The guard paused, then disappeared into the room without replying - but within a few seconds, he reappeared and beckoned us inside!

> "Wait here. Stevie will be with you in a moment."

I held my breath, thinking to myself 'If you are afraid to ask a question, you'll never get anywhere in this world,' when who should appear in the inner doorway of the apartment, but my idol, Stevie Wonder! After telling the guard he needn't stay, he walked towards us and I held out my hand to shake his. However, I was suddenly acutely aware that he was, indeed, totally blind, when he held out his hand in a slightly different direction to mine and I had to move my arm so that our hands would meet. But, he was truly friendly, with no airs and graces, and after a brief introduction, we chatted amiably for several minutes during which I complimented him on his performance with Third World and told him how impressed I was, especially with the rendition of 'Happy Birthday'. He smiled modestly and paid tribute to the backing band for how well the musicians had 'jammed' the song, with virtually no practice beforehand. I then told him about Sonic Salvation and my plans for our recording in

254

a few weeks' time, at which point, he beckoned us to follow him into an adjacent room where he had set up his 'mobile studio'. He explained that this always went with him whenever he was on tour, in case he got any inspiration for a new song and wanted to record a rough version to carry back with him to the big Motown recording studios in America.

For me, it was like stepping into heaven! From floor to ceiling it was stacked with all the latest keyboards, synthesizers, effects-racks, tape recorders drum machines, amplifiers, monitor speakers and other equipment, the like of which I had never even seen. He must have read my mind;

"Hey man, have a go with the gear. Help yourself."

I didn't even know how to turn most of his state-of-the-art equipment on, let alone get it to function! Again, he must have sensed my apprehension.

"This is the master power switch, and then each device has its own on/off switch in the usual place."

And with that, he flipped the master switch, turned on the keyboard and started to play. I just couldn't believe that he could have played with such ease, yet be totally unable to see what he was doing! Then he turned on the drum machine so that I could play along with his keyboarding. I would have been happy to have continued all day, but after a few minutes of our jamming together, he bade us farewell, having remembered there was something he had to do. He invited us to stay as long as we wished, experimenting with this array of incredible equipment, and as he walked out of the door he called,

"Good luck with the recording. Nice meeting you both. Just close the door when you go."

I was completely taken aback that anyone could be so trusting with a total stranger. How could he have known I wouldn't leave with any of his priceless studio equipment? I felt simultaneously humbled at his trusting personality and

255

elated to have had the unique opportunity to meet him. It was a meeting I would never forget; playing music in the personal studio of one of the greatest musicians and song-writers of the 20th century. I had actually jammed along with the amazing Stevie Wonder!

* * *

As soon as the summer holiday started, after a hectic Summer Term, I enlisted my trusted and enthusiastic helpers, Zyn and Tookuma to assist me in creating our novel Sonic Salvation recording studio in my increasingly multi-purpose Physics Lab at Compre, using the adjacent prep-lab as the control room. The first, crucial task was to transform the lab into an 'acoustically dead' region by minimising unwanted reflections from hard surfaces such as walls and the floor. Then the room needed insulating from any sources of unwanted sound such as that from truck horns (as the trucks approached the nearby, one-way Angel Bridge), and from the incessant sound of the cicadas in the trees around the school, particularly in the evening and at night time. All of this was achieved by draping every tent and groundsheet we possessed in the Scout storeroom over the inside of each of the closed louvre windows, over the door arch, and all over the floor. The polystyrene ceiling tiles were already ideal as sound absorbers and so needed no further modification. Although it was going to be like an inferno in the daytime, with the louvres all permanently closed, this was a price we would have to pay in order to achieve the sound properties that the room required.

Then we set about creating a makeshift vocal booth in one corner of the lab, using screens from the recent Science Exhibition, tables stood on end and odd pieces of plywood, all of which were lovingly covered with any remaining tents and some old blankets from home. The prep-lab was rearranged so that the tables were

256

conveniently positioned to create easy access to the large, heavy items of equipment such as the Teac and the Ferrograph tape-recorders, and the Studiomaster mixing console.

After that, it was multiple journeys in the Chariot from the cottage to the lab to transport all the necessary equipment. This included the recording machines, mixing desk, and the monitors, which were to be located in the prep-lab, while all the instruments, amplifiers, drums, bongos and mic-stands, were strategically positioned around the perimeter of the main lab.

Finally, everything had to be wired up and tested, with XLR cables neatly running round the sides of the recording room, from the microphones to the mixing desk in the prep-lab, and mains cabling kept separate to eliminate any hum pick-up. In the end, we also had to completely screen off the drum-set from the rest of the room, thus minimising 'bleed through' of the high volume sound from the drums into the microphones dedicated to the vocals and other instruments. Then we had to check that everything was working and adjust the levels at the mixing desk so that all the inputs were appropriately balanced. After Week 1 had been spent setting up and getting everything functioning effectively, the Sonic Studio was complete and ready to go!

The musicians and vocalists had all agreed beforehand that we would commit Week 2 of the holiday to recording the musicians' parts, and Week 3 to recording the vocalists. Since the Teac tape recorder had only four tracks and we were going to be using vastly more than four microphones and instrument inputs, my plan was to do a certain amount of pre-mixing via the desk, so that each of the four tracks would contain a blend of instruments or vocals, as follows:

Week 2
Track 1 - all the drums, bongos, tambourine and bass guitar
Track 2 - keyboard(s) and rhythm guitar

Week 3
Track 3 - Lead vocals
Track 4 - Backing vocals and lead guitar

Week 2, the first week of recording, therefore required all the musicians except the lead guitarist, to play along to a rough, 'dummy' vocal track (recorded earlier by the lead vocalist), while Week 3 required all the vocalists plus the lead guitarist to sing or play along to the instrumental tracks that had been recorded in Week 2. Some band members, however, such as Floyd and Prince, who both played *and* sang, would be needed for both weeks. Since I would be tied up playing the drums during Week 2, I recruited yet another Compre student, Clive, to operate the tape machine while I was otherwise engaged. Joan, by now busy with Head of Department, and Senior Teacher duties at Compre, was still perceived by the band's younger members, as 'Mother of the band'. As selfless as ever, she took on her shoulders the *mammoth*, full-time task of cooking and serving daily meals for 15 band members during the entire two weeks of recording! All in all, a very substantial degree of planning and organisation was involved, but the project was a great success - and we had a whale of a time! - even though we had to do numerous 'takes' on some of the more musically intricate songs.

When everyone except my helpers had done their bit and we had cleared up the lab and returned all the equipment to its home in the cottage, it was then my turn, during Week 4 of the holiday, to do the mix-down from 4-tracks to 2-tracks, which I could do at the cottage. Then, in Week 5, I had to get the labels typed up and the outer

258

jacket for our first Sonic album, 'Jesus is the Way', designed and proofed for errors. For this latter task, I sought the help of a graphics design company in Kingston who were able to print an enlargement of a nice photo of the whole band on the front, with all the details of the songs and the credits on the back. Finally in Week 6, I took my treasured master tape into Dynamic Sounds for mastering engineer, 'Spider', to create the metal master disk, from which all the vinyl disks would be made in the pressing plant.

While I was working with Spider that day, during a short break, I was curious as to what was happening elsewhere in the studio complex and, in the adjacent main recording studio, chanced upon none other than Bob Marley and the Wailers, who were in the middle of recording their latest album! Not wishing to disturb the musicians during their recording session, but unwilling to let such a fortuitous opportunity pass me by, I pushed open the heavy, control room door and, as bold as brass (but rather cheekily) invited myself in. Since I had met the sound engineers after my tour of the complex a few months ago, they simply gave me a quick nod of acknowledgement from their seats at the huge mixing desk, and continued with their numerous tasks - although the other onlookers who were standing around in the control room didn't seem too pleased at my presence. Maybe they thought I might steal some of Bob's original tunes, but they needn't have worried as I was only able to remain for just a few seconds anyway; the smell of 'weed', which most of them were smoking with abandon (as was typical of Rastafarians), I found so strong and so completely overpowering, that I thought I was going to faint and so I had to make a hasty (but reluctant) exit into the relatively fresh air of the reception lounge. That brief spell in the control room brought back too many unsavoury memories of performing in smoke-filled places, as I had sometimes had to do when playing drums with Third Generation band a few years before.

As far as Sonic Salvation's first album was concerned, all that remained to be done now was to collect (and pay for!) a thousand LP vinyl disks, labels and sleeves, and then distribute and sell them via the band members and a few selected retailers in Kingston. My hope was that I might recoup at least *some* of my expenses, but even if I had got back nothing, the experience, the excitement and the fun of it all would have been worth it! As it happened, that first album proved so popular nationally that we actually had to do a second pressing, which surprised and silenced even the most cynical amongst us!

* * *

Without going into too much detail and repeating myself, what follows is a quick summary of Sonic Salvation's further recordings.

During the summer of 1980, we went through the whole process again in order to create our second album, 'Gospel Journey'. After recording the 4-track master tape in our makeshift studio, I had to make an unforeseen trip back to the 'motherland'. So, sensing a possible opportunity, I took along with me the 4-track master-tape, and had the unforgettable experience of getting it mixed down to 2-track stereo at a professional studio in Luton, just outside London. The 12 original songs on this album were also hugely popular back in Jamaica, and the whole album sounded so good that Dynamic Sounds even offered us a deal to distribute the album throughout the whole Caribbean! However, the amount we were being offered per album, with the band still being responsible for providing sleeves and labels, would have meant us actually making a *loss* on each record, so I reluctantly had to decline. It would have been of great benefit to Sonic Salvation but, by mid-

1980, the Jamaican economy was starting to waver and the dollar was rapidly devaluing. I just didn't have the spare capital to stand the loss that we would have had to suffer and so I had no choice but to say 'no'.

In the summer of 1981, we recorded our final album, 'Our God is the Greatest', which contained a further 10 original songs. In addition, we recorded two double-sided 45s, containing four original Christmas songs. By then we had been joined by Dennis and Suzanne, both gifted songwriters in their own right and who had both contributed original songs that had been included on the album. But in spite of its popularity and the fantastic quality of some of the songs, the further decline in the value of the local currency and the subsequent increase in all the costs involved, meant that this album failed to make a profit and I even had to borrow some money from one of Frankfield's wealthy businessmen in order to get it completed and ready for distribution.

On the positive side, Sonic Salvation songs were now playing frequently on the radio, and we even performed several of the songs on national television. Fortunately, I had encouraged our three key songwriters, Floyd, Prince and Sheila to join the Performing Rights Society in England so that they might collect any royalties due as a result of any of their songs being played on TV or radio. We were also still performing at concerts and in churches across the island most weekends and sometimes played at bigger 'Gospel Extravaganzas' with other gospel groups such as The Grace Thrillers.

By 1984, the band had been around for over 10 years and we had performed in almost every town in rural Jamaica. The number of band members (including our two 'roadies') had increased significantly, as had the amount of sound equipment we needed to carry around with us. The Chariot was just about able to cope when Prince was able to travel alongside and carry some of the band members in his jeep. On the odd occasions when Prince was unable to be with us, however, and everything and everybody had to be crammed like sardines into the Chariot, it made the travelling experience more like a trip in a sauna, which was particularly disliked by the ladies in the band! Clearly, a solution to this dilemma was needed, particularly when we had a concert at a distant location.

As always, God came to our rescue. One day, out of the blue, someone I had never met or even heard of, appeared at the door of our cottage and introduced himself as Calvin, a long-time fan of Sonic Salvation. After we had been talking for a while, he came to the point of his visit which was to freely offer his expertise in finance to assist with the general administration of the band, should we want it, and in the organisation of new, large-scale 'Gospel Extravaganzas'. Furthermore, he also had his own Ford motor car, in which he offered to help with carrying band members to and from concerts, despite my admonition that we were a non-profit-making organisation and that we could, *at best*, only reimburse him with travel expenses for his efforts.

We were now blessed with three vehicles; the Chariot, Prince's jeep and Calvin's car, which all travelled in convoy to and from our concerts. This was an ideal arrangement as the band members no longer had to travel like sardines in a tin, while help was immediately on hand should one of the vehicles succumb to any sort of incident or problem such as a mechanical breakdown.

One such memorable incident occurred in early 1984 on our long drive back to Frankfield after playing at a gospel concert in Montego Bay. As usual, I was leading the convoy in the Sonic Chariot, containing all the equipment and a few band members, while Calvin was driving his Ford car with Howie, Ozzie and Daphne (one of our new lead vocalists) for company, followed by Prince with more band members (including Mikey, the other new lead vocalist) in his jeep.

262

The concert had finished late and by the time we had packed all the equipment back into the Chariot, it was well past midnight. We had decided to drive back via Westmoreland and St Elizabeth and then along the main west-east highway through Mandeville to May Pen, where some of the band members such as Sheila would leave the rest of the group to continue on her long nocturnal journey back home to Port Antonio.

Every few seconds I would glance in my rear-view mirror to make sure Calvin was right behind me, while valiantly trying to keep awake by chatting to Sheila (God bless her), who would generally sit in the front with Joan (who invariably fell asleep on long, late journeys home). Suddenly, while driving along a flat, straight section of the highway in St Elizabeth, the lights in my mirror veered violently to one side before disappearing completely. I immediately slammed on the brakes and screeched to a halt with Prince pulling up immediately behind me.

"Lawd a mercy! Calvin gone off a di road!"

With our hearts in our mouths, we all piled out of the two remaining vehicles and ran over to the far side of the road. Peering into the darkness down the substantial embankment and over the top of the fence at the bottom, which now had a large hole in it, we could just make out through the trees beyond the fence, the dim headlights of our lost vehicle.

"Come quick, man! Mek wi run go help dem an check w'appen to di car", [*Come quickly! Let's run and help them and see if the car is ok!*],

I shouted, as all the men ran down the embankment. I was dreading the outcome of our search as we must have all been travelling at about 60 mph along the smooth 'barber-green' section of highway immediately before the accident, and if you were to run into one of the very large trees beyond the fence at that sort of speed, serious injury would be inevitable - at best.

263

But on reaching the car, which had travelled about 100 yards beyond the fence, we literally could not believe our eyes. There, nestled between two huge cotton trees, was Calvin's red Ford. The four passengers had already climbed out and, although clearly shocked and frightened, were praising God in excited voices that no one had suffered even a scratch or bruise. Not only that, but the car also had neither dent nor scratch. If ever I had seen a miracle, this was it! We were all shouting in disbelief and amazement, hugging the driver and passengers and giving thanks to God for his mercy. Whilst one of the men helped Daphne back up to the road to let the rest of the convoy know everyone was safe and uninjured, Calvin gingerly climbed back into the driver's seat and the rest of us either pushed or pulled the car as it reversed between the trees, through the hole in the fence and back up the embankment onto the road. To our further amazement, not only was the car undamaged, but it was still driving as if nothing had ever happened! Surely a guardian angel must have had his hand on Calvin's steering wheel as the car had careered down the embankment and passed between the trees beyond. I took this as a clear sign that God's endorsement must have been on the band and our mission to spread the Christian gospel throughout Jamaica.

Once we had all calmed down, we joined in a group prayer before continuing, in convoy, on our long journey home. At least no one would fall asleep now, with the amount of adrenaline that was pumping through our veins!

Our most exciting adventure as a band, however, was our week-long foreign tour to Grand Cayman, a nearby island in the Caribbean, in the summer of 1984. For several of the band members, this was their first experience of leaving Jamaica and flying in an aeroplane, so it caused tremendous excitement. The tour was organised by one of the local Christian denominations in Cayman and involved our playing in their main church and also at an outdoor

264

concert in the main square of the capital. Grand Cayman is a relatively small island, so in our free time during the day, we had the opportunity to get to their lovely beaches for a swim and to explore our new environment. Since our equipment was travelling with us on the plane, we could only take the absolute essentials, but at least this meant that setting up for a concert in Cayman was not the usual, massive and time-consuming task that our concerts back in Jamaica involved. We had a truly wonderful, memorable time and the local inhabitants absolutely loved our songs and our ministry.

* * *

I thank God for all the adventures and experiences that we were privileged to be a part of during my 12 years as leader of Sonic Salvation Gospel Band. When I eventually left Jamaica and the band unfortunately folded, as the members went their separate ways, at least we could all look back on a multitude of happy memories. We had played throughout the length and breadth of Jamaica; we had recorded no less than 35 original gospel songs; we had been featured on TV and our songs were still being played frequently on the radio airwaves; we had gone on a foreign tour and played our part in spreading the Christian message abroad. And wherever we ended up in life, across the world, we would always be a part of the 'Sonic family' - the nicest group of people you could ever hope to meet.

265

Chapter 17: The End Of An Era

I trust that the reader will forgive me for briefly going back in time at this point, to 1977, the year that Joan and myself got married. When you are young and in love, with your whole life stretching out before you, it is all too easy to just live for the present and leave the future to deal with itself. This is especially true when one is enjoying life and involved in myriad, time-consuming activities - such as leading Sonic Salvation Gospel Band!

Joan and I were starting a new life together and getting to know each other in a more intimate way; we had the cottage to set up and organise as our new home; I was eager to explore my new Christian faith and was even doing some lay-preaching in the local area, while Joan had taken on the role of Sunday School Superintendent at our local Church of God; we both had enjoyable but increasingly demanding jobs at Compre, and my hands were full to overflowing with Head of Science Department responsibilities, Science Exhibition and Scouts, while Joan was, by then, a Senior Teacher and Head of the General Studies Department, in addition to teaching History and Geography; and Sonic Salvation Gospel Band was just beginning to blossom and flourish. We were busy as bees, and happy as larks.

In spite of the theft of the Chariot, we had managed to make ends meet, and were rarely short of food or basic necessities. We had lots of friends to socialise with, took romantic drives to the beach and trips to Westmoreland in the MGB, and visited England to see my side of the family whenever possible.

Since we increasingly felt 'established' as a married couple, by 1978 we felt it was time to be thinking a bit more seriously about starting a family of our own. Both of us were from big families and accustomed to having our own brothers and sisters to grow up with; so if we were aiming to have several children, we needed to get moving. Furthermore, some of our friends were starting to drop subtle hints, and asking Joan, particularly, about when they might expect to see some young 'Skiplets'!

Of course, as young newly-weds, we were doing everything that we needed to do *physically* that might have been expected of us, so surely it was just a case of being patient and waiting for the news we wanted - that a baby was on its way.

But by the summer of 1979, there was still no sign of a 'Skiplet' so we thought it might be worth making a visit to see Dr McPherson, a well-known and highly respected gynaecologist in Mandeville. Although it was only Joan that was actually going for an examination, I thought it appropriate that I accompany her and, in the process, get to meet the doctor.

The first thing that stood out a mile was that I was the only male out of about 20 people in the entire waiting room. Feeling a little conspicuous, I awkwardly tried to make small talk with Joan, hoping it would soon be our turn to be called in.

'Doc' was a really amiable, genuine sort of a guy whom I warmed to immediately and who was soon quite naturally referring to me by my Jamaican pet-name, 'Skip'. As a Physicist, I wanted a thorough scientific assessment as to why it might be taking so long for us to conceive, and barraged him with question after question. He did his very best to detail all the possible causes that might be responsible, and also pointed out that, sometimes, the problem was with the man rather than with the woman but that it could also be with both. However, he assured us that Joan seemed fit and healthy and with no obvious, major problems; it was 'early days' and we should just carry on doing what we were doing anyway. If Joan still didn't get pregnant during the next year, we should then come back and look into the possibility of both of us having a number of further tests.

We were both reassured and returned home to carry on with our busy lives as usual. I lamented to Joan that young, unmarried, teenage girls seemed able, somehow, to get pregnant with apparent ease, while ironically, we, as a married couple who were longing for children, were experiencing such frustrating problems with conception.

We prayed about the matter and asked some of our close friends to keep us in their prayers but, by the summer of 1980, we were still no closer to our desire to start our own family and so headed back to Mandeville for another appointment with our friend, Doc McPherson.

After three years of waiting since we got married, I knew Joan, particularly, was starting to get concerned about our perceived infertility problem and wanted answers. Doc was very sympathetic and reassuring and, with the help of Pauline, my former Physics student (who was by then a nurse at University Hospital in Kingston), we were booked in for some further tests. Joan would have various scans and other checks, including a laparoscopy, while I would have a sperm count.

Once again, in an even larger waiting room at the University Hospital, I was the only man present, along with a large number of women, most of whom I guessed to be in their early 30s. We were both ushered off to do our respective tests and were advised that the results would be forwarded to Doc McPherson who would be able to explain them to us. We just had to be patient and wait to be contacted by the Doc.

A couple of weeks later, sitting in the Doc's office we learned that our infertility problem was two-fold. My sperm count was on the low side while Joan had fibroids growing on the outside of her uterus. On seeing our dejected faces, Doc assured us that such issues were not uncommon but that neither problem would necessarily *prevent* conception, even if the *likelihood* of Joan becoming pregnant was reduced. After all, it only needed *one* sperm, out of the millions present, to fertilise an egg, and the fertilised egg only needed to find *one tiny spot* on which to attach itself to the uterus wall for a baby to be conceived. He once again advised us not to worry and to continue 'doing what we knew we needed to do'.

It wasn't the outcome we had wanted. I was fully aware that, in a country like Jamaica, it was almost a forgone conclusion that children would follow marriage; an *expectation*, even. To still have no children after more than three years of marriage was likely to lead to all sorts of people asking all sorts of further questions, some innocently hurtful and others deliberately provocative and demoralising. With my thick skin, (or so I thought), I could laugh off such questions with a joke or a witty response, but I knew Joan would suffer more with her greater sensitivity and lovely, gentle nature. Although I tried to be as supportive and reassuring as possible, I felt powerless to solve our dilemma. Alas, all of my accumulated knowledge of Physics and Maths, which had been so helpful in other situations, were utterly useless in resolving this particular problem!

Fortunately, we did have some really concerned friends like the members of Sonic Salvation and our Christian brothers and sisters at church, with whom we could talk and share our deepest feelings without fear of rebuff or ridicule. So, with every week that passed, there were more and more people praying for us and encouraging us not to lose heart. Moreover, I reassured myself, the power of prayer should not be underestimated (as I had already experienced), especially when the prayers were coming from lots of people, all asking God for the same thing. Sometimes, it seemed, one might just have to wait a while for an answer.

269

But by the summer of 1982, five years into our marriage, our hopes of having a child of our own were beginning to fade. Even the Doc was beginning to appreciate our frustration and despondency and, in one of our friendly chats, he suggested that we might consider the possibility of our seeking further tests and possible treatment in England or America, where several new procedures for infertility were, by then, being trialled.

I was already aware that after teaching for seven or more years in Jamaica, a graduate teacher was eligible for a one-term sabbatical, and I realised that this, in fact, could all work out to our advantage. By the following school year, commencing in September 1983, Joan would have completed eight years as a full-time teacher, while I would have completed 12, so we would both have met the necessary criteria. If we could both be granted the sabbatical *simultaneously* for the 1983 Christmas Term, we could spend the available four months teaching in England, and hopefully take advantage of any available infertility treatment while there. At the earliest opportunity, I went to see Mr Latty to ask for his assistance in petitioning the Ministry of Education to approve a joint request. I also shared with him our intention to seek any medical help we could obtain which we hoped might solve our infertility problem, while we were over in England.

I am quite sure Mr Latty must have had sincere doubts about our returning to Jamaica at the end of our proposed four-month trip, but to his credit, he gave our proposal his blessing and managed to obtain the approval we were seeking from the Ministry of Education. Although we had almost a full year to get ready for the trip, a million and one things needed to be done or arranged prior to our departure. A temporary cover teacher would have to be found for Joan, while I was hoping that a former Compre student of mine who would have graduated from CAST by then, would be willing to fill my post for the four months that we would be away. The annual Scout summer camp would need to be brought forward from its usual time at the end of August to the start of the summer holiday, so that we could travel as early as possible after school broke up for the summer. I would also need to find someone to run the Scout group in my absence during the Christmas Term. Sonic Salvation would just have to have a four-month 'holiday' when we would decline any requests for concerts. And most important of all, we would need to make the necessary contacts and appointments with the top infertility scientists in the UK.

* * *

By mid-July 1983, we were on the plane bound for England. We had decided that, after a week or so at my parents', attending some pre-arranged appointments with infertility specialists in nearby Sheffield, we would head back down to London where we could rent a small flat for the duration of our stay and be on spot for any medical appointments down there. Meanwhile we could take up any temporary teaching posts which we might be able to secure for the Christmas Term in the capital.

Without too much searching, we found a cute little bed-sit in West London, quite close to Wembley Stadium. Having both applied for as many advertised temporary teaching posts as we could find, we sat back and waited for replies. Ironically, in view of the dire shortage of Physics teachers in London at the time, it was Joan who was offered a job first, as Temporary Teacher of History and Geography at a secondary comprehensive within walking distance from where we were living. But then, a couple of weeks later, I finally got offered a post of Temporary Physics Teacher at a nearby secondary school for 'disadvantaged' boys. Although the job was probably going to be a bit 'rough' and required a short bus journey to get there, I reckoned I could cope with this in the short-term and accepted the position.

It would take another novel to describe our experiences at our respective schools. Suffice it to say that we both made it through (just!), despite the problems we encountered, working in the British Education system in inner-city schools in West London at that time. It was certainly an eye-opener, after coming from the disciplined environment we were accustomed to at Compre.

To our great disappointment, our medical investigations at the research departments of some of the biggest London hospitals were useful, but failed to reveal much more than we had already found out at the University Hospital in Kingston. In vitro fertilisation was not yet a common procedure at that time so, in the end, we were just getting the same advice as we had been given in Jamaica; *'keep trying, don't give up, and hope for the best.'* When we pointed out that we also had many people praying for us back in Jamaica, we got blank stares. We were experiencing, and not for the first time, the relative apathy and disinterest in the Christian faith that seemed to us so prevalent in England at that time. I didn't find *that* particularly encouraging either.

However, our time spent in London did have many positives. We got to see several, fantastic London shows and musicals, we were able to visit most of the awe-inspiring museums and art galleries, and we enjoyed bus trips around the capital and boat trips on the River Thames. All in all, it was an enjoyable, educational trip, even though not particularly useful from a medical perspective.

After spending a lovely but wintry Christmas back at the family home in Derbyshire with my parents, we set off on the long trip back to our island in the sun. Getting back to a warmer clime would certainly be welcome!

* * *

It felt good to be back in Frankfield and once again living in our own little cottage. Everything was just as we had left it, along with the MGB and the Sonic Chariot (which Mas' John had promised to guard with his life!). He was overjoyed to see us, as was Mr Latty. Clearly many people had just assumed we would have remained in England and not come back at all! So, we started the new 1984 Easter Term, once again in Jamaica, only a little older, but with quite a lot more experience of the wider world. Although we were undeniably disenchanted by the lack of success in our medical investigations, we were still happy to be 'home'. In six months' time we would have been married for seven years, but alas, still with no sign of any little 'Skiplet'.

After just a couple of days to recover from our trip, we were both immediately immersed in the hectic lifestyle of a typical Jamaican Secondary School Teacher, along with all the catching up that was needed to make up for our time away. Our teaching rooms needed reorganising, registers transferring, class lists updating and work schemes prepared for the new term. Preparations for the 1984 Science Exhibition weren't far away.

But the thing that we probably noticed most when we got back was the further drastic down-turn in the Jamaican economy which had clearly occurred while we were away. We learnt that, apparently, the then Jamaican Prime Minister Michael Manley's befriending of Cuban president, Fidel Castro, had not gone unnoticed by government officials in the United States. Wanting to avoid the possibility of a second communist island in close proximity to the USA, they had, in response, massively reduced their purchase of Jamaican bauxite (from which aluminium is produced) and were now even discouraging American tourists from visiting the island! With foreign exchange in short supply, the Jamaican dollar had shrunk in value and there was now a thriving black market in US dollars. Petrol prices had rocketed, so that just filling the Chariot's tank for

273

a single Sonic concert trip was now taking a very significant part of my month's salary. Similarly, the cost of a weekly shop at the Frankfield supermarket had almost *doubled* since we had left for our trip to England only a few months before! There was nothing that we could do, however, but 'grin and bear it' and get on with our daily lives.

With everything that was going on, therefore, I was quite concerned when, around Easter 1984, Joan announced that she was feeling a bit 'under the weather'. I had hoped this was just the result of the rather hectic few months since our return, but then, after eating breakfast one morning, she had a bout of nausea. Given that she was about to take a trip to Kingston to purchase some prizes for the upcoming Speech Day, I thought it best to find out what was wrong as soon as possible, and tried to make an appointment for her with the local doctor in Frankfield. When I was informed that no appointment slot was available for several *days*, I decided we might as well check with Dr McPherson in Mandeville. We just hadn't had time to see him since our return, so we could also get the information he had received from England about the medical tests we'd done whilst there, and kill two birds with one stone.

Doc was really glad to see us when he stepped into the waiting room, and, immediately instructing the receptionist to let us jump the queue, he beckoned us to join him in his office. I briefly shared our experiences at the London hospitals and he, in turn, promised to share all the test results with us presently. Before going into these details, however, he thought it best to first find out what was causing Joan's current sickness, and asked her to lie on the couch provided for a quick medical examination. After a couple of minutes, he turned and came over towards me with what I perceived as a rather stern expression on his face.

"Skip, I have to inform you that..."

274

He paused, and I was immediately worried that Joan might have some serious medical problem, or that he had received bad news from one of the hospitals in London,

"...your wife is pregnant!", and then his face lit up with a huge smile.

What he had just said didn't register with me for several seconds. It was the last thing I had been expecting. And then I realised that I had just received the news we had been longing to hear for almost seven years: *Joan was expecting a baby!*

I was ecstatic beyond my wildest dreams and was sure Joan must also have been completely overjoyed with this unexpected news. After an agonising seven-year test of our faith, God was finally answering our prayers and those of our many friends who had also been praying on our behalf.

However, Doc cautioned, the chances of the pregnancy reaching full term, were slim indeed. Joan's fibroids had already increased significantly in size since our last visit and as the baby grew, so would the fibroids, leaving less and less space for the baby to develop properly. Joan would need to take it really easy over the next seven or eight months, to minimise the possibility of a miscarriage. And, he ventured, we would also 'need to pray really hard for a successful outcome'. It was strange hearing the last piece of advice from Doc since he was not, as far as we were aware, a Christian believer himself. But pray we certainly would, even though I just couldn't imagine that our loving God would bring us all the way to this point in our marriage, having tested our faith for a baby to be conceived for *seven years*, only to snatch our joy away before our prayers were fully answered.

Having now a special interest in our developing little 'Skiplet', Doc wanted to see us at least once a month from then onwards, to check on the baby's development. But irrespective of such regular appointments, which we had every intention of keeping, I knew in my heart that our baby reaching full term and being safely born, depended entirely on God's infinite love and benevolence. And without delay, we would get *every* 'prayer warrior' we knew, at church, within Sonic Salvation, amongst our wider circle of friends and within our families, all praying to God with us, for the safe development and well-being of our unborn child.

By the summer of 1984, Joan was just starting to get a little 'plump' around her tummy. I kept feeling the bump to see if there was any sign of kicking from within, but could detect nothing as yet.

The Sonic Salvation tour to Grand Cayman that summer had been arranged months before, which presented us with some difficult choices. Should we cancel the trip and all stay at home; should I go on the trip with the rest of the band, leaving Joan behind with a close friend or one of her sisters for company; or should we both go on the tour and pray that nothing would happen to adversely affect Joan's pregnancy. In the end, and despite the very vocal objections of some of the band members, we decided on the latter. As it happened, the sea air and warm water, and the opportunity to get plenty of rest during most of our Sonic tour to Grand Cayman, probably did Joan more good than harm. Added to which, she got vast amounts of attention and assistance whenever she needed it from everyone in the band.

On our return home, after a really delightful and blessed week, we immediately scheduled a trip to see Doc. He was pleased with Joan's good health and the progress of her pregnancy, observing with a smile that,

"It looks like pregnancy suits you, Joan!"

Before we left, he whispered to me, perhaps not wanting to cause Joan undue concern,

"The baby seems to be developing well and has a strong heartbeat, but the fibroids are also growing so you can't be too careful. So far, everything is ok, but

276

make sure she gets plenty of rest and continues to take it *really easy.*"

(I had deliberately withheld the fact that we had just returned from a Sonic Salvation tour abroad!)

Based on Doc's sound advice, I decided there and then that Joan really should take it easy from this point on, and therefore, it was time for me, once and for all, to learn how to cook. Over the next few days, I experimented with several recipes and endeavoured to prepare a variety of culinary delicacies. However, after a number of minor mishaps, including almost burning down the cottage when I forgot that I had left a pan of rice on the lit stove, we thought it might be more expedient and definitely safer to get some assistance. We decided to ask two of our delightful Grade 11 students at school, Dacia and Judith, who were already close friends with Joan, to come and stay with us for a while to help out. If their parents were agreeable, we would look after the girls, and help them with their GCE studies as necessary, in return for them assisting with the cooking and helping to care for Joan's needs. They could use the spare bedroom and would be good company for each other. Their parents were delighted and took it as a compliment that their daughters had been asked. This arrangement suited everyone.

Month by month, Joan grew bigger and bigger and some of her teaching colleagues, on feeling two firm bumps in her tummy, thought she might be going to have twins. They weren't aware that while one of the bumps was the baby's head, the other was, in fact, one of the several fibroids growing alongside!

Doc was almost as elated with the progress of the pregnancy as we were, having had very strong misgivings in the early stages that it was most unlikely to come to full term. He had already committed to being in attendance at the birth of the baby, even if it occurred in the middle of the night.

When Joan's waters broke in the early hours of the morning in mid-December and she went into labour, I had the Chariot ready and waiting for the 40-minute drive to the hospital in Mandeville. Given that this was a relatively deserted route and the labour had begun unexpectedly in the middle of the night, Joan was rather nervous, but I assured her that our faithful Chariot would soon have her at the hospital and that there was no need to worry.

On our arrival at the maternity ward, we checked in and were soon joined by Doc who, fortunately, lived close by. Joan could now relax (*at least in some regards!*), and just follow Doc's instructions. However, in our rush to get to the hospital, I had forgotten to bring a number of things that she needed so, since she was now safely in the maternity ward with Doc at the ready, and since labour had only just started, I offered to nip back home to pick up the missing items - I would soon be back!

The road from Mandeville back to Frankfield is made up of a long, downhill section, descending to the bottom of the valley below the town, followed by a long climb uphill to Spaulding, before descending once again to the Rio Minho valley where Frankfield is located. Just as I reached the valley bottom, way below Mandeville, the Chariot came to a rather sudden stop and refused to go any further. When I put the gearbox in neutral, the vehicle could free-wheel without any problem, but as soon as I engaged any of the gears, the engine locked solid. A cursory inspection of the engine revealed nothing, however, so, mindful of the fact that my wife was in the middle of labour, and bearing in mind that it was the middle of the night, with me in the middle of nowhere, I was at a loss to know what to do. Thank God the problem had not occurred an hour earlier on our way *to* the hospital. That really would have been a disaster, with my non-existent knowledge of midwifery!

However, I desperately needed to get to Frankfield and back to the hospital without delay and before Joan started to worry that some disaster must have befallen me. For a moment, my mind ran back to my hold-up experience at gunpoint near Six Miles bridge a few years before, but I quickly dismissed that nightmare and got out of the Chariot to be ready to flag down whoever might be driving by. Maybe it was another test of my faith, but somehow I sensed in my heart that all would be well. Within a matter of seconds I saw another transit van coming towards me, in the same direction in which I had been travelling. When it stopped, to reveal one of the more friendly Frankfield minibus drivers, I couldn't believe my eyes. Not only was the minibus returning to Frankfield, but the driver was more than willing to give me a tow behind him. Maybe he was an angel in disguise!

Having no choice in the matter, I had to leave the Chariot on the roadside by my garden gate, but I took the precaution of alerting Mas' John to its presence all the same. At that point in our lives we could really do without another stolen vehicle. Then I hastily collected the items I thought Joan would need (having forgotten the list at the hospital in my haste to leave) and jumped in the MGB. At least the drive back would be a bit quicker.

By the time I got back to the hospital after all my adventures, the labour was 'in full swing' so I decided to spare Joan the details of having yet another problem with the Chariot. But this baby was determined to take its time in coming and it wasn't until 4 o'clock in the afternoon, after a 12-hour labour, that our baby finally entered the world outside the womb. I couldn't contain my elation and was inwardly spellbound to witness the birth of a new human being:

God had blessed us with a perfect baby boy -
we had decided to call him David.

Moreover, after the birth, my darling wife and our miracle baby were both doing really well; and Joan was overjoyed to be able to hold her new-born son in her arms for the very first time. Given the difficulties the fibroids might have caused, Doc was relieved, and amazed that everything had worked out so favourably, against all the odds. The broken-down Chariot back in Frankfield paled into insignificance; it would be sorted out in due course.

God had answered all our prayers. We were now a family of three. Most of our friends, and perhaps even Doc, had expected our new baby to be quite dark in colour but, as it turned out, he was actually whiter than I was! When I nervously held him for the first time, afraid I might drop this wonderful 'gift from God', looking so perfect and peaceful, I knew that every minute of our seven-year wait for this child had been worth it. Nothing could compare with becoming a father for the very first time!

When we eventually got back home, it was as if we were celebrating an early Christmas! The girls were enthralled with our new family member and over the next week, there was an almost constant stream of visitors and well-wishers at our cottage. I must have taken hundreds of photographs to send to all my family and friends over in England. At that time there were only three telephones in the whole of Frankfield, one of which served the school and its Principal. However, Mr Latty was kind enough to let me use the school phone to call Mummy and Baba with the good news. We decided to have four godparents, Sheila, Suzanne and Mikey from the band, along with Harry's older brother Cleve. After a memorable christening service at our church a few weeks later, all our guests and well-wishers headed up to school for a sumptuous meal, prepared in the school canteen. It was a truly joyful time, which I shall never forget.

Unfortunately, my life's myriad activities soon had to resume, but I had insisted that Joan take an extended maternity leave to fully recover from giving birth and to give her ample time to bond with our new baby. Dacia and

Judith were delighted when we asked them to continue with us at the cottage and remained for almost the rest of the school year, so they were able to fuss over David to their hearts' content. Meanwhile, I had managed to find out what was wrong with the Chariot and to get it fixed. To my utter disbelief, I discovered that my new crankshaft had actually *broken in half* - something I had never even heard of happening before! But it was a costly repair and had not come at the best time now that we had all the additional expenses of looking after a new baby. The purchase of baby food and diapers alone was using up a massive proportion of our joint salaries, as the local currency continued to diminish in value. And filling the petrol tank of the Chariot accounted for almost one whole month's salary now. Things were looking increasingly difficult.

By the time we got to the 1985 Easter holiday, we were seriously suffering economically, despite the fact that both Joan and myself were, by then, Heads of Departments and Senior Teachers, up at the top of the salary scale. A few years before, we had given serious thought to either making an offer to buy the cottage we were renting or, alternatively, buying a plot of land and building our own home on it, but both of these aspirations were now clearly impossible.

Our salaries were not going to rise much further and even with the extra income I was, by then, receiving for doing some part-time teaching at Knox College in nearby Spaulding, we were still struggling financially.

One evening after the girls had gone to bed, Joan and I sat down to have a serious discussion about our futures. I loved living in Jamaica with its friendly people and its beautiful mountains and coastline; I loved my jobs teaching Physics at Compre and Knox; I loved the musical ministry of Sonic Salvation Gospel Band and all the wonderful members of the band; and I loved all the energising, outdoor activities encompassed by our Scout group.

But if we had reached this stage in our working lives and could barely meet the costs of having just one child and paying for petrol to power our means of getting around, something had to give. Joan presented similar arguments but was clearly upset at even *considering* the possibility of having to leave the land of her birth. However, weighing up all the pros and cons, we realised that there was only one viable option. We were going to have to leave Jamaica in the summer at the end of the school term and allow God to lead us elsewhere.

* * *

That night, my mind was in turmoil and I could not sleep. I kept reflecting back over the years I had spent in this beloved, enticing island; how I had found my first year of VSO so enjoyable and why I had decided not to return to England. Without doubt, choosing to take a year out from my studies to work overseas with this organisation was one of the best decisions I had ever made. The experience had opened my eyes, and my heart, to a different culture and a different way of life to what I had been used to. Working alongside colleagues and friends of a different race now felt completely natural. Interacting with people of all ages who had a different skin colour to my own was how the world ought to be; and I had come to realise that the colour of everyone's heart was the same.

I was now more aware that there were different ways to tackle a problem and that different societies perceived things very differently. I had discovered that the vast majority of Jamaicans had big hearts and friendly dispositions. They were people with a strong belief in God and humanity.

Although I would be leaving, I had a new-found and ever-deepening Christian faith, God had provided me with a wonderful Jamaican wife and I had been further blessed with an adorable son. I now felt part of a wider family, many of whom were students I had taught and who were now some of my closest friends. Several of these former students like Spenga and Clifton were now in influential positions both in Jamaica and abroad. Floyd felt like a family member while Tookuma almost felt like an adopted son, just as he thought of me as his adopted father.

Through my work in the Physics Department, I had helped Compre to establish itself as one of the leading Secondary Schools in the island and, hopefully, fewer people now thought of Frankfield as just some little backwater town in the middle of nowhere! My Gospel band, Sonic Salvation, had established a new direction in Jamaican gospel music, providing an outlet for the creative talents of Floyd, Prince and Sheila to compose music and pen contemporary lyrics for most of the original gospel songs that we had recorded. Hopefully my Jamaican legacy would last for at least a little while after I was gone.

All in all, I had lived an almost idyllic life for the last 14 years. I had grown to more deeply understand, and also to love and embrace, Jamaica's motto, 'Out of many, one people'. Despite my foreign origins, I truly felt I was now part of the culture and its people, and no one would miss Jamaica more than me. But, sadly, it was clearly the end of an era.

I had no idea where we would go but, with God's help, I was sure we would make a success of it. Hopefully, there would be others who would take up the mantle and carry on where we left off.

Farewell Jamaica, our Island in the Sun.
Farewell to our many beloved friends.
Our happy memories will remain with us forever,
But our hearts we leave with you.

About The Author

The first child of a Turkish father and an English mother, Deniz 'Skip' Önaç was born and raised in the beautiful Peak District National Park in England. After completing his secondary education at Lady Manners Grammar School in Bakewell, where he was House Captain and Head Boy, he moved from rural Derbyshire to pursue his undergraduate degree in Physics at University College, London. He then served with VSO for two years at the Edwin Allen Comprehensive High School in Frankfield, Jamaica as a volunteer teacher of Physics. After a further 12 years' teaching in Frankfield, he then relocated to Kingsway Academy in Nassau, Bahamas where he was High School Principal for 10 years. In 1995, he returned to his birthplace in the UK with his wife, Joan, and son, David, and the final years of his 44-year career in education were spent as Head of Physics at Denstone College. Having now retired from teaching, Skip once again lives in a peaceful and picturesque Peak District village. He and Joan will soon be celebrating their 44th Wedding Anniversary, and their enduring love for each other is a powerful testimony to the case made in this book, that the colour of all human hearts is the same.

As this book demonstrates time and again, music has always been a significant part of Skip's life. He began playing drums at age 11, continuing to do so right up to the present day, and he still enjoys drumming regularly in the worship band at his local church. In addition, he has had a lifelong interest in audio engineering, and often works on musical projects in his home studio, including transferring all the original *Sonic Salvation Gospel Band* songs recorded in Jamaica from vinyl to CD. He still maintains frequent contact with almost all of the former members of the band. Skip and Joan's son, David, himself an accomplished pianist and composer, is now Musical Director for *Voices Beyond*, a pioneering Gospel Collective based in the UK.

Get In Touch

The author would welcome any comments or feedback; please email him at denizengyn@btinternet.com.

Alternatively, you can email him via his publisher at info@ltyvpublishing.co.uk

If you have enjoyed reading *"The Colour of my Heart."* please leave Deniz 'Skip' Önaç a good review.

Thank you in advance.

Printed in Great Britain
by Amazon